SANDY

SANDY

THE AUTHORISED BIOGRAPHY OF
SANDY JARDINE

TOM MILLER

BLACK & WHITE PUBLISHING

First published 2016
by Black & White Publishing Ltd
29 Ocean Drive, Edinburgh EH6 6JL

1 3 5 7 9 10 8 6 4 2   16 17 18 19

ISBN: 978 1 84502 991 3

Typeset by Iolaire, Newtonmore
Printed and bound by CPI Group (UK) Ltd, Croydon, CR0 4YY

CONTENTS

ACKNOWLEDGEMENTS

Sincere thanks to the Jardine family, Shona and Steven for their support in putting together this tribute to not just a fantastic footballer but a wonderful man.

To all Sandy's friends, colleagues and teammates who shared so many memories and emotional moments with me, it was a real privilege and pleasure to roll back the years with you all. I hope I have transferred your affection and relayed treasured tales in a fashion that fully captures the special relationship you all clearly had with Sandy.

For the Rangers fans and the poignant second minute applause during matches at Ibrox to show support for Sandy when he needed it most. It really was something special and highlighted the esteem Sandy was held in by the Rangers family. It was a hugely significant gesture.

To Patricia, as ever, keeping me grounded even when I have my match day "wiggle" on and Big T whose help was invaluable. I could not have got this one over the line without you both.

Thanks too for the faith shown in me by Campbell Brown and his team at Black & White Publishing. It is greatly appreciated.

To young James Wilson from the East Enclosure you are a genuine hero and a real true blue. Keep enjoying Rangers TV.

And for Dennis Nicholson – this one came too late for you but your love of books and sport was an inspiration. A fantastic man who will be greatly missed by all.

FOREWORD BY ALLY McCOIST

I will be forever grateful that I had the good fortune to have played and also managed Rangers. It is impossible to explain how proud and honoured I feel to have served what has always been and always will be a fantastic club with such an incredible history.

When I consider the regularity with which this club attracted the best players down through the decades it is an absolute privilege to be able to think that I wore the Rangers jersey. But I must say that when I was asked to write this foreword for the late Sandy Jardine, I was truly humbled.

Throughout its 144-year history there have been many illustrious names associated with Rangers – Jim Baxter, John Greig, Willie Henderson, Davie Cooper, and Walter Smith to name but a handful – and in my view Sandy is right up there with the legends who graced the Ibrox pitch or who guided the club to success and silverware from the dugout.

Sandy is, and will always be, a true legend in every sense of the word. He was a world-class footballer in his time but, more importantly, he was a world-class human being.

I cannot over-emphasise the qualities and character this man displayed in his life as a footballer and as a thoroughly decent, honourable person. His love of life always shone through but his probity and his desire to do the right thing were truly inspirational.

Of course I used to watch him playing for Rangers when I was a boy, never for a second thinking I would be given the opportunity to work so closely with him, but the great pleasure of doing precisely that was what I experienced when I returned to the club in 2007. Undoubtedly, Sandy was a remarkable man.

His achievements both on and off the pitch are second to none and I was honoured to regard him as a friend. He gave everything for Rangers and worked tirelessly in a number of roles because he wanted to ensure the traditions, history and standards at the club were maintained.

In fact, he was the epitome of a great Ranger. A man of dignity and class who was respected not only by the supporters who idolised him when he pulled on the famous light blue jersey but also among the wider football community.

It is not an exaggeration to say my admiration and respect for Sandy grew daily during those dark and diffi-cult days of administration. He stepped forward when the club needed a focus and direction and he played such a key role in holding things together. His presence and his words had a galvanising effect on the staff at Ibrox and Murray Park.

He went out of his way to make sure spirits remained as high as they possibly could at a time when it would have been easy and understandable for some to feel that they couldn't take any more. His performance in those times when it felt as though each new day brought another trauma was astonishing and he won the respect of every member of staff.

However, he also had the respect of Rangers fans and it was hardly surprising to see Sandy at the front when thousands of Rangers fans marched to Hampden to protest at the sanctions imposed on the club, which threatened

Rangers' very existence just as much as anything that had been perpetrated by a succession of detestable characters who had gained influence over the club.

Sandy was also one of the driving forces behind the creation of the Rangers Hall of Fame and he looked after the club's memorabilia, including the trophy room and club archives. He was on the board of the Rangers Youth Development Fund, a key member of the Former Rangers Players' Benevolent Fund and a key figure behind the Rangers Fans' Fighting Fund.

Before he passed away, he told me he was so proud to be a Ranger and wished to be remembered as such. His wish is assured. There is no doubt that Sandy is a huge loss to Rangers and football, and we may never see his like again.

Dignity is the quality that probably epitomises Sandy best and he displayed it every single day during his struggle against his illness. Despite his pain, he was even able to return to Ibrox and unfurl the league flag and just watching him walk out on to pitch that day is a moment I will never forget.

It was a proud moment for Sandy and I know he was also touched when the club decided to name the Govan Stand in his honour, a wonderful gesture and totally deserved. It is such a pity he didn't survive to witness the unveiling ceremony, ironically against his old club Hearts where he is also fondly remembered for his phenomenal contribution.

The term "legend" is often overused in sport but it certainly applies to Sandy. He gave five decades of service to Rangers as a player and then as a vital and hugely influential member of staff.

He is gone but he lives forever in the hearts and minds of his family and friends. And in those of every Rangers fan.

I have my own memories of a fantastic player, friend and man. And my life has been enriched though knowing and learning from him. Hopefully this book captures the essence of Sandy Jardine and by reading it you may also come to know and understand exactly what a wonderful human being he was.

1

RANGERS ARE BACK
2016 PROMOTION

On the 5th of April 2016 Rangers Football Club secured the Championship with a single goal victory over Dumbarton.

Rangers were back in the top flight of the Scottish game after a four-year journey, having been positioned in the bottom tier of the Scottish League pyramid following their liquidation of 2012.

It took four managers and four seasons of trips to Peterhead, Annan, Airdrie and East Fife among others with some horrific performances, results and challenges to test an incredibly impassioned and loyal support but on a wet spring Tuesday night at Ibrox, it somehow all felt worthwhile.

James Tavernier's goal in the fiftieth minute sealed the points and gave Rangers an unassailable seventeen-point gap at the top of the table. It was Tavernier's thirteenth goal in his first season as a Ranger. The right back, signed from Wigan, had been a revelation since scoring on his debut against Hibernian back in July and had become not only an absolute fan's favourite, but a first pick ever present under new manager Mark Warburton. That league-clinching strike took Tavernier to one goal off the goals record for a

Rangers full-back in a single season. The record of fourteen was shared by the man voted the greatest ever Ranger John Greig and the late great Sandy Jardine.

Tavernier would go on to claim two more goals before the season was out including the goal of the season volley in the Petrofac Training Cup final at Hampden, but that night against Dumbarton with 48,568 inside Ibrox celebrating the Light Blues' title success, many were thinking of absent friends who started the journey but sadly were no longer with us with the return to the Premiership now complete.

In the aftermath of the ninety minutes and as the Rangers squad perambulated the track inside Ibrox stadium, Club Director John Gilligan broke down in tears live on Rangers TV not just in the knowledge that he and his co-directors, who had overthrown the previous boardroom regime just over a year before, had achieved a major milestone in their vision for Rangers going forward, but John knew that his lifelong friend, Sandy Jardine, had made a massive contribution to ensuring Rangers were still alive and kicking to make this day happen right up until Sandy lost his own battle and succumbed to cancer almost one year before.

It was a very poignant moment.

Live on air, John Gilligan shared a tribute to Sandy and a global Rangers audience knew exactly why the part Sandy played to protect and promote his beloved Rangers should never be forgotten or understated.

The Rangers fans inside Ibrox knew it too as thoughts drifted back to the march to Hampden of April 2012 when Sandy rallied the troops and led over 8,000 loyal and true to the steps of the national stadium in an effort to highlight sanctions including fines and transfer embargoes that threatened the very future of the club.

William Pullar Jardine was not going to let that happen.

Almost four years to the day later Sandy may not have been around to see it, but his efforts were still fresh in the minds of the massive Rangers support. Many say that Sandy was there that night the league was won if only in spirit and you can be assured his presence will be felt again as Rangers take their place back in Scotland's major league and go all out for title fifty-five in their glorious history.

2

FOLLOW FOLLOW
MARCH TO HAMPDEN

Rangers Football Club was a stricken business. Craig Whyte had effectively taken a wrecking ball to a footballing institution that was successful on the park, and was managing its financial affairs prudently despite some potential issues inherited from misguided decisions being taken on players contracts, and the mechanism for financial rewards that HMRC were far less than comfortable with.

Administration in February 2012 meant uncertainty and a threat to the very existence of the club. Sanctions were being threatened from every quarter but the Rangers fans were determined to make a stand and show the authorities that they would not let their club die. They were prepared to go to any lengths to prevent it.

In a renowned Rangers public house, Annie Millers, just off the Clydeside in Glasgow city centre, a bunch of fans got together and a plan was hatched to marshall the support and march on the Scottish Football Association (SFA) headquarters at Hampden Park in a show of unity and force that would reflect the mood of the massive Rangers fan base. That would reinforce their message and belief that Rangers were being treated unfairly, with an example recently being an SFA judicial panel deciding to impose a twelve-month transfer embargo on the club and levy a £160,000 fine.

The fans were convinced that such negativity from Scotland's football authorities was disrupting the club from going forward and effectively restricting interested parties from making their final decision to purchase the assets of the football club.

Two takeover bids were on the table of administrators Duff & Phelps. One was from the consortium known as the Blue Knights led by former director Paul Murray, the other from American transport tycoon Bill Miller.

The bids were subject to numerous conditions but bidding parties were troubled on what they were actually buying if sanctions as threatened were indeed imposed.

Meanwhile, the future for all Rangers employees was also looking bleak and Ibrox and the club training complex at Auchenhowie were not happy places, with morale low as people went about their daily duties.

That situation sparked Sandy Jardine, who was effectively the father figure for playing staff and non-playing staff alike and the man almost everyone went to for advice and guidance, into action.

The fans' idea of marching on Hampden was growing at pace with social media – the key to galvanising the plan and getting the desired numbers in place to maximise effect. The fans also needed a frontman. Somebody with stature. Somebody that typified everything that was Rangers Football Club and what it stood for. That man was Sandy Jardine.

It took twenty-four hours for the fans to have their strategy in place. It took Sandy less than twenty-four seconds to agree to front proceedings.

It was to be a peaceful protest and designed to show the world the depth of feeling the fans had for the club.

Strathclyde Police had strict guidelines on stewarding and the route the fans were to take. In meetings with the police, Sandy Jardine put his name and reputation on the line by giving the authorities all the assurances necessary, and they were equally comfortable that the marchers would not let down one of the greatest players to ever pull on the light-blue jersey.

Later, Sandy admitted that despite a stellar and well decorated career, that day of the march to Hampden remained one of the proudest moments of his life.

However, not one of the 8,000-plus that made the journey behind Sandy that day in April 2012 could conceive that this fit and healthy Rangers icon would no longer be with us just two short years later.

The plan was to deliver a formal letter of protest signed on behalf of the Rangers support in an attempt to have the SFA accept that the turmoil at Rangers and the negativity surrounding the club was not of the fans' doing, and that with support and not sanctions, they would endeavour to get the club back on an even keel for the long-term good of everybody involved in Scottish football.

Unfortunately in the passion and excitement of the day as the marchers, led by Sandy and his good friend and Rangers supporters liaison manager, Jim Hannah, gathered at Queens Park it was realised the actual document to be handed over on the steps of the national stadium had been left behind on Sandy's desk within the Argyle House office suite of Ibrox stadium!

Unperturbed and with a degree of black humour that was a feature of those days, a pen and paper were rapidly produced from the crowd and a hand-written replacement was hastily crafted.

The impact captured for history was not about the letter. It was all about 8,000 people and more determined to make their position clear that Rangers should be treated fairly and appropriately in line with whatever misdemeanours they had committed.

The fans and Sandy Jardine were not prepared to have their beloved club killed off in any circumstances.

After the letter was delivered, Sandy addressed the

fans from the steps of Hampden and received a rousing reception.

Later, and recalling events and the way the day unfolded, Sandy remembered: "To lead the march was a tremendous feeling and I was honoured and privileged. There were around 8,000 people in the march and the same number on the streets supporting us.

"From that day I had no qualms that the club would survive with everybody behind us. Given the passion and the size of our support there was no doubt."

Remembering previous troubles at the other half of the Old Firm Sandy went on: "Probably only Celtic fans, because they have the same backing and support, would understand and have an inkling about what we went though."

There was, however, a high level of ill feeling towards Rangers from other clubs in their most serious period of uncertainty yet what was perceived by many Rangers' fans as a degree of vindictiveness about the way matters were dealt with at the SFA was something Sandy too could never understand or get his head around, claiming: "If Rangers are successful, and they are most years, it's denying other clubs so their fans can get vitriolic and perhaps they have seen this as a chance for some revenge and there is no doubt some were vindictive. Even if you don't support Rangers you have to understand they are a huge part of Scottish football and if you don't have a successful Rangers, you don't have a successful Scottish football."

Sandy was adamant when he forcibly made his point: "You have to put your petty jealousies out of the way."

He also recognised that not everyone did all they could in the circumstance to help. "There's no doubt in my mind the SFA and SPL treated us abysmally. If you look down south at Portsmouth, they went into administration about the same time as Rangers. They were getting help from their FA but I don't think one person from the authorities stepped forward to help us."

With consideration to how Rangers found themselves in this position, Sandy was equally adamant. "The players, staff, manager and supporters did nothing wrong. We had one person who raped our club and we are paying the costs."

The very successful march from Queens Park along Queens Drive, Cathcart Road, Prospecthill Road and Aitkenhead Road to Hampden had Strathclyde Police on high alert, but later Strathclyde Police chief superintendent Andy Bates stated: "There were no arrests and I am delighted at the way the supporters conducted themselves."

The Rangers family were never going to let Sandy Jardine down because quite simply they knew that Sandy Jardine would certainly never let them down.

An SFA spokesman said: "We are now in receipt of the letter signed on behalf of the Rangers support and are grateful that today's event passed peacefully. We appreciate the frustrations of the Rangers support during this period of uncertainty and today's march showed the depth of feeling towards the club.

"The Scottish FA exists to govern with the best interests of the game at all times and will continue to do so throughout this challenging time for the Scottish game."

In effect, the challenges were really only beginning for Rangers Football Club and in a rare look back to Sandy's reference to the man who "raped" the club, he recalled how former chairman Alastair Johnston and his other directors had concerns on the suitability of Craig Whyte. "The old board had flagged up concerns and soon it wasn't a real surprise as to where the club was heading. He was so secretive and kept everything close to his chest.

"He decapitated the club by getting rid of all the directors and was running it himself."

With only the best interests of the club at heart, Sandy went to see Whyte when he first arrived. "I introduced myself and tried to tell him what I did but his body language after two minutes told me he wasn't bloody interested."

Whyte was soon to be hounded out after administration on Valentine's Day 2012.

With survival the name of the game, the fans came up with another plan. This time it was to establish a fighting fund. Again, Sandy was the go-to man to give gravitas to the project and confidence to the fans ensuring the cash would only be used for genuinely worthwhile cases of club needs.

Former Rangers manager Walter Smith stood shoulder to shoulder with Sandy to launch the fighting fund. You could not get two more committed, faithful and true Rangers men and that faith can be demonstrated by elderly fans donating their full weekly pensions and youngsters sending in their pocket money for the cause.

Surely now the football club could move forward, especially with the fund being fully endorsed by the three major fans groups; the Association, the Assembly and the Trust.

It was around this time the Rangers faithful came up with the mantra "In Sandy we trust!"

Again it was a wise choice from the fans and Sandy was ready to do everything in his powers to preserve his beloved Rangers.

3

GREEN FOR GO
RANGERS HAVE A NEW MAN AT THE HELM

Sandy Jardine remains one of the very few people I met at Rangers who was honest and truthful throughout ... his only agenda was Rangers
– Charles Green in a text to Tom Miller 20 January 2015

Despite it being a Sunday morning on the last day of the domestic league campaign, a hastily arranged media conference was held at Rangers training complex Murray Park on the 13th of May 2012.

The reason for the need to alert the media was quite simple: Rangers Football Club had been the subject of an unconditional purchase proposal from a consortium led by former Sheffield United Chief Executive Charles Green and it was an offer considered acceptable to administrators Duff & Phelps.

Green's group had entered an irrevocable contract after paying an exclusivity fee and that process saw the previous preferred bidder, Bill Miller from the USA, now very much out the picture.

Green wasted no time in putting across his vision for Rangers and confirmed he had signed an exclusive deal with previous owner Craig Whyte to buy his eighty-five per cent shareholding for £1. The same price Whyte paid Sir David Murray with the bold Charles also stating: "I gave him a pound out of my own pocket too so he (Whyte) has made a 100% profit!"

In front of all divisions of the Scottish sporting media, Green dismissed reports of previous links between himself and Monaco based Whyte advising: "I met Craig Whyte for the first time a week last Tuesday in London."

As this circus was unfolding, Sandy Jardine sat clearly impassioned but keeping his thoughts to himself as did the others from the Rangers in-house media team.

With time moving on, the media briefing was brought to a close allowing those that were heading to Perth for Rangers' curtain call for the season against St. Johnstone to head north on the A9.

Clearly, many more questions were needing to be answered but what was obviously apparent was that if Green was to succeed, he needed the support of Sandy Jardine and others who knew how the club ticked, those who had the best interests of Rangers at heart and who also had its age-old traditions to uphold.

Head of Football Administration Andrew Dickson joined Sandy and Green for the road trip to McDiarmid Park and the man destined to be next King of Ibrox had a thirst for knowledge of all things Rangers.

Neither Dickson nor Jardine were convinced or taken in by the bluster of the former Sheffield chief, but he was the only game in town.

Prior to kick-off in Perth, Green had been kitted out in an official Rangers club tie and looked every inch the real deal as he took his seat in the Director's box, with Sandy Jardine at his immediate right-hand side.

On the field, Rangers delivered a fine performance that day and signed off for the season with a very comfortable

4-0 victory that saw Sone Aluko claim his first ever senior hat-trick after Lee McCulloch, deployed as a striker that day, opened the scoring.

Barrie McKay, at the tender age of seventeen, made his competitive debut as Rangers finished their season in style with the victory in Perth, making it six wins out of their last eight games.

Three months after entering administration, things were looking up for the Light Blue fans as they travelled home from Perth, relatively upbeat especially as a host of Ally McCoist's playing squad had intimated that they wanted to continue to be Rangers players for the next campaign.

The win had also ensured Rangers' final league position was good enough to qualify for Europe for the following season but UEFA rules would scupper that.

A new owner ... new investment promised ... a good and capable squad of players committed to the club and the likelihood of quality additions to the squad, if not prohibited under SFA red tape: all things Rangers were looking much more positive than they had been only a few weeks ago.

Or were they?

Not many watching events of Sunday, 13th May 2012 would have believed that Rangers would not play top flight league football for the next four years!

History shows the original Charles Green plan to exit administration via an acceptable CVA (Company Voluntary Arrangement) programme failed, and Rangers were plunged into liquidation.

Rangers were ultimately positioned in the bottom tier of the Scottish game. All the promise and positivity of that end of season day at Perth had gone – just like many of the players who had previously pledged their commitment to the cause just months before.

As Rangers stitched a makeshift side together to contest a Ramsdens Cup tie at Brechin City's Glebe Park on 29th July 2012, Sandy Jardine, the directors, manager McCoist and the fans knew Rangers were starting at the bottom and as they entered their 132nd season in competitive football, their quest to come through the leagues would start at the north-east of Scotland footballing outpost of Peterhead on 11th August 2012.

Looking back to the day in Perth, and the players who were involved in securing a league position that under normal circumstances would have delivered European football, only Kirk Broadfoot, Lee Wallace and Lee McCulloch started the match at Balmoor Stadium against the team from the Blue Toon.

The harsh realities of liquidation meant Rangers could not perform on the European stage that season, having been unable to meet the presentation of accounts deadline that ruling body UEFA insisted upon. That fact may have been influential as players chose to exercise their rights not to transfer allegiance, and indeed, their playing contracts to the new regime.

This clearly had a hugely negative effect on the plans of manager Ally McCoist, but it was Sandy Jardine who was most vocal and critical of those that left, claiming the players had reneged on a previously satisfactory arrangement. "There was an agreement reached over wage cuts and they got a great deal because they could leave for rock-bottom prices," he said. "And now they have seen an opportunity. In many ways, it's greed."

Sandy Jardine believed the players' motives were purely selfish and cash-driven which meant that their actions would deny Rangers vital funds to aid the rebuild process. Remember too that Sandy had been a vital cog in the recruitment process, working closely with previous managers, and Chief Scout Ewan Chester regularly sought Sandy's advice and support when trying to get transfer targets to commit to the Light Blues.

In his role as club ambassador, Sandy was quoted as saying: "I am dismayed and disappointed by the actions of the players who have chosen to leave. What they have done is seen an opportunity, whether it is them or their agents, and it's all about maximising their income.

"The players took a salary sacrifice. But in return, they got clauses in their contracts which would allow them to leave on rock bottom prices if clubs came in for them."

A visibly upset and frustrated Sandy continued: "I have to be honest and say I think the players have used our predicament for personal gain."

With Rangers' position still far from clear, Sandy did compromise, saying that he understood international players would not be comfortable dropping down the divisions, and while he admitted he would be reluctant to see them go, he could relate to their position. But all Sandy really wanted was for the club to be paid a reasonable fee for their services, and while it was likely to be bargain basement rates, Sandy had hoped the club would secure as close to market value as possible.

Sandy again reflected on the many previous meetings and discussions with the players and said: "What we don't have an answer to is why the players simply did not adhere to the original deal and allow the club to make money from those reduced fees." Prior to Rangers being confirmed as a League Three club, Jardine added: "What we have to do in the current situation is to get everything sorted out, know what players are staying and then start to build from there.

"If we don't have money from fees for players leaving, which we are completely entitled to, then what are we supposed to build on, fresh air?"

In those days of uncertainty, Jardine's already iconic status in the eyes of the Rangers faithful was growing by the day, and the figurehead and spokesman for the club that 100 per cent of the support fully trusted was being positioned as the man to lead the club out of the darkness and mess of recent times.

Let's look back to that team that won 4-0 at Perth and where they were as Rangers finally clinched a return to Scotland's Premier elite …

Allan McGregor

Left in the summer of 2012 for Turkish outfit Bursaspor where he had one sensational season before joining Hull City.

Kirk Broadfoot
Left in the summer of 2012 for Blackpool and signed for Rotherham at the expiry of his contract with the Seasiders.

Lee Wallace
Stuck with Rangers throughout the turbulent years and is now proud skipper of Mark Warburton's talented side. After promotion to the top league, he was rewarded with a contract that will keep him at Rangers until 2019.

Steven Whittaker
Jumped ship in the summer of 2012 and alienated a large section of the Rangers support with a misconceived media conference to justify his Ibrox exit alongside close pal Steven Naismith. Joined Norwich City and continued to be a Scotland regular.

Ross Perry
Highly-rated defender who has been transient since being released by Rangers in 2014. Struggled with a knee injury that seriously restricted his ability to fulfil his potential.

Kyle Bartley
Was on loan from Arsenal and on returning south moved on to Swansea and most recently hit the loan trail again with a switch to Leeds United.

Lee McCulloch
Stayed for the challenges despite a host of offers to move on and a player who regularly went to Sandy Jardine

for advice. Left Rangers after failing to win promotion through the play-offs in 2015. With his playing days running out and at the age of thirty-seven, Lee moved to Kilmarnock to take up the position of Assistant Manager.

Maurice Edu
Headed back to the US after indifferent spells with Stoke City and Bursaspor.

Sone Aluko
Came to Rangers from Aberdeen and left in mid 2012 for Hull City. His contract expired in 2016 and despite a history of injury problems there were suggestions of a Rangers return.

Alejandro Bedoya
The American internationalist struggled to make an impact at Ibrox but after penning a contract with French outfit Nantes in 2012, he has enjoyed a successful career.

Rhys McCabe
A controversial departure after breaking into the Rangers side in 2012. The Rangers support was very disappointed when he chose to leave without a fee and signed for Sheffield Wednesday. He later came back north and won promotion with Dunfermline.

Substitutes
Andy Little
Stayed to secure the Third Division championship and was also a League One winner in 2014. Moved on to Preston where injuries limited his opportunities and loans at Blackpool and Accrington Stanley followed.

David Healy
Fulfilled a boyhood dream by playing for Rangers. Moved on to Bury and is now managing Linfield in his

native Northern Ireland.

Barrie McKay

A real roundabout route to success. After his Perth debut and scoring Rangers' first goal in the league campaign of 2012/13, he found opportunities limited under Ally McCoist so went on loan to Morton and Raith Rovers to gain experience. Came back and flourished under the management of Mark Warburton, making himself a fan's favourite in the Championship-winning season and scoring a scorcher of a goal against Celtic in the epic Scottish Cup semi-final of 2016. Made his Scotland international debut in the summer of 2016.

As Sandy Jardine educated Charles Green on Rangers, it would have been impossible to envisage that such a major transformation would be evident from that day in May 2012.

Nobody too could have anticipated the boardroom strife that was to be all too evident and would bring such serious distractions to the club in its time of need.

Interestingly, Rangers Club historian David Mason recalls Sandy's black humour when things were going a bit wrong under Green: "We used to meet on the morning of match days to plan who would do what to entertain all our corporate guests with former players like Willie Henderson, Alan McLaren, Colin Stein and Bud Johnston always looking to take instruction from Sandy who would 'meet and greet' in whichever lounge while I would be giving tours of the trophy room. One Saturday, even before questions were being asked about Charles Green and his board's intentions for Rangers, Sandy came into the Blue Room singing 'there may be trouble ahead!' My goodness we all laughed at the time, but he had the measure of Green, that's for sure."

Soon, Charles Green was to lose the trust of the Rangers support and again the constant – the man the fans could relate to despite a host of characters coming and going in many guises in the club and in the boardroom in particular – was William Pullar Jardine.

Sandy Jardine had the trust of everyone with an interest in the Rangers situation.

His battle for Rangers was only starting.

4

JUST WILLIAM

On the last day of 1948, twin sons were born to proud parents Jimmy and Peggy Jardine. William and James Junior were born five minutes apart around midday on the 31st December 1948 with William first to arrive.

Dad Jimmy Jardine was a bus driver in Edinburgh while mum Peggy was a school dinner lady.

The Jardines lived in White Park, just off Gorgie Road, in the west of Edinburgh and when the twins started primary school at Balgreen, the family moved to Whitson Crescent. Now, while the distance between the two council houses was little more than a stone's throw, the move was significant in as much that it became the catalyst to launch a football career for young William and although James Junior also showed promise, Billy was the one that would go on and make a major impact on Scottish football, his skills being honed on the grass pitches of Saughton Park which was directly opposite the new Jardine residence.

Both Jardine boys were key members of the teams at Balgreen Primary and Tynecastle High School that won the Edinburgh Schools Cup at each level, with the finals of both tournaments being played at Tynecastle Park, home to Heart of Midlothian FC. As a young Hearts fan, this made the wins extra special for the lad who was to become Scottish football legend Sandy Jardine.

It was while playing primary school football that John Murphy first met Billy Jardine and a friendship was forged for life.

John Murphy would make the grade in professional football himself with Hibernian and at the age of just seventeen, travelled to New York for a seven-week tour with the Easter Road club, being drafted into the squad after Colin Stein, who would later be transferred to Rangers, pulled out through illness. But it was at Meggetland playing fields that John and Billy Jardine first crossed swords before either of them were teenagers. John remembers the occasion: "It was an Edinburgh Schools cup game. Billy was playing for Balgreen as was his twin brother Jamie and I was playing for Stenhouse Primary. We lost 5-2 and Billy scored two goals. He was playing outside right that day and I remember him being fast and wiry with a real shock of red hair, but most of all, I remember his determination. Even after all these years it sticks in my memory and despite Billy being so young, his determination was incredible. I had never seen such determination in my life before. I may have been on the losing side on the day but we were soon best friends and we played together on those Saughton pitches every day – all day – no matter the weather."

On Sundays, the Jardine boys would also join in for a match, sometimes of up to fifteen-a-side on the rugby pitch at Saughton. Good pals David Ross, Ian Cruikshanks and, of course, John Murphy, would all be there to make up the numbers. Incredibly, the four youngsters who were inseparable as teenagers all succeeded in playing football at a professional level. David Ross signed for Dundee, Ian Cruickshanks was taken on by Hearts with Murphy joining their biggest rivals across the city at Hibernian. Jamie Jardine played in Rangers' third team a few times in the old Combination Reserve League but was never offered a full-time contract but to be fair, by the age of fifteen and just out of high school, he had embarked on an apprenticeship as a joiner.

Jamie's twin, William, joined Rangers and was promptly nicknamed Sandy because of his flame-coloured locks.

John Murphy says in those days there were no other distractions for kids; it was just all about playing football. "Sundays were special, no age barriers or limit to the numbers that played and you had to grow up quickly in that school. We all worked on our skills and even if there were only three of us down the park we would play one versus one and one taking turns in goal. Sometimes we played 'barrie' where the trick was to play the ball off the crossbar from as many different angles as you could with both feet and controlling the ball as it came back to you off the woodwork. It definitely helped us all to improve and progress in the game."

John was delighted that Billy was given the chance at Rangers, especially as he had already been assured of a contract at Hibernian, but he also took a bit of a ribbing from his pal as Billy Jardine was a huge Hearts fan.

Sometimes Hearts would train on Saughton Enclosure which was adjacent to the park, but being fenced off, it was considered hallowed ground, as John confirms: "We would get chased if we tried to play there but when Hearts some-times trained at the Enclosure, we used to run on when they were finished and fire our cheap Woolworths footballs into the goal that always had nets up. What a thrill that was. I remember Billy asked Hearts legend Willie Bauld to sign his plastic football and he refused. Billy was devastated, but many years later when he was by then playing for Hearts, he reminded the man known as "The King" to Hearts fans and while he ribbed him, Billy (Sandy) never really forgave him."

John found it strange to get used to calling his friend Sandy rather than Billy. "He was Billy to everybody in Edinburgh, cronies, family and friends and while it was Davie Kinnear, the Rangers trainer, who first called him Sandy, it was Jim Baxter who made it stick, never calling Billy anything but Sandy and that was it. But to me he was Billy and it was the same for his wife Shona, she never called him anything but Billy. If the phone went at home and the caller asked for Billy, it was family or friends. If they asked for Sandy you could be sure it was a football related call."

John Murphy moved from Hibernian to sign for Morton and travelled with his good pal on the train every day from Haymarket to Queen Street. John Greig, Willie Mathieson and fringe player at Rangers Derek Trail were also regular travelling companions and again football was always the topic of conversation on the journey. "It was a bit surreal with me calling him Billy and the rest talking to him as Sandy but it never bothered him, he just went with the flow." But that was probably what William Pullar Jardine was all about. Sandy never changed from those days at Saughton and friendships that lasted with David, Ian and John right up until his untimely death.

John became Sandy's driver when his illness made getting behind the wheel himself impossible but will always remember the humility and thought that he had for others despite his own condition. "Billy never forgot his roots and while he was a favourite to thousands as Sandy, he was just William or Billy at home. He lived a simple life. Thursday night was dominoes night when we would meet up in the Liberton Inn and Billy would have one pint, or sometimes he would push the boat out and have three half pints. He liked his mince and tatties and every night he had a can of Fanta orange with his dinner. He loved his garden, and his lifestyle was as far removed from that of a top footballer as you could imagine."

John remembers the day his great friend confirmed his illness was terminal. "I drove to the house and as I parked my car I noticed both Billy and Shona's cars were still there. Shona opened the door and she was in tears. Billy then came over and confirmed the sad news. I gave him a huge cuddle and I was in tears as well. Billy then said 'dinnae be daft. If anything happens to me, as long as Shona and the kids are all right – that will be fine.' I have never met a stronger person in all of my life. I am privileged to have been his friend – Sandy to many but Billy to me. If I were ever in the trenches and wanted someone in the battle with me it would have been William Pullar Jardine. He was a very special person and I miss him dearly."

5

OUT OF THE BLUE
SIGNING FOR RANGERS

William Pullar Jardine was brought up within the distance of a long goal kick of Tynecastle Park, home to his boyhood heroes Heart of Midlothian FC, and he went to school at Tynecastle Secondary.

At the age of twelve, football dominated Billy Jardine's thoughts and while he held his own academically and 'O' Levels were within his grasp, he was determined to leave school at fifteen.

Billy was also captain of the school football team and had been converted from his first position as an outside right to centre forward. He was a regular goalscorer for his school and his under-15 team, North Merchiston Boys Club. In his autobiography of 1987 with former *Scotsman* journalist Mike Aitken, Sandy recalled scoring twelve goals in one match with twin brother Jamie scoring four in the same game and the story featuring in Edinburgh's Saturday sports special the *Pink News*. But Billy bettered this with an eighteen-goal haul, all in the first half, as his team set a half-time 36-0 advantage. The opponents that day refused to come out for the second half and young Billy was unable to add to his first-half goal-fest.

Billy tasted footballing success early when, as part of the

Edinburgh Primary School select, he won the Scottish Cup and at Tynecastle Secondary he won the National Schools Cup again for that age group.

It wasn't long before Billy Jardine was catching the eye of Hearts' scout Mr Tam Aitken who just happened to be the janitor at young master Jardine's school. Billy was soon training with the team he supported as a boy. However despite the obvious affinity to Hearts and being on their doorstep, the Gorgie club never offered even ground-staff terms to the fifteen-year-old. Billy started to consider that a career as a car mechanic may be a good option until out of the blue one Sunday evening his father came home and proclaimed, "You have the chance to become a professional footballer!" Billy was astonished when his father told him the club he would be joining was Rangers!

At fifteen years of age in 1964 and being from Edinburgh, Billy knew very little about Rangers and was, in his own words, "quite naive!" He had never even been to Ibrox and also knew nothing of the club's then signing policy. What Billy did know, and again in his own words, was that "they were the biggest and most powerful club in the country."

Billy had to report for pre-season training as part of the ground staff and he travelled by train from Edinburgh to Glasgow with George Rennie who was another youngster heading to Ibrox for the first time. Going through the front door and up the marble staircase – the same staircase where a bust of Sandy was positioned fifty-one years later – was an imposing task for any rookie and when he was introduced to Rangers manager Scot Symon, Billy could only whisper, "Hello, sir."

Symon looked at his latest new recruit and immediately intimated that Mr Jardine had broken the first rule of the club by not wearing a tie! Billy didn't own a tie and despite turning up in his only suit and wearing a brand new casual sports shirt his Mum had bought specially for the occasion, Billy made sure he borrowed a tie from his dad James before he returned for his second day at Rangers.

He didn't make the same mistake again.

Soon young Billy had new travelling companions from Edinburgh when he joined the train at Haymarket station. Already on board for the 08:30 from Waverley were first-team stars and Ibrox icons John Greig, Ralph Brand and Jimmy Millar. What an experience that was. Every journey was spent listening and learning about what Rangers were about and what it was like to play in Scot Symon's first team.

Week one of training was fairly relaxed with baseball, basketball and crab football the order of the day. Even the second week didn't prove overly taxing with runs or pounding the track, but passing drills were the highlight with players from all three Rangers teams, including the third team who played in the Combination Reserve League, out in force in the Albion training ground across the road from Ibrox. Billy Jardine couldn't believe it when he was teamed up with Jim Baxter for the routine that saw the two players stand around thirty yards apart and bounce passes back and forth in rhythm to each other. Even Billy knew Baxter! He was the most famous player in Scotland at the time and the man who had scored two goals at Wembley just one year before as ten-man Scotland beat England after another Ranger Eric Caldow had been carried off with a broken leg.

Billy diligently upped his game and consistently delivered inch-perfect passes to 'Stanley' as he was known to his teammates, but the accuracy of the return balls from Slim Jim saw young Jardine chasing the wayward and often overhit balls, and it took some time for the penny to drop with Billy that it was a deliberate ploy on Baxter's part to minimise the effort he had to put in on the training ground. It was fairly public knowledge that Jim Baxter – genius that he was – was not a particularly industrious trainer. Of course, Billy was expending energy and ultimately returned a pass to Jim that went astray, Baxter was quick to give the youngster dog's abuse! It was a steep learning curve being a Ranger!

It wasn't all about spending time with international foot-ballers though and all the traditional duties and chores had to be attended to. Cleaning boots was a task that took time and woe betide anyone who didn't get the perfect shine on the size nines of skipper Bobby Shearer or Captain Cutlass as he liked to be called.

Full-time professional contracts were not available to players until they turned seventeen and at the age of fifteen, Billy was paid the going rate for his age of £5 per week wages and an additional £5 travelling expenses.

Rangers decided to farm young Jardine out to juvenile side United Crossroads and that brought about its own challenges. Since his school days, Billy was in the habit of winning games often by crushing margins but at United, it was a different story as they struggled in most matches even with the talents of young Jardine, now operating in their midfield. Regular Saturday defeats were never mentioned when Billy went back to Ibrox on a Monday.

In 1965 and at the age of sixteen, young Jardine was called up to Rangers' third team after his first year apprenticeship on the ground staff, and made his first appearance in light blue in a pre-season friendly on the island of Cumbrae. Millport was the venue.

Rangers travelled with the great Jock 'Tiger' Shaw in charge. Jock had been a Rangers player for fifteen years before he retired and captained the club for twelve of those years. He was later to serve the club as the groundsman after his stint as trainer with the third team but he basi-cally committed himself to Rangers for what was almost a lifetime.

Billy incurred his wrath on his first match day just like he had with Scot Symon on his first day at Ibrox. This time, however, Sandy managed to miss the start of the match having been accidentally locked in the toilet when the teams left the dressing room. No damage was done and Rangers' third eleven headed back for the ferry having won 3-2.

Over that second season on the Rangers payroll, Sandy

featured fairly regularly in the third team as did young Aberdonian Colin Jackson, who also ultimately made the transition to the first team, and the pair shared many successes together over all their years at Rangers. Willie Johnston was also part of that group for a short spell but he was more than a year older than Sandy and progressed to the second team and was, in fact, soon in Scot Symon's first team and was representing Scotland as a full internationalist at just eighteen!

On Hogmanay 1965, William Pullar Jardine turned seventeen and celebrated his birthday by signing a full professional contract at Rangers. The deal was agreed when James Jardine accompanied his son William up the marble staircase to the office of Scot Symon. A signing on fee of £750 was agreed and his weekly wage improved to £11. His £5 travelling expenses remained unchanged. It seemed a handsome reward to a young man who only wanted to play senior football and was certainly not motivated by money.

However, before the terms were finalised, Sandy, with a number of third-team players, had visited the famous St Enoch hotel in Glasgow which was often used as a base by Rangers where members of the first team and even some from the second team were allowed to dine from the à la carte menu. This privilege did not extend to members of Rangers' third-tier playing staff. As the boys were tucking in to a veritable feast, manager Scot Symon and the first-team squad came into the dining room. Aghast at the sight of his youngest players enjoying the finest the hotel had to offer, Scot Symon declared all were to see him in his office in the morning.

Next day the manager confirmed all the boys involved were to be fined one week's wages. The only exception was young Mr Jardine who got off scot-free. Symon's decision may have been influenced by the commitment Rangers had in securing Billy's signature on that professional form.

In those days of the '60s, the young Rangers players got to train with the top team, and senior professionals were always quick to encourage and pass on tips to those who wanted to learn. Billy Jardine was hungry for all the knowledge he could glean from guys like Jimmy Millar and Davie Wilson and even John Greig who wasn't that much older than Billy himself.

It was now time for Billy to make the step up to the reserve side. It was a team full of emerging young talent and included Willie Mathieson, Colin Jackson and Alex Willoughby with experienced campaigners like goalkeeper Billy Ritchie, Davie Wilson and George McLean also featuring regularly when they couldn't find a place in the first team.

Jardine had caught manager Symon's eye and he highlighted the youngster to the media as the young player most likely to break through in season 1966/67. It was around this time that the nickname 'Sandy' was struck. Trainer Davie Kinnear christened Billy as Sandy because of the natural colour of his hair and thereafter it just stuck. Willie or Billy was a pretty common name at Ibrox with Ritchie, Henderson & Johnston all with the same Christian name so Sandy made sense to differentiate, and it was how Billy began to be addressed at the club and in games. It did cause confusion with fans who wanted autographs and when they noticed the signature said Billy Jardine and not Sandy, it wasn't just this author who thought Rangers had two Jardines on the playing staff.

Rangers reserves was another key part of Sandy's football development and his performances there soon had him being invited to train with the first team. With each session improvements in his game were evident.

In fact, so impressive were young Jardine's performances in training games that John Greig, who was not only club captain but Scotland captain, was convinced Sandy was destined for the top and bet his young protégé £1 – and remember, Sandy was only earning £11 per week so it was a fair amount of money – that he would make the breakthrough soon and certainly before his nineteenth birthday.

Sandy was less than convinced and had set his own goal of playing first-team football by 1968. Sandy's call to arms in February 1967 after the Berwick fiasco may have been a dream come true for the Edinburgh youngster but it also cost him £1 as he lost his wager with skipper Greig.

Before that first start against Hearts at Ibrox on 4th February 1967, Sandy had been gradually introduced to the first-team squad, often travelling with the team as the spare man, but he did make the bench and again it was Hearts in opposition. This time the game was at Tynecastle and it was a momentous day for the young Jardine who had played football in the streets all round the famous Hearts stadium not that many years before, usually pretending to be Hearts legend Willie Bauld. Now he was actually lining up against his team but unfortunately, this time as twelfth man he wouldn't get the call from the bench. This was the stadium where Sandy used to stand on the terraces in awe of the players in the famous maroon jersey. It was much later in his career that Sandy actually got to wear Hearts colours himself.

Sandy's inclusion in the first-team squad was being carefully engineered by manager Scot Symon and he soaked up all the experience with every minute spent with players like Greig, Provan, McKinnon, Dave Smith and Davie Wilson. Scot Symon continued Sandy's development with a place on the bench in the 1966 League Cup semi-final at Hampden and although it took two games for Rangers to overcome Aberdeen, winning 2-0 in a replay after the sides had been tied at 2-2 in the first match, Sandy Jardine's services were not called into action and he had to settle for being an unused sub.

When Rangers contested the final against Celtic just five days after the second Aberdeen match, Davie Wilson replaced him as twelfth man.

The first full debut was surely only a matter of time and in confirmation of Sandy's growing confidence and involvement with the first team, he summoned up the courage just after his eighteenth birthday to request a pay rise from manager Symon. Sandy was astounded when the manager said he would consider his request and was even more taken aback when his wages were almost immediately increased to £15 per week.

In the week leading up to Rangers' visit to the border town of Berwick for the now infamous cup tie, Sandy Jardine had been struggling with a flu virus and was unable to turn out for the reserves on the same day. Instead, Sandy accompanied his father James to Tynecastle to take in Hearts' match with Dundee United. Very quickly after the full-time whistle at Gorgie, word was coming through about the shock result from Berwick. Nobody could believe the scoreline at first but it soon became apparent that Scottish football had just delivered the shock of the century with lowly Berwick Rangers knocking the mighty Glasgow Rangers out of the Scottish Cup.

As Sandy made the short walk home from Tynecastle, little did he think what significance that infamous Rangers defeat would have on his career.

On Monday morning, Sandy reported to Ibrox for training in the normal fashion and it was a gloomy atmosphere that met him. However, he was immediately told to lift his kit from the reserve changing room and take a peg with the first team. The ill wind of Berwick was to provide a welcome window of opportunity for William Pullar Jardine.

For the next match in the wake of the Berwick disaster and which by a strange quirk of fate saw Heart of Midlothian coming to Ibrox, Sandy Jardine was given his first starting jersey.

A soon-to-be-great Ranger was taking his first steps in a stellar career that would see him play a further 673 games for the club and secure a well-deserved place in the Rangers Hall of Fame.

6

BERWICK BOMBSHELL
TRANSITION TIME AT IBROX

The 28th of January 1967 will go down in the history of Rangers Football Club as one of their blackest ever days on a football field, and the result from the cup tie that day in Berwick sent shock waves throughout football and left a scar of a scoreline that Rangers will carry for life.

Thirteen thousand, three hundred and sixty-five people witnessed it, in Shielfield Park in the town of Berwick that straddles the Scottish and English border: Berwick Rangers 1 Rangers 0.

Berwick should have been lambs to the slaughter. Rangers had nineteen times previously won the Scottish Cup while the 'Wee Rangers' had only joined the Scottish Football League in 1955, a mere twelve years before this epic first-round tie when Rangers travelled south to start the defence of Scotland's foremost cup competition, and only a matter of months after they had wrestled the cup back from Celtic the previous year taking a replay and a single goal. The only goal in 120 minutes of football came from Danish full-back Kai Johansen. Celtic had lifted the trophy in 1965 but Rangers had almost made it their own with three consecutive wins in 1962, 1963 and 1964.

It was only the fourth ever meeting between the sides and the Glasgow giants had never lost to their namesakes, previously having scored ten in their previous encounters and conceded only two.

To book their place in the history-changing cup tie, Berwick had to negotiate two previous preliminary rounds which they did with great aplomb, beating Vale of Leithen 8-1 away from home and following up that win with a comfortable 2-0 success over Forfar Athletic just three weeks before they entertained Scot Symon's side with experienced and seasoned internationalists in every department.

At the time of the match, Rangers were in second place in the Scottish League Division One while Berwick were struggling in tenth spot in League Division Two.

Berwick Rangers were, of course, a team entirely composed of part-timers.

Rangers started with a team that had been over the course before. A team Symon had total trust in.

Norrie Martin in goal, Kai Johansen and Dave Provan as full-backs, a halfback line of John Greig, Ronnie McKinnon and the cultured Dave Smith who had been signed the season before from Aberdeen. Flying wingers Henderson & Johnston were expected to fire the ammunition for Alex Smith, Jim Forrest and George McLean who were a very capable goal threat and completed the Rangers starting eleven who were shoehorned into the cramped visitors' dressing room, a far cry from the luxury of Ibrox. Davie Wilson was on the bench and highlighted the Rangers' strengths with ten of the twelve players stripped all being full internationalists.

In the home dressing room, a former jungle fighter was plotting Rangers' downfall. Jock Wallace was manager of the home team. Yes, the same Jock Wallace who was later to have a sensational career as manager of Glasgow Rangers: among a host of trophies secured during his tenure, his double winning trebles achievements – delivering a clean sweep of domestic honours in Scotland in seasons 1975/76 and again in 1977/78 – remains a record no Rangers manager since has been able to equal.

Not content in managing the Wee Rangers that day, Wallace engineered the win while keeping a clean sheet in goal despite Rangers throwing everything at him as they chased the game, having gone behind to a goal from former Motherwell inside forward Sammy Reid with the clock showing thirty-two minutes.

For the record that day Berwick lined up:

>   Jock Wallace
>   Gordon Haig
>   Jim Kilgannon
>   Ian Riddell
>   Russell Craig
>   Doug Coutts
>   Tommy Lumsden
>   'Goalscorer' Reid
>   George Christie
>   Kenny Dowds
>   Alan Ainslie
>   Andy Rogers was on the bench.

It was a team made up of joiners, sales representatives and engineers among other full-time professionals who played to supplement their income or just for enjoyment. Others had played at a higher level and were winding down their footballing careers.

Jock Wallace was only thirty-one years of age and that January day was to propel him to a full-time career in coaching and football management.

Rangers started brightly and attacked their second-division opponents from the first whistle. Three corners in the opening five minutes confirm the Light Blues' supremacy. Henderson, Alex Smith and Johnston all went close to claiming the opener but a combination of inspired goalkeeping from Wallace and a timely intervention from Coutts kept Rangers out. Referee Eddie Thomson also waived away appeals for a penalty when Willie Henderson was upended by Jim Kilgannon in the box. Kilgannon's two brothers, Bill and John, had played for Rangers' biggest rivals Celtic and now sibling Jim welcomed the opportunity to mix it with the big boys, but he was given the benefit of the doubt by the Edinburgh-based man in the middle and Berwick took full advantage by scoring at the other end shortly after.

Winger Kenny Dowds combined with former East Fife frontman George Christie to carve open Rangers' dithering defence, allowing Sammy Reid clear sight of goal to blast the ball beyond the despairing dive of Norrie Martin and into the net, having taken a deflection off the inside of the post.

It was all against the run of play and thirteen minutes short of the interval. It could have got worse for Rangers just two minutes later but centre forward Christie half hit his shot from close range and Martin was able to make the save.

Rangers were shell-shocked and offered little to trouble Wallace in Berwick's goal for the remainder of the first period with the exception of a drive from John Greig that went narrowly wide of the target.

Things got even worse for Rangers after the restart when they lost the services of Willie Johnston whose pace had been causing problems for the home side. Johnston raced in on goal and as he looked to get his shot away, he was blocked by the huge presence of the out-rushing Berwick Keeper-Manager Jock Wallace. Willie Johnston collapsed in the collision and the chance was lost. More worrying for Rangers though was that Johnston had broken his leg in the clash and had to be stretchered off. There was no question of Wallace's challenge being illegal, it was two committed players going for the same ball but Johnston took the brunt and landed awkwardly. Wee Bud's (as Rangers teammates called him) match was over. But surely his replacement from the substitutes bench, Davie Wilson, would be the talisman Rangers needed? After all, Wilson had scored all three goals against Berwick when the teams met here at the same venue in Rangers' 3-1 cup victory in 1960.

Wilson weaved his magic and, along with McLean and John Greig again, came close but could not penetrate the home side's goal.

It wasn't all one-way traffic however and Berwick were playing with confidence from their single goal lead. Left winger Alan Ainslie brought out a fine save from Norrie Martin then the same player looked on in agony as he slammed his close-range shot against the post. At the other end, Wallace was struggling to see properly as the second half wore on as he had lost a contact lens on the mud heap of a pitch as he bravely battled to keep Rangers at bay.

Rangers were desperate and with the clock showing ninety minutes, John Greig pleaded with referee Thomson to add on another couple of minutes but was dismissed by the official with the suggestion that he had already played four minutes over time.

When the final whistle blew and Berwick were confirmed winners by that solitary Sammy Reid first-half strike, it was the first time in thirty years that Rangers had lost to a second division club. After the match, Ibrox Captain John Greig sportingly shook hands with every Berwick player as they left the field of play before proclaiming the result as 'probably the worst result in the history of our club.'

National newspaper *The Scotsman* went further and reported the events of Shielfield Park from the 28th January 1967 as "the most ludicrous, the weirdest, the most astonishing result ever returned in Scottish football."

Dave Smith, who was to remain at Rangers for a further seven seasons and later managed Berwick Rangers himself recalls: "No doubt about it, Berwick played out of their skins that day. The pitch didn't help as it was like a quagmire but no excuses, we didn't turn up and paid the penalty.

"Big Jock had them fired up and organised while we just maybe took it that we only had to turn up to win. The bus journey back to Glasgow is one I'll never forget. The supporters, too, were in a state of disbelief. This just didn't happen to Glasgow Rangers."

Dave's namesake Alex Smith, who had joined Rangers from Dunfermline only five months before, remembers: "It's not a game I want to remember but it's impossible to forget. It was a terrible game and we got what we deserved."

The fallout from the result down Ibrox way was huge and it signalled the end of careers at Rangers for strikers Jim Forrest and George McLean. Neither would ever play for Rangers again and within a matter of weeks (no transfer windows in those days) they were shipped out to Preston North End and Dundee respectively.

Both Forrest and McLean had been prolific goalscorers in their time at Rangers but they carried the responsibility for the shameful cup exit and were effectively made scapegoats for the defeat.

However, this knee-jerk decision may have had further serious ramifications for the club before the season was out and a number of senior players believed axing two instinctive goalscorers and regular match winners was a mistake. Midfield schemer Dave Smith was one who was in that corner. "It was a real blunder. Between Jim and George we lost probably more than forty goals that season. We just didn't have the quality to replace them immediately and that was never more obvious than when we made it to the European Cup Winners' Cup final later that year. We just had no fire power and I believe it cost us the trophy."

Alex Smith agreed with his teammate. "The two boys carried the can but everybody was to blame. Scot Symon made Jim (Forrest) and big George (McLean) the scapegoats."

The Berwick loss probably signalled the beginning of the end too for Rangers manager Scot Symon although it was a number of months later that the board of directors made that decision.

Symon was scathing in his after-match comments telling the assembled press: "Our prestige has received a shattering blow. This is the worst result in the club's history and it's there now in the record books and these players took part in the game. That cannot be forgotten."

Two players out of the squad was to create opportunities for others.

Step forward one William Pullar (Sandy) Jardine who was immediately promoted from the reserve dressing room to fill the gap and it came within one month of him celebrating his eighteenth birthday.

The squad was also augmented later that year when Scot Symon used the Forrest and McLean funds to purchase Alex Ferguson from Dunfermline Athletic for sixty-five thousand pounds and set a new record transfer fee between two Scottish clubs.

But that January day belonged to Berwick and although he didn't know it at the time, Jock Wallace had put himself in the shop window as a young coach with plenty to offer. Many years later and after a spell at Heart of Midlothian, Wallace was with the big Rangers of the Scottish game and the disaster of Berwick was still a major carbuncle on the tapestry of a rich Rangers history.

Sammy Reid, who made his own mark in history that day, was back at his 'day job' within twenty-four hours of the epic win for a Sunday shift in an engineering business in Lanarkshire. He had to make up for time he had been given off during the previous week to train for the cup match against Rangers.

For the record, Berwick Rangers were eliminated from the cup in the next round going down 1-0 to Hibernian at Easter Road.

Meanwhile, elsewhere in the capital, young Sandy Jardine was now very much part of manager Scot Symon's first-team squad and laying foundations for a career that he could only have dreamed of when he put pen to paper as a Ranger at the tender age of fifteen.

Seven days after the bombshell of Berwick, Jardine got his Rangers first team start against his boyhood heroes Heart of Midlothian. Rangers showed great character and bounced back in that match at Ibrox with a 5-1 win against the Tynecastle side, with Jardine making his debut at right half.

Sandy went on and made nineteen appearances that season, scoring two goals and he even made the starting eleven as Rangers contested the European Cup Winners' Cup final in Nuremburg against crack German outfit Bayern Munich.

It was a baptism of fire for the flame-haired youngster and not many would have suggested that Sandy was set to be a Ranger for just about the rest of his life.

Allan Herron, Scotlands foremost football writer then with the *Evening Citizen*, recounts the event that stunned Scottish football: "When Sammy Reid hit his left foot shot past Norrie Martin in the Rangers goal on the English turf of Berwick on January 27, 1967, in the thirty-fifth minute, it proved to be not only the biggest upset in Scottish Cup history but a soccer tsunami in the minds of those who were in control at Ibrox and the many thousands who pledged their support.

"Defeat by a single goal in the first round of the Cup from a wee team, somewhere near the river Tweed! A disaster, humiliating, embarrassing and totally unacceptable to those who pounded the pavements of Copland Road, week in and week out. However for one Rangers player, an eighteen-year-old reserve, it proved a defining moment.

"The Cup defeat meant that heads would roll. The scapegoats were strikers George 'Dandy' McLean and Jim Forrest. They had failed to put the ball past Berwick's player manager, 'keeper Jock Wallace, so they had to go. No credit then for Jock, later to become the Ibrox manager, for keeping a clean sheet?

"McLean, sold to Dundee, and Forrest, sold to Preston North End, had played their last game in a Rangers strip.

Was the decision made by manager Scot Symon? Maybe not. The Rangers Press Officer was Willie Allison, a former sports writer. It was he who met with Chairman John Lawrence and insisted that McLean and Forrest must never again play for the club.

"Symon had no alternative but to reshape his team. Sandy Jardine, a very promising versatile reserve, suddenly found himself a first-team player, making his debut at right half against Hearts at Tynecastle in a 5-1 victory. It was the start of an historic and quite legendary career. He finished that season as a first-team pick, scored his first goal against Ayr United, hit a twenty-five-yard screamer in a 2-2 draw with Celtic at Ibrox in front of a 78,000 crowd and played against Bayern Munich in the final of the European Cup Winners' Cup in Nuremberg. And there was more to come. Much more.

"Was the winter of discontent now over for Rangers? Not quite. In that European final Rangers found themselves without a recognised centre forward, and used the powerful, hard-working Roger Hynd as their main striker. It didn't work. One wonders what would have happened if Jim Forrest, a fleet-footed natural striker and the main victim of the Berwick defeat, had not been sent packing and given the chance of a rehab?

"We'll never know. But what we do know is that Sandy Jardine went on and had a most wonderful career."

7

EUROPEAN CAMPAIGN
THE ROUTE TO ANOTHER FINAL

After being drafted into Scot Symon's first team squad following the humiliation of Berwick, Sandy Jardine played nineteen games until the end of that season and scored two goals. His first goal came on the 18th of March 1967 in a league match against Ayr United in front of a crowd in excess of 11,000 at Somerset Park.

By the time Jardine was making his mark, Rangers were already progressing in Europe and five of Sandy's nineteen appearances in that debut season came against European opposition as Rangers carved a track to their second ever European final.

Experienced teammate Alex Smith wasn't at all surprised by Sandy's elevation to the first team after Berwick. "Sandy was a raw young laddie but that enthusiasm was just what was required after being knocked out the cup," he said.

"John Greig had kind of mentored Sandy so he fitted in easily and while he wasn't short of confidence, he was never cocky and soon Sandy gained and deserved respect just as he had always shown such great respect for the people he played with."

Sandy's first taste of continental opposition came on the

1st of March 1967 in the European Cup quarter final first leg tie against top Spanish side Real Zaragoza at Ibrox.

Leading up to that double header against the Spaniards, Rangers had beaten Borussia Dortmund in the previous round after starting the campaign against Northern Irish opposition in the form of Glentoran.

In Belfast, Rangers settled for a 1-1 draw with George McLean's strike cancelled out by a late counter from Glentoran's Sinclair, but the Light Blues quickly got the job done at Ibrox with a 4-0 rout, with Willie Johnston, Dave Smith, Dennis Setterington and George McLean all on target.

That set up a two-legged second-round tie against German opposition – just like Rangers' previous European sojourn that led them to the final six years before. On route to that 1961 final, they had demolished Borussia Mönchengladbach 11-0 on aggregate. This time it was the Borussia of Dortmund they faced. It was a real end to end encounter in the first leg at Ibrox with Rangers winning 2-1. Kai Johansen and Alex Smith were scorers for the home side but Trimholdt pulled one back for the visitors to set up a precarious return meeting in Germany. Rangers put in a really determined defensive shift to protect their single goal advantage and even after losing Bobby Watson to injury and playing the match out with ten men, they managed to keep Borussia out and were relieved when the final whistle blew with the teams still tied at 0-0.

That match against Mönchengladbach was played in December 1966 and the tournament went into winter cold storage until March of the following year.

The bombshell of Berwick would change things at Ibrox by the time Real Zaragoza came to town.

Willie Henderson thought that was to Rangers' advantage. "No doubt about it, we were all despondent after being knocked out the Scottish cup but it didn't last long. Sandy coming in helped and Scot Symon certainly stirred things up by a couple of his changes.

"Sandy was always positive, whatever he was doing, and while he was still a teenager, I was only twenty-three myself, I like to think we both had old heads on young shoulders. Sandy had slipped into the team like he had played there all his life and he wasn't fazed at all by the prospect of moving up a gear to play in Europe."

For Sandy Jardine's first continental game, the atmosphere was electric under the old Ibrox floodlights. Two goals in the first half from Dave Smith and Alex Willoughby put Rangers in a strong position for a trip to northern Spain. It was almost a fairy tale start to European football for Jardine on a night when the elements made flowing football impossible with driving sleet enclosing Ibrox. With only five minutes on the clock, Sandy fired a speculative shot on target that the Spanish goalkeeper managed to push on to the post before it was cleared to safety.

The starting line-up that night showed only two changes from the team that later would contest the final, with Davie Wilson in for Willie Johnston who was recovering from a broken leg received in the match at Berwick, while Alex Willoughby led the line. Like Jardine, Willoughby became a fixture in the Rangers side after the Scottish Cup elimination that year and despite notching seventeen goals between his introduction and the European final scheduled for Nuremberg in May, you can understand the bemusement of many that Hynd got the nod against Bayern Munich and Willoughby wasn't even stripped.

Three weeks after the first game against Real Zaragoza, Rangers went down by the same scoreline in La Romareda Stadium as they had recorded in their favour at Ibrox. Lapeta fired home a first-half free kick then the tie was levelled by Santos from the penalty spot after John Greig had handled in the box. 2-0 for the Spaniards meant 2-2 on aggregate and it would take a toss of a coin to determine which club would go through to the semi-finals as neither side could score in the thirty minutes of extra time. However, Dave Smith did miss a penalty kick in time added on and nerves were on edge as the referee brought the captains together to spin the decisive coin.

John Greig and manager Scot Symon got together and collectively elected to call 'tails', which was represented by the side of the two-French-franc coin that had the figure '2' as its centrepiece.

The referee spun the coin and it floated in the wind before he grabbed it almost as it touched the ground. Both captains looked on anxiously and as the referee opened his palm the number two of the French coin was facing skywards. Greig and Symon hugged and leapt in the air while Trainer Davie Kinnear ran to the dressing room to pass on the good news to the players who had chosen not to watch, that Rangers were in the semi-final! Willie Henderson had a ringside view of proceedings and set off doing cartwheels of joy when he realised his skipper had called it correctly. After the initial celebrations, somehow Davie Kinnear managed to persuade French referee Michel Kitabjian to part with the coin that came down luckily in Rangers' favour and presented it to John Greig as a special memento from a special night in Europe.

Midfielder turned frontman, Alex Smith, was one who couldn't watch the toss of the coin escapade. "Can you imagine nowadays tossing a coin for a place in a European Cup semi-final? We were exhausted as it was a warm evening in northern Spain and some of us couldn't bear to watch after a demanding 120-minute game so we headed off to the dressing room to cool down.

"Next thing I remember was the door bursting open and wee Willie Henderson shouting 'We're through! We're through!'"

Next up for Rangers was a trip to Bulgaria where PFC Slavia Sofia were the opposition. Davie Wilson scored in thirty-six minutes after Alex Willoughby forced an error from the home goalkeeper, but Rangers had to weather a storm from Sofia who were playing in an all-white playing kit in homage to the great Real Madrid side of that era.

Norrie Martin was in inspired form between the sticks for Rangers and, against all odds, kept a clean sheet in the Vasil Levski National stadium to give Rangers a slender but valuable advantage to take into the second leg at Ibrox three weeks later.

A packed Ibrox watched Rangers play a high line pressing game with the athletic Jardine wearing number four and covering every blade of grass for the cause. Rangers' pressure paid off and it was Willie Henderson who fired the ball high into the Slavia Sofia net on the half hour mark after good combination play by Roger Hynd and Willie Johnston. Added to the first leg counter, it was enough to send Rangers into the final with a fine 2-0 aggregate victory, and the sense of achievement was not lost on the 71,000 crowd, many of whom invaded the pitch to celebrate.

Willie Henderson remembers the campaign. "It was incredible. We just felt at ease playing in Europe and Sandy had been a great addition to the squad. We were still quite a young team and we only operated with a small squad of players with Sandy coming into the group for the quarter finals, but we had some good results in the tournament even before then."

Rangers had booked their place in their second ever European final.

It was looking like a bizarre but welcome end to a season that had been turned on its head on that January day at Berwick, which was without question widely acknowledged as Rangers worst-ever result.

Now pretty much the same group of players had the chance to make amends.

It had been a whirlwind introduction to the European football scene for Sandy Jardine. He had played four games, and despite experiencing defeat in Spain, the aggregate result and progress in the tournament more than made up for that disappointment.

8

BEATEN BY BAYERN
ANOTHER FINAL DISAPPOINTMENT

The final months of the 1966/67 football season truly were the halcyon days for the Scottish game.

Rangers had booked their place in the final of the European Cup Winners' Cup for the second time in their history and the shock Scottish Cup defeat at Berwick surely felt like a lifetime away.

However, on the domestic front, it was a barren season for the Ibrox men as it was an all-conquering Celtic side under Jock Stein that swept everything before them to claim all five trophies they contested that season.

Celtic defended their League title and added both the Scottish and the League Cups to secure the treble. Rangers had been beaten by the Parkhead side in the League Cup final with the only goal of the game coming from Bobby Lennox. With Rangers' early elimination from the Scottish Cup, Celtic marched on and saw off the challenge of Aberdeen in the final. It was Celtic's nineteenth success in the Scottish Cup and brought them level with Rangers who were also nineteen times winners.

It wasn't a bad end to the season too on the international front with Bobby Brown in charge. Scotland were inspired by a virtuoso performance from ex-Ranger Jim Baxter to beat World Cup holders England on their own patch. The records show a 3-2 win for the Scots, but the margin of victory was much wider than the scoreline suggests. Law, Lennox and McCalliog were the Scotland scorers with Rangers represented by John Greig and Ronnie McKinnon while Simpson, Gemmell, Wallace and Bobby Lennox were the Celtic players in evidence.

In the rapidly advancing European arena Scottish clubs also excelled.

Celtic became the first British club to win the European Cup beating Inter Milan 2-0 in Lisbon on the 25th of May 1967 and Rangers were scheduled to try and deliver the double for Glasgow, with their Cup Winners' Cup final due to be played in Nuremburg against emerging giants Bayern Munich just six days after that huge Celtic success.

In the third European tournament in those days, the Inter-Cities Fairs Cup, Kilmarnock reached the semi-finals before losing out to Leeds United who themselves failed at the final hurdle to Dinamo Zagreb, while Dundee United in their first European sojourn, eliminated cup holders Barcelona both home and away before going out to Italian giants Juventus in the next round.

On League business, Rangers could only finish second to Celtic with the gap a mere three points but it's no coincidence that Rangers finished with nineteen fewer league goals scored than their biggest rivals, and minds drift back to Dave Smith's comments about a lack of fire power with Forrest and McLean being jettisoned after the embarrassment of Berwick. Perhaps a case of what might have been? For the record, Clyde finished third that season in Scotland's top flight league albeit they were a distant fourteen points adrift of champions Celtic.

Rangers still had the opportunity, however, to rescue something from their season. The European Cup Winners' Cup final beckoned.

On the way to the final Rangers had beaten Glentoran,

Borussia Dortmund, Real Zaragoza & PFC Slavia Sofia with a young Sandy Jardine a fixture in the side since his introduction in February.

This was Rangers' second tilt at Europe's second club trophy having lost their previous final of 1961 to Fiorentina in what was the tournament's inaugural season, and indeed, the only time the final was played over two legs. Unfortunately, Rangers lost both home and away, going down 2-0 at Ibrox and 2-1 in the Comunale Stadium in Florence.

Rangers fans travelled in hope that this would be their year although Bayern had the advantage of the game being played on their home soil albeit in Nuremburg, but the Städtisches Stadion was only 170 kilometres away from their own home in Munich.

To get to the final, Bayern defeated TJ Tatran Prešov from the then Czechoslovakia, Ireland's Shamrock Rovers and Austria's SK Rapid Wien in the quarter finals. Then they booked their place in Nuremburg, winning home and away with a 5-1 aggregate victory over Belgium's Standard Liège.

It was to be Bayern Munich's first ever European Final and their team included a number of players who were to become legends on the world stage. These included Sepp Maier, Franz Beckenbauer and Gerd Muller.

That night on the 31st May 1967 the teams lined up:

BAYERN MUNICH
Sepp Maier
Peter Kupferschmidt
Werner Olk
Franz Roth
Franz Beckenbauer
Hans Nowak
Rudolf Nafziger
Rainer Ohlhauser
Gerd Müller
Dieter Koulmann
Dieter Brenniger

RANGERS
Norrie Martin
Kai Johansen
Davy Provan
Sandy Jardine
Ronnie McKinnon
John Greig
Willie Henderson
Dave Smith
Roger Hynd
Alex Smith
Willie Johnston

In effect, manager Scot Symon had made only two changes from the team that lost to Berwick four months before, with Roger Hynd coming in for Jim Forrest and the teenage Jardine replacing George McLean.

The pressure was on the Light Blues, with Celtic having broken new ground by lifting a European trophy less than a week before. Jock Stein had used a team of totally home grown talent all born within a thirty-mile radius of Celtic Park. Scot Symon deployed one foreigner in his ranks that night, Danish internationalist Kai Johansen.

Alex Smith (no relation to teammate Dave), signed from Dunfermline less than a year before, was given the job that night as the second striker to support Roger Hynd who was really a defensive midfielder by trade. Although Alex had finished top scorer in that season with twenty-three goals, he was not an out and out centre forward in the old fashioned way. Hynd had scored a few goals for Rangers reserves in the final weeks of the season and the twenty-five-year-old journeyman – whose uncle was legendary Liverpool boss Bill Shankly – was given the starting jersey ahead of natural frontman Alex Willoughby who had been in fine scoring form in the preceding period.

Willoughby was also a full cousin of the discarded Jim Forrest and took his relegation from the side as a personal slight, and later left Rangers for Aberdeen where he again teamed up with his cousin Forrest.

Roger Hynd had been a PE teacher and had the build of a light heavyweight boxer. Scot Symon appeared to prefer the physical presence of Hynd to the cuter and silkier skills of Willoughby against the athletic German defenders. It almost paid off when Hynd had the ball in the net but it was disallowed by Italian Referee Concetto Lo Bello, who adjudged the Rangers man to have handled the ball before despatching it beyond Maier in the German goal.

Rangers probably had the better of the first-half exchanges while Bayern were stronger in the second. However, after ninety minutes, the scoreline remained blank and the teams were headed for extra time.

Into the second period of the extra thirty minutes, Rangers conceded the only goal of the game and it was enough to ensure the trophy stayed in Germany.

Bayern were strong and physically imposing in the later stages with Franz Roth moving from his midfield role to add power to the attack, and when Rangers failed to clear a ball inside their own eighteen-yard box, Roth saw the opportunity as Rangers defenders hesitated and he forced the ball beyond Norrie Martin from close range.

Roger Hynd had a great chance for Rangers after Dave Smith set him up but the auxiliary frontman snatched at it and effectively the game was lost.

Alex Smith, who was asked to provide the goal threat that night with Roger Hynd, admits: "I had no pace, and you need pace up front especially against that calibre of opposition. Big Roger was the same, as we weren't natural centre forwards. Jim Forrest and George McLean were but maybe Symon was too quick to get rid of them." With 23 goals and, despite finishing that season as Rangers' top scorer, Alex Smith was sold on to Aberdeen where he finished his career, not as a striker, but as a midfielder as he would be called in the modern game.

After the event, then Rangers Chairman John Lawrence

was critical of the Rangers side and manager Scot Symon's selection, describing the Light Blues' forward line as "make-shift" and containing "three out of position half backs."

Lawrence may have had a reason to be frustrated as he had high hopes that a Rangers win may have seen him awarded a knighthood as had happened at the other end of the city when Celtic Chairman Bob Kelly became Sir Bob Kelly after his side triumphed in Lisbon.

For Scot Symon it was another huge disappointment and of course left Rangers further in the shadow of Celtic.

Despite summer signings of Alex Ferguson for a record fee far higher than the Rangers Directors believed his market value, Swedish hit man Orjan Persson from Dundee United and Danish goalkeeper Eric Sorensen from Morton, Scot Symon was to remain in charge of Rangers for less than six months from the Nuremburg final and despite Rangers being top of the league table at the time, Symon was relieved of his duties in controversial fashion in November 1967.

Dave Smith recalled his thoughts in the aftermath of that January day at Berwick. "I said it then and I can say it again now moving on Jim Forrest and George McLean was a huge mistake by Mr Symon. I don't doubt if we had those players in our side in that European final against Bayern we would have won the cup. We just didn't have anybody in our ranks that converted the numerous chances that we made. We had Willie Henderson on one wing and wee Bud Johnston on the other, any centre forward worth their salt would have prospered and scored goals aplenty with the service these guys provided."

As for Sandy Jardine, Smith recalls: "Sandy settled into the side immediately. He was quiet but he was quick. He had football intelligence and he had the stamina of a teen-ager that allowed him to run all day, but he had an old head on young shoulders and knew how to play the game by keeping the ball. It was right up my street to have another player in the team who wanted to play the game the right way.

"We were all hugely frustrated that we couldn't win in Germany but it wasn't for the lack of chances. What was criminal was that we didn't take them. Alex Smith passed up a chance that night that he wouldn't normally miss while Big Roger gave all he had for the cause, but it wasn't his fault that he was thrown in at the deep end against Franz Beckenbauer at the heart of the Munich defence."

Many years later, Sandy Jardine himself said that he never really appreciated how big an achievement it was to get that far in a European competition then and it certainly made him appreciate the 1972 victory over Dynamo Moscow even more.

Nuremburg and the steep learning curve from his introduction in February of that season were all part of the still eighteen-year-old Sandy Jardine's apprenticeship.

Sandy had originally arrived at Rangers as a centre forward, and had experienced game time as a wing half and as an inside forward. Much later, under Willie Waddell, Sandy would be converted to a modern-day wing back and all these experiences were put to good use as he grew in stature as a Ranger and went on to make an incredible 674 appearances for the club.

9

SILVERWARE AND TRAGEDY
LEAGUE CUP SUCCESS BUT
NEW YEAR NIGHTMARE

Rangers Football Club had not lifted silverware in four years.

Scot Symon had departed the managers' office. David White had also come and gone as his replacement without delivering a trophy and in doing so he became the first Rangers manager in history not to win anything. It was left to former player turned journalist Willie Waddell to answer an SOS from the Rangers board to put away his pen and come back to steady the ship.

Changes in the playing staff were obvious with other youngsters such as Colin Jackson, Alex Miller and Alfie Conn joining Sandy Jardine as regular starters in the first team.

But it was another youngster, who had only played three games for the club and had only been a professional for three seasons, that scored the only goal of the League Cup final against Celtic on the 24th October 1970 to make history and position himself in Rangers folklore.

Derek Johnstone was sixteen years and 354 days old when he rose above Celtic skipper Billy McNeill to bullet a header beyond Evan Williams in the Celtic goal as 106,263 people squeezed into Hampden Park to witness the end of Rangers' barren spell.

Admission that day for a North Stand ticket cost the princely sum of sixteen shillings or eighty pence in todays' cash terms.

Rangers had lost 2-0 at home to Aberdeen in the match before the final, and when iconic skipper John Greig was ruled out with injury, the bookmakers made Celtic outrageous favourites.

Perhaps Celtic boss Jock Stein was over confident as he left out some big hitters, and gave starting jerseys to Jimmy Quinn at left back and Lou Macari in attack. Glasgow had suffered heavy rain in the week leading up to the final and a further deluge on the day meant it was heavy going underfoot. It soon became apparent after the first whistle that Rangers were able to adapt more quickly to the challenges of the Hampden turf on the day.

Willie Waddell had converted Sandy Jardine to a full back, encouraging him to use his pace and ball-playing skills to get forward almost as an auxiliary winger in the knowledge that that same pace would be a huge asset in recovery if an attack broke down.

Of Waddell's starting selection that October day against Celtic, seven players went on to lift the European Cup Winners' Cup at the third time of asking in the 1972 team that beat Dynamo Moscow in Barcelona in what remains Rangers' finest hour.

Rangers lined up:
        Peter McCloy
        Sandy Jardine
        Alex Miller
        Alfie Conn
        Ronnie McKinnon
        Colin Jackson
        Willie Henderson

Alex MacDonald
Derek Johnstone
Colin Stein
Willie Johnston

On the way to the final Rangers had won their group section against Morton, Motherwell and Dunfermline. They then beat Hibernian by the same 3-1 scoreline both home and away before cruising past Cowdenbeath 2-0 in the semi-final.

The game was dominated by Rangers but they could not find a way to beat Williams in the Celtic nets until five minutes before half time. Willie Henderson started the move with a pass to Alex MacDonald who fed left winger Willie Johnston who had switched flanks to put pressure on Celtic rookie Quinn. When he swung over the perfect cross, sixteen year old Johnstone timed his leap to perfection climbing majestically over his marker McNeill to win the hearts of the Rangers faithful and win the cup for Rangers. It was a cup that Celtic considered their own having won it in the five preceding seasons.

Rangers had laid the ghost of failing to win a trophy to rest and for twenty-one-year old William 'Sandy' Jardine, he was able to claim his first winners' medal in senior football.

Derek Johnstone was to go on and score 210 goals in two spells at Rangers but it's unlikely that anyone would argue that his goal on that October day at the national stadium was anything but the most valuable.

For Alex MacDonald, who had arrived at Ibrox from St. Johnstone eleven months previously and had struck up a great friendship with Sandy Jardine, this was also his first winners' badge, but the pair would have many successful days ahead in their Rangers careers together. In fact, by the time MacDonald left Rangers in 1980, 503 appearances later and two years ahead of Jardine, the pair had collected three League winners medals and four Scottish Cup medals and added a further three League Cup wins to the success of 1970.

Alex MacDonald looks back on the managerial changes as a good thing. "Waddell replacing Davie White turned out to be the best thing that happened to me although it took a while for that penny to drop," he recalled. MacDonald had been signed by White and had been with Rangers less than a year when he was dismissed and, like his pal Jardine, MacDonald was destined to have his style of play altered to meet the team shape Waddell was after. Alex remembers: "My game was about grafting, running, I liked to get on the ball too but my new instructions were to push and run, push and run. It was about pressure on the ball and tempo."

For the League Cup final on the 24th October, Rangers were without talismanic skipper John Greig and while the public statement claimed it was because of a flu bug, the situation was much more grave than that. A gash on Greig's shin picked up in the previous week's defeat to Aberdeen had turned sceptic and some suggested it could even have been career threatening. Celtic were clear favourites going into the game having won the competition for the previous five successive seasons.

Derek Johnstone knew the tide had changed for Rangers. "It was my first winners' medal and to score the only goal of the game was immense, surreal even being just sixteen.

"I went on to win many other medals and even the European medal from Barcelona is extra special, but you never forget your first medal, and it was the first for a number of that 1970 team including Sandy, who was adapting to his new right back role. He was such an athlete that he never looked out of place and he still had all the instincts of a midfielder and always saw a pass early.

"I think Kai Johansen had decided to retire at the end of the previous season and Sandy was the man Willie Waddell and Big Jock (Wallace) turned to and what a decision that was!"

Ronnie McKinnon captained the side to that League Cup triumph in the absence of John Greig and he remembers

Sandy Jardine always asking him how long was there to go? Ronnie said: "We were an emerging team but we were out the winning habit and you could see some of the younger guys like Sandy, Derek, Alex Miller and Alfie Conn start to get edgy, and nerves were creeping in. Concentration was strained, but we held out and when the whistle blew it was a case of shear elation."

Like Johnston, Sandy Jardine cherished the moment and his performance that day probably removed any doubts about his best position and further established him as a Rangers first-team regular.

It was just what Jardine needed, having married Shona Baxter in St. Catherine's Argyle Church in the Meadows area of Edinburgh less than a year before the cup win. Sandy Jardine had cemented his position in strong foundations on and off the park. He was twenty-one years old.

Rangers played a total of fifty-three competitive matches during the 1970-71 season with the League Cup win the highlight.

They finished fourth in the league campaign and runners up to Celtic in the Scottish Cup albeit it took two games to settle the tie.

Sandy Jardine missed that final and the replay through injury with Alex Miller switching to right back for the first game, and Jim Denny getting the jersey in the replay.

On the Saturday, a 120,092 crowd saw the teams battle out a 1-1 draw with Bobby Lennox scoring for Celtic while Derek Johnstone was again on target for Rangers.

Four days later and back at Hampden, Celtic claimed the cup with Harry Hood and Lou Macari the marksmen for Jock Stein's side and an own goal from Jim Craig the only consolation for Rangers. An incredible crowd of 103,332 packed Hampden Park for the midweek fixture.

The season was to be totally overshadowed, however, by events of the 2nd January 1971 when sixty-six people perished on stairway thirteen at Ibrox Park at the end of the New Year Old Firm fixture.

It was an uninspiring match on a grey Glasgow day with 80,000 inside Ibrox with all the notable action coming in the last few minutes. Jimmy Johnstone broke the deadlock and almost with the last touch of the game, Colin Stein claimed a late equaliser for Rangers.

As the players from both teams enjoyed a relaxing bath back in their dressing rooms after full time, they were totally oblivious to the chaos going on in the right-hand corner of the stadium. Whether it was confusion with fans trying to get back to see the action after Rangers scored and possibly clashing with others trying to exit the ground has never been fully determined as the cause of the tragedy, but what was apparent was steel barriers on the stairway had given way under stress, and people were falling on top of others with horrific consequences. Fans leaving from other areas of Ibrox stadium had no idea either of the catastrophe that was unfolding at stairway thirteen.

Alex MacDonald had come off the bench as a late substitute for the Light Blues that fateful day and was still in the home dressing room when manager Willie Waddell came in and shouted that all players still in the dressing room had to get out now! Alex recalls: "I was still trying to get my breath back from the frantic action at the end of the game but when Willie Waddell bellowed OUT again even more forcibly, we knew something was amiss.

"I think Sandy was still in the bath as he was usually one of the last out but we were told to get dressed quickly and go home.

"Within minutes ambulance men were bringing people in on stretchers. The injured were in the dressing room, the treatment room and even in the gymnasium."

It took some time for the absolute scale of the tragedy to unfold as radio bulletins and television reports increased as the evening wore on, but it was confirmed all too soon that sixty-six fans had lost their lives and 145 were injured.

It was a dark day in the history of Rangers Football Club. Football was irrelevant.

Sandy Jardine had just celebrated his twenty-second birthday, two days before the disaster, but he faced his responsibilities with extreme courage as did all his team-mates who attended every funeral, and made many visits to the injured in hospital. Sandy attended fifteen funerals as the squad split into groups to ensure the club was repre-sented at every service.

Rangers' season was closed down with training cancelled and games postponed. When Rangers did take the field again in competitive action, it was a sombre occasion with the game against Dundee United on the 30th of January, four weeks after the tragedy, finishing 1-1 at Ibrox.

Rangers manager Willie Waddell said at the time, "These have been black days at Ibrox ... days of grief and anguish. The scar is deep."

Waddell also made a pledge in the wake of that 1971 disaster that never again would anybody's safety be endangered at Ibrox, and committed an initiative and revolutionary plan to revitalise Ibrox Park by converting the stadium to a modern all-seated arena. It was effectively the blueprint for Rangers' stadium as it stands today.

A fund was also set up to support the families directly affected by the tragedy and a benefit game was arranged to further boost the finances. Hosted at Hampden Park, an Old Firm select took on a Scotland international side and a host of top football stars from further afield than Glasgow were quick to commit to the cause. Although it was Scotland who ran out 2-1 winners, the crowd of just over 82,000 enjoyed the spectacle and a very worthy cause benefited from the cash generated on the day.

Sandy Jardine may have picked up his first Scotland cap in November 1970 coming on as a substitute for David Hay against Denmark in a European Championship qualifying tie, but this benefit match was a step up in company again.

The Scotland team to face the Old Firm select was:

> Jim Cruikshank (*Hearts*)
> David Hay (*Celtic*)
> Tommy Gemmell (*Celtic*)
> Pat Stanton (*Hibs*)
> Ronnie McKinnon (*Rangers*)
> Bobby Moncur (*Newcastle*)
> Peter Lorimer (*Leeds*)
> Archie Gemmill (*Derby*)
> Colin Stein (*Rangers*)
> John O'Hare (*Derby*)
> Charlie Cooke (*Chelsea*)

While the select lined up with a few guests included:

> Peter Bonetti (*Chelsea*)
> Sandy Jardine (*Rangers*)
> John Greig (*Rangers*)
> Bobby Murdoch (*Celtic*)
> Billy McNeill (*Celtic*)
> Dave Smith (*Rangers*)
> Willie Henderson (*Rangers*)
> John Hughes (*Celtic*)
> Bobby Charlton (*Manchester United*)
> Willie Johnston (*Rangers*)
> George Best (*Manchester United*)

It was a hugely entertaining and fast-flowing game. Archie Gemmill and Peter Lorimer scored for Scotland and George Best replied for the select.

The players' commitment to this fundraiser was testimony to the true depth of feeling that touched everybody in the football world.

10

ANOTHER EUROPEAN CAMPAIGN RANGERS AND BAYERN AGAIN CROSS SWORDS

With the history between the clubs and with both progressing well in the European Cup Winners' Cup campaign in 1971/72, it was inevitable that Glasgow Rangers and Bayern Munich would be paired with each other at some stage in the tournament.

You could almost say Rangers were only in the tournament through default as they had lost the Scottish Cup final to Celtic in a replay, but with their Old Firm rivals also winning the domestic league, Rangers as runners-up qualified to compete for Europe's second trophy.

The teams needed extra time to determine a winner in the same tournament final in 1967, with Franz Roth's goal in 109 minutes enough to see Bayern lift the trophy.

Roll on three years and the teams were again paired to play together in the opening round of the now defunct Inter-Cities Fairs Cup. In the first leg, Rangers gave a credible performance and real hope of progressing by only losing 1-0, with Franz Beckenbauer on target for the Munich giants thus setting up a real nail-biter for the second leg in Glasgow, two weeks later.

Colin Stein gave Rangers the lead but with extra time on the minds of everybody inside Ibrox "Der Bomber", Gerd Muller, popped up with an equaliser and that was enough to see Bayern progress and Rangers be eliminated. It was close from Rangers but again, they just fell short against the slick and organised German outfit.

Now in 1972, Bayern Munich stood between Rangers and a place in The European Cup Winners' Cup final.

John Greig, Willie Johnston and Sandy Jardine had played in all clashes with Bayern and despite Greig being the senior of the trio at twenty-nine – Bud Johnston was twenty-five and Sandy a tender twenty-three years old – they could well be described as veterans of the fixture.

Willie Johnston confirms: "We were very much more streetwise when we played Bayern in 1972. Willie Waddell and Big Jock Wallace saw to that."

Rangers' campaign started with a potentially dangerous tie in France against the wonderfully technical Stade Rennes FC. Rangers gave themselves a real chance of progressing, picking up a very favourable 1-1 draw with Willie Johnston claiming the vital away goal.

The Ibrox men were heavily criticised for their performance in France, with the Rennes Manager claiming it was "anti-football" and that Rangers had come to "stop us" from playing and "we will show them how football should be played in the second leg." In truth, Rangers had deployed tactics that were probably a bit ahead of their time for the Scottish game with the game plan relying on a high tempo and pressure on the ball from the front. This requirement was carried out to perfection by the physical and powerful Colin Stein and the cute and quicksilver Willie Johnston. Behind the front pair, Alex MacDonald snuffed out their midfield general in a man marking masterclass while Sandy Jardine and Willie Mathieson matched anything the Rennes wingers had for pace.

In the second leg at Ibrox, Rangers again had their

preparations pay off in a real team performance with a goal from the dynamic former St. Johnstone midfielder MacDonald, who showed his ability to defend when Rangers didn't have the ball, but got forward to support the front players when they did.

Next up, Rangers were drawn against tournament favourites Sporting Lisbon.

In the first leg at Ibrox, the Light Blues were three up at half-time with Colin Stein notching a double and Willie Henderson also on target. However, the Portuguese side raised their game in the second half to score twice meaning Rangers travelled to Portugal with only a single goal advantage while Sporting had two away goals to call upon in the event of a draw.

It was a challenging journey to Lisbon for Rangers with fog and a baggage handlers strike at Heathrow making it a full day and a half's travel time, meaning Willie Waddell's side only arrived in the Portugal capital twenty-four hours ahead of the scheduled kick-off.

Héctor Azalde broke the deadlock to see the teams tied at 3-3 but Colin Stein cancelled it out within a minute. João Laranjeira scored on the stroke of half-time to even things up again. Sixty seconds after the turn around, Stein again found space in the Sporting rearguard to claim his second of the night making it 2-2, with Rangers still in the box seat to go through by a single goal. Then disaster for Rangers. Elegant and dominating centre half Ronnie McKinnon went down in a sickening clash with a Sporting forward and his leg was broken in two places.

McKinnon was stretchered off. The severity of the injury meant that he would never play for Rangers again. The game was destined for extra time after Pedro Gomes scored, meaning the teams were locked on a 5-5 aggregate scoreline. With both teams having scored two goals in their respective away games, that meant the normal method of determining the winner by away goals counting double was effectively redundant.

Into the extra thirty minutes and Willie Henderson converted to make it 5-6 to Rangers, but again, the Portuguese hit back with Fernando Peres scoring to reflect a 4-3 home win on the night and 6-6 on aggregate over the 210 minutes of football.

So a penalty shoot-out was the call from referee Laurens Van Ravens.

Rangers missed three of their first four efforts – including a double miss from the normally reliable Dave Smith who had to suffer the ignominy of a retake after fans invaded the field when he struck the first. Sporting scored all of their first four kicks from the mark and jubilation for the home fans saw goalkeeper Damas carried off shoulder high as the hero of the hour.

Rangers were out! Except they were not!

In a dejected visitors' dressing room, morale was low and not helped by concern for distressed teammate Ronnie McKinnon whose badly broken leg was not getting attention as the local medics lacked experience or the confidence to offer immediate or suitable treatment. Willie Johnston recalls: "I remember sitting with our heads down. We were out." While the other Willie, Henderson, said: "It was hellish and we were all low but there was a knock at the dressing room door. The manager opened it and one of the Scottish press contingent was standing there. He took Mr. Waddell away and we didn't know what was going on." What was going on was that John Fairgrieve, a well known Scottish sportswriter, had checked the rules and despite the Dutch referee's belief to the contrary, away goals scored in extra time DID also count double and in effect, Rangers were victors on the away goals rule and the sham of the penalty kicks was just that and totally unnecessary!

Willie Waddell and Fairgrieve challenged Referee Van Ravens and the UEFA Officials who were present who immediately agreed and awarded Rangers the tie.

Rangers were into the quarter finals and Italian cracks Torino would provide the opposition.

The first leg against Torino was away in Italy and eighteen-year-old Derek Johnstone stepped back into defence to partner Dave Smith with the absence of leg-break victim Ronnie McKinnon. Rangers defended like lions and Willie Johnston again showed his knack of scoring goals on the big occasions (and that would be further substantiated in stunning style in the final) by giving the Light Blues the lead after twelve minutes with a close-range finish when he got on the end of a Willie Mathieson cross. There was an onslaught to the Rangers goal thereafter and eventually the Italian pressure paid off with Pulici scoring for the home side just after the hour mark.

For the game against Torino, skipper John Greig had been instructed by Gers coach Jock Wallace to put Italian wonder kid Claudio Sala "out the game." Rumour has it that the Rangers iron man Greig retorted, "is that just for this game or for good?" Suggestions are John was only half kidding.

The teams reconvened at Ibrox two weeks later on the 22nd March 1972, and a solitary goal from Alex MacDonald just after half-time was enough to send Rangers through and set up the epic semi-final clash against old foes Bayern Munich.

Rangers were drawn away from home in the first leg.

Since the 1967 final, Sepp Maier, Franz Beckenbauer and Gerd Müller had all developed into genuine inter-national superstars of the game while exciting younger talent, including Paul Breitner and Uli Hoeness, had come through to further strengthen the German squad since the Inter-Cities Fairs Cup meeting of the previous season. Light Blue legend Derek Johnstone had the utmost respect for his semi-final opponents and admitted: "Going into those games, Bayern had the Indian sign on us. We had run them close but we just couldn't get that win."

You can understand Johnstone's admiration for a team that was to contribute the bulk of the side that would win the next European Championship and the World Cup less than two years later. That season, Bayern Munich went on to win their own domestic league competition. They claimed it again in each of the next three seasons, and competed in three consecutive European Cup finals between 1974 and 1976. This was a very special emerging side, not just the best of that particular era, but arguably one of the very best in the history of club football.

The first leg was in the Grünwalder Stadium which also hosted home games for neighbours 1860 Munich as Bayern would only move into the new Olympic Stadion in time for their last game of that season.

Rangers fielded the same starting eleven as delivered the desired result away in Torino in the quarter finals.

Willie Waddell again had his team totally prepared to withstand the expected German pressure and with Hoeness pulling the strings in midfield, Rangers duly conceded with Paul Brietner scoring midway through the first period. But after forty-nine minutes, Rangers got that bit of luck you sometimes had when on your travels in Europe. It was down to the tenacity of Colin Stein pressurising Bayern defender Rainer Zobel, and he could only turn Stein's delivery behind his own goalkeeper to level the scoring.

Sandy Jardine afterwards was quoted as saying: "That was the biggest hiding I've ever had in my life but after we scored, they shot their bolt. We were exceptional and it paid off for us again."

After the game, Derek Johnstone was singled out for a mature defensive performance beyond his teenage years, but manager Waddell was also quick to qualify his comments by acknowledging that it was an all round great team performance.

Rangers stood ninety minutes away from the final.

In the return leg at Ibrox on the 19th of April 1972, Glasgow hosted two European Cup semi-finals. That same night on the other side of the city, Celtic played host to Internazionale but while Rangers got the desired result, Celtic were eliminated in a dreaded spot-kick decider after both semi-final games ended goalless.

A crowd of 80,000 packed into the Rangers ground and they did not have long to wait for something to cheer about. Fans were still coming into the ground when Sandy Jardine gave Rangers a dream start. Sandy drove on from his right wing back role before cutting inside on to his left foot and curling an unstoppable effort into the net. It was an incredible start to such a high pressure game. Derek Johnstone takes up the story: "We went into the game without our skipper John Greig, and Derek Parlane had come into the side to replace him, but what Derek lacked in experience, he made up for with energy. Greigy was a big miss. He was our leader. He was the boss on the park but we were determined not to let him down."

On the way to the semi-final stage, Bayern had eliminated Steaua Bucharest of Romania, beaten a very talented Liverpool side at Anfield after a no score draw at home, having started their campaign with a huge aggregate 7-1 win over TJ Skoda Plzeň of the then Czechoslovakia.

But on the night, Rangers were relentless. Colin Stein crashed a header off the crossbar from a Willie Johnston corner, then eighteen-year-old debutant Parlane doubled Rangers' lead and the game was still only twenty-one minutes old! That strike meant Rangers were 2-1 ahead on aggregate. It was a stunning half volley strike from Parlane that shaved the underside of the crossbar and went into the net leaving Maier helpless to do anything about it.

Derek remembers his introduction to the side. "I was asked, no I was told – it was Big Jock of course – I had to do a marking job on a guy called Franz Roth who played in their midfield and was a big player for them in more ways than one. Now as a skinny eighteen--year-old playing my first ever game in Europe against a team who arguably were the best in Europe at the time, marking an experienced twenty-five-year-old with the nickname 'The Bull' was, as you could imagine, a somewhat daunting task." Roth just happened also to have been the player whose extra time goal in the 1967 final broke Rangers hearts and gave the German side the cup.

Derek Johnstone admitted: "Strangely, we never really missed John Greig but I think our good start played a big part in that. When Sandy sank to his knees after firing home the opener it was confirmation that he was as surprised that his swinger had gone in, but taking nothing away from Sandy, he was brave enough to try it and it came off." Sandy's strike was also scrutinised by Bud Johnston but he was a bit more charitable than Derek Johnstone. "Sandy's goal may have caught Bayern cold and they didn't appreciate that he had the technique to score like that, but Sandy was capable of scoring all sorts of goals and remember he started off in the game as a centre forward."

Legendary broadcaster Archie Macpherson captured the moment perfectly in his television commentary as Sandy scored with: "And it's there … A sensation!"

Rangers were never going to relinquish a two-goal lead in front of a fervent home crowd, and were so much on top later in the game that Willie Johnston tormented and teased the German rearguard, and even had the temerity to race clear of his full-back before sitting on the ball in an act of defiance. Johnston's supreme act of confidence fully deflated Bayern and their challenge was effectively ended.

Derek Johnstone remembers his namesake teammate being chastised by Jock Wallace for his showboating. "Big Jock told wee Bud that it was disrespectful but followed that up with a wink and a pat on the head and a well done wee man!"

For Parlane, he will be eternally grateful for the assistance Sandy Jardine gave him that night. "Sandy settled me down by never stopping talking to me and encouraging me, telling me when to go tight and ensuring I was in the right position whether it was to defend in the team shape or to be in the right place to receive a pass. After that game we were celebrating back in the dressing room and I have a picture of Sandy and I with our arms round each other drinking some bubbly. It's a picture I'll treasure forever."

Another hero that night was stand-in Captain Dave

Smith who gave an outstanding performance at the heart of the Rangers defence. On his day, Smith was an elegant and cultured footballer who was also very modest about his own talent. Smith said: "It was a privilege to captain Rangers that night and I have a picture with me exchanging pennants with Franz Beckenbauer before the game. After the game he signed it 'To my friend Dave Smith'. He was a better player than me no question but over those two big games, I maybe just had the edge!"

Rangers could look forward to another final, with Barcelona the venue and Russian giants Dynamo Moscow the opponents.

Derek Johnstone sums up the mood of the Rangers camp at that time. "The draw in Germany gave us real confidence for the second leg and, with hindsight, the two games against Bayern were probably harder than the final itself."

11

BARCELONA BEARS
EURO GLORY AT LAST!

Rangers had made it through to another European final.

It had been a terrific campaign but it came at a cost. One of Scotland's most cultured defenders and a stalwart in Rangers' rearguard since the early '60s, Ronnie McKinnon, would miss the Barcelona final having suffered a broken leg in Portugal in the second round tie against Sporting Lisbon.

Other than McKinnon, only Sandy, Dave Smith, John Greig and Willie Johnston were still first-team regulars from the eleven who had lost narrowly in the final of the same tournament five years previously.

More than 25,000 Rangers fans made the trip to the Nou Camp stadium and hopes were high that it would be third time lucky and the cup could come back to Glasgow.

The date is forever etched in Rangers history: 24th May, 1972.

Today, Ibrox stadium has its own BAR 72 to commemorate the occasion. The bar was opened in 2006 in what was then the Govan Stand which has since been renamed the Sandy Jardine Stand, and in season 2012/13, Rangers' home kit was a replica of the iconic 1972 strip of all blue shirt, white shorts and red and white socks.

Dynamo Moscow were the opponents and it was the first time a Soviet team had reached a European final.

The Russian side had pedigree and had booked their passage to the final with a 3-1 aggregate winner of Greek side Olympiacos, comfortable wins both home and away against Turkish outfit Eskişehirspor and they had seen off Belgrade's finest, Red Star, to set up their semi-final tie with Dynamo Berlin. So both teams faced German opposition to book their place in the final with Rangers facing old foes Bayern Munich as the Muscovites took on Berliners from the east side of that country's dividing wall.

Dynamo Moscow took a very credible 1-1 draw back to Russia from their trip behind the Iron Curtain and after another 1-1 draw at home, Moscow progressed, winning the tie in a penalty shoot-out.

Rangers and Dynamo Moscow had locked horns on one previous occasion and it was a match that was controversial in many ways.

In 1945, Dynamo were on a British tour and a game against Rangers was arranged at Ibrox. It was played in November and the Second World War had only ended in August so it truly was a groundbreaking fixture. Ahead of the Glasgow clash, Dynamo had played Chelsea, Arsenal and Cardiff and were unbeaten in all three games.

It was a foggy day in the Empire's second city and the weather did not improve as kick-off time approached. The match carried so much intrigue that nearly 90,000 were inside Ibrox when the game started. Rangers were forced into a change of kit as Dynamo were wearing dark blue shirts so Rangers took the field in light blue and narrow hoops! The game ended 2-2 but Dynamo had fielded twelve players for a long spell in the second half and because of the fog, no one – including the referee – had noticed!

It was perhaps the pioneering nature of this game and the three previous fixtures on Dynamo Moscow's tour that set the prelude to European football becoming a regular feature in the sporting calendar fully ten years later, with the European Cup being established in 1955 and Real Madrid being the first winners, while the Cup Winners' Cup tournament saw Rangers compete in its first ever final in 1961. Now, eleven years later, they were in the final for the third time.

But as the teams were set to do battle for Europe's second most prestigious club prize, this time Rangers gained the psychological advantage by claiming the right to play in their regular blue kit, forcing Dynamo into changing to white.

Rangers had made their way to the final by beating Stade Rennes, Sporting Lisbon, Torino and Bayern Munich, all cup holders in their own countries and were undefeated, with the exception of the 4-3 extra time reverse in Portugal, but it was academic. As Rangers had scored three away goals in the match they were through to the quarter finals and effectively rendered the penalty shoot-out a farce. It was bizarre in the extreme that the referee had to have the rules brought to his attention by Rangers officials and a member of the travelling Scottish press pack.

To the final itself in the sweltering Catalan heat. Captain John Greig who still sported the goatee beard that he had grown to cover a cut from a previous on-field battle and had refused to shave off while Rangers were still in the European Cup Winners' Cup, led his charges on to the Camp Nou field. His thoughts were straying to Rangers' last European final of 1967 where they lost out to Bayern Munich, whom they had secured revenge against in this year's tournament.

Greig remembered Roger Hynd hurling his runners-up medal into the Nuremburg crowd saying second was of no interest to him, while Greig himself through frustration and disappointment bounced his own medal off every wall back in the dressing room in the aftermath of defeat.

Five years had elapsed and this could be John Greig's last chance of European success as he was to celebrate his thirtieth birthday later in that year.

Rangers were forced into fielding a makeshift defence. With McKinnon injured, Colin Jackson, who had been doing sterling work as his replacement, turned his ankle in a light training session on the morning of the game ruling him out of contention. Derek Johnstone, whose headed goal in the League Cup final two years before ended four years without a trophy for the club, was shunted back to centre half to play alongside Dave Smith. Johnstone was still only eighteen!

Rangers started as if they meant business, adopting a high tempo and pressing game like they did in previous rounds and in doing so, were managing to defy the heat of the balmy Barcelona evening.

More than 25,000 vocal Rangers fans had made the journey to Spain, most without tickets, and it was clear from their exuberance that the sangria had been flowing pre-match. Those that had managed to get into the ground were making it a real carnival atmosphere.

Rangers opened the scoring in twenty-three minutes and it was no more than their play deserved. Dave Smith despatched a long ball into Dynamo territory and Colin Stein hared after it with two Russian defenders in his wake. Stein steadied himself then rifled the ball into the net beyond the despairing dive of Vladimir Pilguy in the Moscow goal. Rangers fans spilled onto the pitch as they celebrated but that was only a taste for what was to follow. Five minutes short of the interval and Rangers doubled their advantage. The crucial second goal was a thing of beauty and was engineered by not one, but two marauding ball playing centre half's! Derek Johnstone and Dave Smith, with scant regard for their defensive duties, combined to play through the Dynamo midfield before Smith with the cutest of drag backs and showing exquisite ball control, clipped an inch perfect centre that Willie Johnston happily headed home.

Half-time and Rangers were two up.

Four minutes after the restart it was three. Towering goalkeeper Peter McCloy, who was known as the Girvan

Lighthouse, launched an Exocet missile of a kick that went straight to the heart of his opponents' territory and was totally misjudged by two Dynamo defenders. The predatory Colin Stein saw the opportunity and reacted with lightening reflex before conjuring up a deadly accurate finish which put Rangers in what should have been easy street. Rangers 3, Dynamo Moscow 0.

Suggestions were that Dynamo Moscow froze on the occasion and only found their form after going three behind, but they had been missing experience in the form of Kozlov and Kozhemyakin who were both out through injury, and with the game slipping away from them, the Russian sides' manager Konstantin Veskov replaced number eight Yakubik for Vladimir Eshtrekov who carried more of a goal threat than his industrious teammate. He reduced the arrears within four minutes of coming off the bench. Then, with Rangers fighting a desperate rearguard action with tired legs and minds in evidence, the Light Blues conceded again as Dynamo stepped up a gear to finish with a flourish, although Aleksandr Makhovikov's strike was too little too late to take the game to extra time.

Rangers, at the third time of asking, were winners of the European Cup Winners' Cup.

Peter McCloy, who made 535 Rangers appearances and, like Jardine, is one of an elite club of only eight players who played more than 500 games for Rangers in the post-war years, remembers Barcelona as his finest footballing hour. "Undoubtedly our European Cup Winners' Cup success was special but we were a special team with a fantastic team spirit. The biggest disappointment, and it was something Sandy and I spoke about often, was the anticlimax after the final whistle when the fans invaded the park. They didn't mean any harm or to cause problems but the Spanish police did not handle it well and we were back in the dressing room as things escalated."

With the Nou Camp playing field totally swamped by fans in a sea of red, white and blue, Rangers were presented with the trophy and medals behind closed doors and not even were they presented together. Captain John Greig, who had led the team to victory despite not being fully fit, was ushered into a room that resembled a broom cupboard and without ceremony was handed the silver trophy. Undoubtedly events on the field tarnished the occasion but Rangers' reputation would be tarnished too. Dynamo Moscow even petitioned for the game to be replayed and demanded Rangers be stripped of the cup but common sense prevailed. However, through the act of a minority of mindless fans, Rangers suffered a twelve-month European ban the following season meaning they were unable to defend their trophy. UEFA originally imposed a two-year ban but Rangers had it reduced to one year on an appeal led by Willie Waddell, who had moved upstairs to his new position of General Manager.

Peter McCloy remembers the key part Sandy Jardine played in that successful European campaign that ended on such a sour note in Barcelona. "Willie Waddell and Jock Wallace meticulously prepared us for European games. We were each given pictures of our expected direct opponent and if it was a man-for-man marking job, Big Jock left nobody in doubt with his usual comment that 'if he goes to the bloody toilet … you go with him' while I was usually given a detailed in depth dossier of things like set pieces and corners they had taken from their previous games.

"But we also had a very modern team shape that let the ball flow and nobody was better suited to playing the continentals than Sandy Jardine. Sandy had balance, poise and elegance of movement. He was a thoroughbred who never sold himself in the tackle, just a terrific all round footballer and if the occasion called for it, he was outstanding in a man marking role. Even as a sweeper, I remember Sandy giving a masterclass in that position against Juventus in 1978 when we won 1-0 in Italy. Sandy Jardine was the best in that position I ever played behind and that includes Dave Smith who was a fantastic reader of the game and sweeper too.

"When I joined Rangers from Motherwell, Kai Johansen was the regular right back and Sandy was in and out the team, sometimes playing half back, but when he was converted to a full back, he really came into his own. But he really could play anywhere.

"Leaving aside Sandy's goal in the semi-final against Bayern that set us on our way to Barcelona, he was an inspiration and cornerstone of the team."

Of course that team will be forever known now as "The Barcelona Bears." For the record the team that night against Dynamo Moscow was: Peter McCloy, Sandy Jardine, Willie Mathieson, John Greig, Derek Johnstone, Dave Smith: Tommy McLean, Alfie Conn, Colin Stein, Alex McDonald and Willie Johnston. The eleven men who started the match finished the match and none of the listed substitutes were used: Gerry Neef, Jim Denny, Graham Fyfe, Andy Penman and Derek Parlane, but everyone in the squad was a hero.

After things died down, there was the usual post-match banquet when the players did get a chance to celebrate and let their hair down and it's recorded that even Alex MacDonald – who was usually teetotal – had a bit of a hangover the next day before the team flew back to Glasgow.

A crowd met their returning heroes at the airport, and later in the evening, a bigger crowd assembled at Ibrox where the trophy was displayed properly as the players paraded round the track on the back of a flatbed lorry.

Rangers had made their mark in Europe but at home they were still struggling for domestic success, and cups and league titles that were almost annually retained in the Rangers trophy room in the early '60s were proving very hard to come by, with old rivals Celtic continuing to dominate.

12

CZECH MATE

It was a full-house 100,000 crowd that celebrated Scotland reaching their first World Cup finals in sixteen years with an historic win over Czechoslovakia.

It was a night of high drama on the pitch and equally dramatic, but contrasting, commentary from the legendary mic man Arthur Montford who captivated a massive television audience with his passion and desire for Scotland to succeed. Such was the fervour for the game, even *Coronation Street* was moved from its regular slot to allow live coverage of the crunch qualifier from Hampden.

Wednesday the 26th September 1973 will go down in history as one of Scotland's greatest triumphs on the football field.

Scotland came back from a goal down to win 2-1 and their place in the 1974 finals to be hosted by West Germany was assured.

It was Sandy Jardine's eighth appearance in the dark blue of Scotland and one of his most memorable.

The highly talented Czechoslovakians would win the European Championships just three years later, but having drawn away in Copenhagen against Denmark, who made up the three-team group in the tie ahead of the Hampden visit, it meant a win for either side would guarantee them safe passage to the finals scheduled for the summer of 1974.

Scotland started their campaign with Tommy Docherty at the helm having been recruited by the SFA from Hull City and tasked with taking the nation to the finals, but when Manchester United came calling for his services, "The Doc" was soon on the move to Old Trafford and his unlikely replacement mid tournament was St. Johnstone boss, Willie Ormond.

Ormond wasn't long in putting his own stamp on the squad, especially after getting his reign off to the worst possible start, going down to England in a five goal thrashing seven months previously in a match arranged to celebrate 100 years of the Scottish Football Association. The game effectively signalled the end of the international careers of centre back Eddie Colquhoun of Coventry City and Aberdeen goalkeeper Bobby Clark. Alex Forsyth, then of Manchester United, had lined up at right back against the auld enemy with Sandy Jardine not involved, but this pair would later play together as a full back partnership in the light blue of Rangers after the emergence of a certain Jimmy Nicholl as a red devil saw Forsyth join Rangers. He was originally on a loan arrangement, before the arrangement was made permanent by Ibrox manager John Greig.

Sandy Jardine meanwhile had found it difficult to become a first pick under Docherty, largely down to being deployed more often in marking roles as the manager saw fit rather than the attacking full back position that Sandy had perfected at club level. However, all that was soon to change and Sandy was to become a fixture under Ormond. Sandy was first capped by Bobby Brown and his qualities were also recognised by Ally Macleod and Jock Stein, meaning he played under five Scotland managers before bringing the curtain down on his international career in December 1979.

For the crucial game against Czechoslovakia, Ormond

fielded Jardine at right back with Danny McGrain showing his versatility by switching to left back, and the relatively untried Coventry winger Tommy Hutchison was thrown in for his first cap playing as a genuine left winger. Denis Law, at the age of thirty-three, was recalled to lead the attack.

Jim Stewart was a nineteen–year-old rookie goalkeeper but he was receiving rave reviews for his performances between the sticks for Kilmarnock, to a level that he was called into Ormond's squad as third-choice keeper. Stewart, now Rangers' goalkeeping coach, remembers Hampden being an emotional place that night. "It was a night of mixed emotions. I was in the stand with the other players who hadn't made the bench, but we felt the anguish the same as the fans all round about us when we fell behind, but we were all out of our seats when big Jim Holton equalised and at the winner, we all went a bit berserk.

"We thought it wouldn't be our night when Billy Bremner hit the post, then Willie Morgan clipped a ball in and Joe Jordan, who wasn't much older than myself, threw himself at it to head us into a 2-1 lead. When the final whistle blew it was a mix of relief and disbelief that we had done it. We were going to Germany although if I am being honest, I wasn't confident that I would be part of the squad."

A teammate of Jim Stewart's at Kilmarnock at that time was teenage wide man Gordon Smith, who was to become Chief Executive of the Scottish Football Association twenty-seven years later, believes that night at Hampden transformed Scottish football. "It was quite spectacular, everyone was so enthralled with Scotland winning and making it to the World Cup finals. It gave the whole game a lift. You look at the team of that era including Law, Bremner and Willie Morgan who were all performing at the top of the English leagues and while Willie Ormond didn't quite create the national fervour or belief that we could actually win the trophy the way Ally MacLeod did four years later, there was belief that we could go to Germany with a chance.

"That night when qualification was assured, not for a minute did I think that I would be in the same Ibrox dressing room as Sandy Jardine just three years later.

"I had an interest in Rangers since the days of Baxter as he was my favourite player growing up although I was a Kilmarnock fan, and remember that my grandfather, Mattha Smith, twice won the Scottish Cup with them, but anybody who liked football usually supported the national team too. I had watched Sandy Jardine excel in Europe during the Cup Winners' Cup run of 1972 in a role that would now be termed a "wing back" before it had been thought of, but against the Czechs, he dovetailed fantastically well with the big power-house centre half Jim Holton and formed a great partnership at the heart of Willie Ormond's defence. Years later, I was fortunate to witness Sandy's qualities in both positions first hand after I joined Rangers from Kilmarnock. For domestic competition, Sandy would normally operate at right back but in Europe, especially under John Greig, he would be deployed as a sweeper and in particular when we played away from home, I lost count of the masterclass displays that Sandy delivered."

Jim Stewart did indeed make the squad as back up to more experienced goalkeepers David Harvey from Leeds United and Thompson Allan of Dundee but bizarrely, Stewart had to wait until 1977 to take his Scotland bow in a match against Chile as Scotland prepared for the next World Cup of 1978.

It really was a night when the nation united. Starved of tournament football at the high profile final stages for sixteen years, could Scotland make it to Germany?

Even TV match commentator Arthur Montford kicked every ball and was almost like an extra coach and his passion and desire came through as he described every piece of action. Derek Rae, now one of the game's top commentators on BT Sport and ESPN, remembers the night well despite being still at primary school. "I watched at home on a black and white TV set and at the time didn't appreciate how special this was remembering that live football on the box was a rarity and, in fact, we only had a choice of three channels to watch back then. It was iconic, if a bit jingoistic, commentary from Arthur Montford who really was a wonderful orator of the game but that night Arthur let his mask slip and he was really a fan with a microphone that was captivating a massive audience watching the action unfold from the comfort of their home! Perhaps at the time, people were less "worldly" and a bit more parochial – an inward nationalism culture almost – and Arthur was no different. I have watched the old grainy footage many times over and I even recall Arthur offering advice in his commentary: "Careful Denis (Law), he's behind you!" It was as if Arthur was oblivious to the fact he was on live television. Maybe though in the 1970s that's how you did it, but football broadcasting has certainly moved on since then. Secretly, however, wouldn't we all have loved to have uttered the words of Arthur that night even after the bad start when he described the Czechoslovakian goal "a shot – and it's a good one – it's a goal! Disaster – it's absolute disaster for Scotland!" And from agony to ecstasy: "Big Jim Holton is going down to the box – Holton's there– and it's there! – Holton scores! – That's the one! A beautiful goal! – Holton a beautiful header up and under the crossbar – and it's 1–1!"

Things got cranked up even further when Scotland scored the winner: "Still dangerous – Morgan flinging in the cross – Jordan – It's there – Jordan scores – Magnificent – Superb goal – the ball is in the back of the net and it's 2-1!" With full time almost on us again, Arthur allowed his passion to overflow: "coming up for the ninety minutes mark – the referee is looking at his watch – that's it! – THAT IS IT! – Congratulations Scotland – Well done boys!" Derek Rae again recalls Arthur`s enthusiasm with true admiration, "Iconic commentary from fantastic days for Scottish football. Such a pity that we are not back at the top internationally and contesting finals of European Championships & World Cups. 1998 in France seems a lifetime ago."

But back then after a gap of sixteen years, Scotland could look forward to the World Cup finals in Germany scheduled for the following summer.

13

SANDY OF SCOTLAND

Having already acquired a wealth of European experience at such a tender age since his first five-match run to the 1967 European Cup Winners' Cup final, it was inevitable that International football would follow.

It was former Rangers goalkeeper Bobby Brown who was in charge of the national team that gave Sandy his first Scotland cap.

Brown was the man who masterminded the sensational Wembley win of 1967 against world champions England but three years on, his squad was in transition. There was also pressure on the Scotland boss because of the number of Rangers players who featured regularly in his squads. The media suggested a bias.

In November 1970, Jardine was introduced as a second half substitute at Hampden Park in a European Championship qualifying tie against Denmark. Scotland were winning 1-0 through a fourteenth-minute goal from Derby County striker John O'Hare when boss Brown swapped like for like by withdrawing full-back for full-back, and the fact that it was a Rangers player replacing David Hay of Celtic, certainly pleased the huge Rangers contingent in the

Hampden crowd. Changing a full-back was highly unlikely to be a game changer and further fuels the fire developing in the media that manager Brown had a Rangers-driven agenda. That night, Jardine was in familiar company and had Rangers teammates John Greig, Ronnie McKinnon, Colin Stein and Willie Johnston in the Scotland starting side. Other than Hay, Celtic's only other representative was Jimmy "Jinky" Johnstone.

Bobby Brown remembers the game. "I had swithered about bringing Sandy into the squad simply because I wasn't sure of his best position. Was he a midfielder or half back as was in those days? He had been playing a few positions for Rangers but appeared to be settling in as right back.

"Remember, Sandy was still just twenty-one and competition for places in the squad was fierce. Tommy Gemmell was still only in his late twenties, Eddie McCreadie was thirty, John Greig gave me options in that role too and David Hay was a genuine emerging talent that took to international football like a natural. Was I showing a bias to Rangers by the number of Ibrox based players in the squad? Not at all! If anything I tended to favour more Anglos than home based players but it genuinely was more about who was on form at the time. Sure, at that time the Tartan Army, although they weren't really known as that then, was made up in a huge part by Rangers supporters but I never let it influence selection policy."

Brown knew Sandy Jardine was destined for a fine career. "Sandy was such a straightforward fellow to deal with. A delight. He just wanted to play but he had an appetite to learn on the training ground too. I'm proud to this day to say that I gave Sandy Jardine the first of his thirty-eight caps."

Sandy may have made his Scotland debut in a winning Scotland team that night against Denmark, but he had to wait almost a year for his next taste of international football. Injury had robbed him of the opportunity to play in

the home international series that year but when the call
came from Tommy Docherty to join the squad for another
European Championship qualifying tie, this time against
Portugal, Jardine was more than ready to grasp the opportunity. By the time of this game, Sandy Jardine was operating as a regulation right back in the new look Rangers side
under Willie Waddell and Jock Wallace. However, Tommy
Docherty, who had been in the Scotland job for a little over
a year, saw more in Sandy's game than "just" a full back.
For the crucial tie against Portugal, Tommy Docherty, The
Doc, handed Sandy a man-for-man marking role on none
other than the legendary Benfica play maker Eusébio!
Typically, Sandy didn't ask questions, no theatrics, he just
went out and did the job that was asked of him. Scotland
ran out 2-1 winners and the great Eusébio da Silva Ferreira
was substituted with twenty minutes of the game to play.
For the record, Tommy Docherty's selection that night was
predominately made up of Scots who played their football
south of the border and Jardine's only Ibrox teammate in
the starting eleven was Derek Johnstone.

One month later, as Scotland entertained Belgium at
Pittodrie, Docherty again deployed Sandy in a marking
role. This time the man in his sights was Paul Van Himst
who was a physically imposing and lightening-quick
forward in a very good Anderlecht side of the day. Again
Jardine showed his versatility, Van Himst was kept quiet
and Scotland won 1-0. Sandy was the only Rangers player
in the side.

Docherty was getting results that mattered with Sandy
Jardine a key part of his team shape but not everyone was
happy about things. Back at Ibrox, Rangers manager Willie
Waddell was of the belief that Sandy had much more to
offer than just stopping the opposition.

However, Tommy Docherty stuck with it and again
handed Sandy the role of the spoiler when Scotland travelled to Amsterdam in December 1971, and this time his
task was to put the shackles on Johan Cruyff who would

have been a candidate at that time for any greatest player in the world accolade. The side that saw Jardine again the only 'Light Blue' in dark blue put in an excellent performance but went down narrowly 2-1 to the total football that Holland were famed for.

The nomadic Tommy Docherty had vacated his Park Gardens office to take up the challenge of reviving the fortunes of Manchester United and his replacement in the Scotland job was an appointment that surprised many. Willie Ormond had been a flying winger in the Hibernian "Famous Five" frontline of the fifties and was now showing his qualities as manager of St. Johnstone. Ormond had taken Saints into Europe for the first ever time through guiding the Perth side to a third place league finish. He had St. Johnstone punching above their weight, of that there is no doubt, and had even taken them to the League Cup final of 1969 which they lost by a single goal to Celtic with Bertie Auld the Parkhead side's marksman.

Ormond was to prove to be a good fit for the Scotland job and one of his first decisions was to make Sandy Jardine his first choice right back. Ormond also had the vision to give regular Celtic right back Danny McGrain the left back beat in his Scotland side. He effectively set up a partnership that gave his side a truly different dimension and probably set the tone for the modern term of "wing backs" before others saw how the pace of both going forward added something extra to the attack, and when the ball was lost, the ability of both Jardine and McGrain to get back to cover was never in question.

Sandy Jardine captained his country on nine occasions. It's fair to say the period playing international football under Willie Ormond brought the best out in Sandy.

In the official match programme for Sandy's testimonial match against Southampton in May 1982, the other Scotland national managers Sandy had worked under all had positive comments to make about the committed and consistent Jardine whenever he pulled on the dark blue of Scotland.

Tommy Docherty wrote: "Sandy impressed me from the first time I saw him – he was my kind of player with so much ability for a full back. I used him in a marking role and he didn't object. In fact he played it magnificently. He was always ready to put the team's interests before his own."

How prophetic that is from Docherty when you consider the events at Rangers Football club thirty years later.

Willie Ormond, who had what for all the world appeared to be such a laid back attitude, moulded a team that would acquit themselves better than any other Scotland side before or since in tournament football, with Jardine a regular in his squads, said: "I always regarded Sandy as a very dependable kind of player. But not only that, he had a good turn of speed and could use the ball from the back as well as make runs and help join in attacks. Probably he hit his peak during our time together in the 1974 World Cup. He was twenty-five then – the age at which many players reach their top standard."

Next was Ally MacLeod who had whipped the nation into a frenzy with the belief that we could actually travel to Argentina and win the 1978 World Cup. "One of Sandy's main assets, I believe, is the fact that he is a deep thinker about the game. If and when he moves into coaching he should do well. When he emerged with Rangers as a full back he was several years ahead of his time as a great attacking player. The best game Scotland played in my time was against Czechoslovakia at Hampden in another World Cup qualifier in 1977, where we won 3-1 when Sandy and Danny McGrain were the full backs."

As we know, the Argentinian tournament didn't go to plan and Sandy only managed to play one game in the tournament in the Group Four match against Iran. The game finished in a 1-1 draw and ended Scotland's hopes of progressing in the tournament.

Jock Stein knew Sandy Jardine's qualities as well as anybody, having been in the Celtic dugout for many Old

Firm clashes, with Jardine an integral part of the Rangers side going back as far as the late 1960s. He noted: "Sandy's position is one in which Scotland have been pretty sound over the years and now, as it happens, Danny McGrain has tied it down. But, in my view, Sandy was always a very capable player, a good professional. At club level particularly he has shown his versatility by playing in so many different positions."

Sandy Jardine also had the distinction of captaining his country on nine occasions.

The first match that Sandy had the captain's armband on in the colours of Scotland was against East Germany at Hampden in an international challenge match in October 1974 under manager Willie Ormond. Scotland ran out 3-0 winners and that match gave international debuts to a twenty-one–year-old Graeme Souness, then making his way in the game with Middlesborough, and Dixie Deans, who would only appear in a Scotland jersey one more time while Souness would go on and amass a total of fifty-four caps. At the time, John "Dixie" Deans was a regular goal-scorer for Celtic but had previously come close to joining Jardine as a Rangers player. Deans had been performing well for Neilston Juniors and Rangers had shown a high level of interest but before they made any attempt to sign him, he had committed to Motherwell who sold him to Celtic in 1971 for £17,500.

Sandy also had the honour of leading Scotland out at Wembley in May 1975 in the British International Championship. It wasn't a happy day however as Scotland went down 5-1 in what was a personal disaster for Jardine's teammate Stewart Kennedy, who looked totally overawed by the occasion. Although it was suggested that the keeper had been injured in a previous match in the end of season tournament, he probably shouldn't have played as goals from Gerry Francis and Kevin Beattie had the auld enemy two up in the first six minutes. Bruce Rioch pulled a goal back for Scotland just short of the interval but any fightback was extinguished by goals from Colin Bell, Gerry Francis again and David Johnson in the second half.

Sandy Jardine managed only one goal in his Scotland career, and that had come one year before the Wembley disappointment in another home international, this time against Wales at Hampden. That day, Billy Bremner was the skipper and Sandy doubled Scotland's advantage from the penalty spot after Kenny Dalglish had opened the scoring. The game finished 2-0 in Scotland's favour.

Sandy picked up the last of his thirty-eight caps in December 1979 in a European Championship qualifier, with Belgium the visitors to Hampden. Jardine was given the captaincy by manager Jock Stein but again the game ended in disappointment with Belgium winning 3-1.

So Sandy's international career was over but it had spanned nine years and one month. If you analyse the average number of games then compared to now, it wouldn't be unfair to suggest that had Jardine been playing today, his thirty-eight caps would have been much nearer eighty or even 100 when you consider the limited number of games he lost to injury over the years.

14

BRING ON THE WORLD

Scotland were about to compete with the international elite of world football for the first time in sixteen years.

It was the summer of 1974 and West Germany was the venue.

The countries would be competing for a brand new trophy, "The FIFA World Cup Trophy". Designed by Italian sculptor Silvio Gazzaniga, it was replacing the previous Jules Rimet prize, which was now the permanent property of the Brazilian FA following their success in Mexico four years previously. That being Brazil's third World Cup win meant the original trophy was theirs to keep.

For Australia, East Germany, Haiti and Zaire, it was their first appearances at the world finals.

Scotland were positioned in Group Two with defending champions Brazil, new boys Zaire and old foes Yugoslavia. The games were scheduled to be played in the German cities of Dortmund and Frankfurt.

After securing qualification against Czechoslovakia, there was a real sense of optimism throughout Scotland that we could do well in Germany, although in typical Willie Ormond style – the polar opposite to the man who took us to the finals four years later, Ally MacLeod – he played it down and concentrated on building a team spirit that would stand us in good stead in the finals. However, in typical Scottish fashion, the preparations and warm-up games leading up to June 1974 didn't quite go to plan.

As ever, the home internationals were to be played at the end of the domestic season and while Scotland should have gone to play Northern Ireland in Belfast, the troubles in the province saw the game hosted in Glasgow meaning Scotland would play all three games on home turf. Despite the Hampden advantage, Scotland lost 1-0 to Northern Ireland but beat Wales three days later with a goal from Kenny Dalglish and a penalty from Sandy Jardine giving Scotland a comfortable win and setting up a showdown with the old enemy England. As it was, Scotland would beat England by the same scoreline as the Welsh game with Joe Jordan on target and an own goal from Colin Todd sealing the Scottish victory.

Leading up to the England game, the press would have a field day as some early morning "high jinks" left the Scotland squad's professionalism in tatters and questions being asked about Willie Ormond's management.

After the midweek win over Wales, a group of players left their base at the Queens Hotel in Largs with full approval of manager Ormond to indulge in a few refreshments. It became a late session and indeed the sun was coming up as the players made their way back to the hotel. Walking along the seafront, Celtic winger Jimmy Johnstone couldn't resist the opportunity to jump into a rowing boat that was berthed half on the shore and half in the water. "Jinky", who was renowned for his fine singing voice, had decided he was ready to serenade his teammates before they headed for bed at the hotel. As Jimmy started his vocals, Sandy Jardine, with a slight sense of devilment, pushed the bow of the small boat with his right foot maybe not as firmly, but just as assuredly as he had connected with the ball to convert Scotland's spot-kick the night before, and next thing, Jimmy Johnstone was heading out to sea having been caught by the tide in a rowing boat that was missing, of all things, oars! A prank that was now a concern. So much of a concern that Erich Schaedler and Davie Hay quickly boarded another boat nearby to go to Johnstone's rescue. The problem for Hay and Schaedler was their craft was leaking and they had to quickly scamper back to shore. Davie Hay recalls: "Looking back, it was funny. Wee Jimmy was heading to America and still singing his head off and by now the whole squad were on the prom killing ourselves laughing but I don't think Willie Ormond, who had been summoned from his bed by now, was. The coastguard was called and they got wee Jimmy in OK and although we all knew we shouldn't have done it, the whole escapade maybe just helped bond us a wee bit more."

The next day papers had the story as the front page splash.

By Sunday it was almost all forgotten as Scotland beat England for the first time since Jim Baxter's virtuoso performance in a 3-2 Wembley win in 1967. The British Championship was Scotland's. After the Hampden win, Baxter's good friend Jimmy Johnstone was warmly embraced on the pitch by manager Ormond, and Jinky gave a V-sign message to the press corps housed high in the stands on how he thought the papers had reported on the Largs boating incident. Davie Hay sums up Jimmy Johnstone's performance. "The wee man was just brilliant that day!"

Scotland warmed up for Germany with games in Belgium and Norway, and even with the finals getting closer, the Scotland camp still managed to find a way of putting manager Ormond under additional stress with another night out story. This time the location was Oslo, not Largs. Again, Jimmy Johnstone was at the heart of it as was Captain Billy Bremner. The squad had been billeted at a university campus and the facilities were fairly spartan. There were also issues on commercial matters, where players had been promised huge potential additional income through various sponsorship schemes that their appointed business manager Bob Bain had promised. These included sponsored boots and a Vauxhall car deal. The car was only for their use for one year and not for keeps and there weren't enough for everyone in the squad and the back-room team to have one each. As for the boots, the players ended up using the footwear of their choice although in some cases, branding was often unstitched where possible or covered over by black boot polish. It's fair to say there were frustrations and distractions leading up to setting up base camp in Germany.

In Oslo, Johnstone and Bremner missed the team dinner on the night of arrival and as things deteriorated, a hastily arranged meeting of the Scottish Football Association hierarchy saw both players severely reprimanded, but allowed to stay with the group despite pressure to have them sent home in disgrace. Suggestions remain that Jinky and Billy Bremner were given leniency as during their drinking session, they were actually joined by manager Ormond who had initially gone to their room to ask them to quieten down but ended up having a refreshment or two himself.

Despite the off-field performance, on the field Scotland summoned up enough to beat the largely part-timers of Norway 2-1 on the 6th of June with second-half goals from Jordan and Dalglish. Eight days later in the Westfalenstadion, Dortmund, Scotland would get their World Cup finals campaign up and running against Zaire.

Scotland started brightly and opened the scoring in twenty-six minutes through Peter Lorimer. They made it two eight minutes later with Lorimer's Leeds teammate Joe Jordan on target, but Scotland couldn't add to their scoreline against the first black African team at the World Cup finals. Scotland celebrated, but were the section to be decided on goals, only two against the side considered the poorest in the group could come back to haunt them. The day before the Zaire tie, favourites Brazil had been held to a goalless draw by Yugoslavia, and five days later, Scotland would emulate that feet with a very credible 0-0 against Brazil and it could have been so much different had Billy Bremner not passed up a great chance from only a yard out with the goal gaping. A win would have all but assured Scotland's qualification. As Scotland were going agonisingly close to beating Brazil, Yugoslavia were doing what Scotland couldn't against the "Leopards" of Zaire, putting nine goals past their opponents without reply with six of them coming in the first hour of the match.

This meant Scotland needed to beat Yugoslavia to make the next round of the tournament. On the same day, Brazil finished their group section with a 3-0 win over Zaire meaning Scotland had scored the least against the African minnows.

Scotland expected and prepared for a bruising encounter against the Yugoslavs and so it proved, although with the advantage, Yugoslavia set out their stall to try not to lose and to hit on the counter-attack. It was indeed the counter-attack that was the undoing of Scotland, and with only nine minutes remaining, Stanislav Karasi skipped away from Danny McGrain to put Yugoslavia ahead. Despite a rousing finish from Scotland and a goal from Joe Jordan in eighty-eight minutes, they failed to conjure up a winner.

Despite an undefeated record of one win and two draws, it wasn't enough to progress. Yugoslavia, Brazil and Scotland all finished the group on four points. Yugoslavia were group winners with a goal difference of +9, Brazil second with +3 and Scotland +2. Undefeated or not, Scotland were heading home.

It was an excellent campaign, even if the build-up to Germany had not been ideal, and it was the tournament that saw Sandy Jardine and Danny McGrain crowned the best full back partnership in the world.

Danny McGrain recalls his first World Cup experience with mixed emotions. "We were pretty much a mishmash group of players and we didn't have much coaching, but on the park we all got on with it. It was great to look back and think that we were undefeated, but maybe if we had known a bit more about opponents and what to expect, even in the conditions, we could have done even better.

"I know Sandy and I were voted the best full backs in the world at the time and that is high praise in itself when you think the Germans had Vogts and Breitner. Holland had Arie Haan and the Italian legend Facchetti was some player too." Danny believes the squad of 1974 team built its own special bond and spirit, adding: "We were friends and had respect for each other. Even when we had death threats supposedly from the IRA, we got through it together laughing like footballers do with their own brand of black humour."

The death threats Danny McGrain alludes to were taken seriously indeed and had come in the form of a handwritten letter with an English postmark, having been delivered to the police in Munich claiming to be from the IRA, and stating that "two killers had been sent with the instruction to kill two 'Scottish Protestant bastards!" This came on the evening before the crucial Yugoslavia clash. Immediately, security was tightened around the Scotland camp as it had only been two years previously, at the Munich Summer Olympics of September 1972, that the Palestinian terrorist group "Black September" had taken nine hostages from the Israeli party, including athletes, officials and coaches. All the hostages perished. In a botched rescue attempt, all the terrorists were killed as well. Two years on, Germany was on high alert to avoid any such repetition, and this supposed IRA threat was certainly not taken lightly by the German authorities.

Footballers are clearly a different breed. Danny McGrain explains, "We were given warnings and told that we had to be careful where we went and who we went with, even if just going shopping, we had security guards with us at all times."

It became public that the two targets to be eliminated were Sandy Jardine and Jimmy Johnstone.

McGrain remembers the reaction of the squad to the news. "Wee Jimmy just laughed and said 'that's me off the hook then – I don't qualify, but Sandy could be in trouble!', but we all made a joke of it although nobody would sit next to Sandy on the bus, saying what would happen if a shot went astray? Actually, we were just typically stupid foot-ballers believing nothing could happen to us. If Sandy was bothered, he never showed it, joining in with the banter and laughing at the jokes at his expense. I don't think players would have the same attitude now.

"As far as the best full backs partnership in the world goes, we were just doing our job. I never thought about moving from right back to left back and it's not for me to say who was better, Sandy or me, but we were both quick and could use the ball well. The press tended to make more of it than Sandy or I did and the manager Willie Ormond gave us minimal instructions, but he did used to say he wanted his best players on the park so making a wee adjustment from my club position was no big deal. I was comfortable on either side and had played on the left for Celtic too. Sandy had played everywhere for Rangers, maybe with the excep-tion of left back, but he was great to play with. I knew that if I got forward on one side, Sandy would tuck in to let one of the centre backs get across to cover and I did the same when Sandy went forward. Gordon McQueen, Jim Holton and John Blackley knew what our game was all about."

Legendary broadcaster Archie Macpherson covered the German finals and is in no doubt that it was as good a Scotland squad as he ever remembers. "We had a real club type mentality in the team Willie Ormond forged. A good mix of experience, pace and that good old Scottish term "gallus" comes to mind. Bremner the beating heart, Lorimer with his piledriver shots and Joe Jordan a real pest to play against. The guile came from the emerging Dalglish and the wily old campaigner Denis Law, but when it came to full backs – wow – we were so lucky to have not just one, but two genuine world-class craftsmen available at the same time. It says so much about Danny McGrain that he could seamlessly step into the left field role and not look out of place, but it also tells you just how good Sandy Jardine was that Danny had had to move over just to get in the team!

"Sure, we ultimately left disappointed and a few more goals against Zaire would have been enough, or had wee Billy put it in the net against Brazil instead of putting it beyond the post we might have made history, but we came home with our heads held high and don't forget, England hadn't even qualified for the finals!"

Sandy Jardine played in all three games in the West German finals as did Danny McGrain. Both players would experience other World Cup final campaigns. Jardine was in the squad four years later for Argentina and while McGrain missed out on that one through injury, he did make the squad for the finals in Spain in 1982 and amassed a total of sixty-two caps for his country, despite being diagnosed with diabetes on his return from the German finals of 1974.

So Scotland were British Champions in 1974 but their tilt at the world title ultimately ended in glorious defeat. So close, yet so far.

That pretty much could still be Scotland's mantra over forty years on.

15

TITLE TIME
1975 CHAMPIONS FOR
THE FIRST TIME IN ELEVEN YEARS

Celtic were heading for ten in a row.

Ten consecutive league titles were on the horizon for Celtic, and Rangers were determined not to let it happen. It was scheduled to be the final season of the Scottish League First Division as we knew it as plans were in place for a revised super sponsorship-attractive Scottish Premier League that was set to transform the Scottish game from season 1975/76.

Jock Wallace had been promoted from his Ibrox coaching role to manager after the European success in Barcelona in the club's centenary year with Willie Waddell moving upstairs.

Wallace had brought revolutionary training procedures into play and he built a squad on fitness stamina and desire, but all players in his charge could play a bit as well. There was much more to Jock Wallace than the rough-edged and often brusque demeanour of the man who had fought in the jungles of Malaysia for his country. Players respected him and believed in his methods which were innovative and tactically astute, much more astute and effective than many gave him credit for.

In his first season in charge, Wallace delivered the Scottish Cup for the first time since 1966. It was an epic final settled by that unforgettable Tam Forsyth goal from under the crossbar with the clumsiest of touches off the studs of his right boot as he forced the ball over the line.

Ian Archer in his after-match report for the *Glasgow Herald* described Rangers' win on the 100th anniversary of the Scottish Football Association as "a landmark for the Scottish game."

Celtic opened the scoring in twenty-four minutes when Deans released Kenny Dalglish who fired the ball beyond McCloy. However, instead of silencing the Rangers crowd, it inspired them to get fully behind their team and raise the Hampden decibel levels through a chorus of defiance. Within eleven minutes of going behind, Rangers were level. MacDonald lost Connelly after Mathieson sent him away and when the terrier-like midfielder delivered a near-post cross, Derek Parlane was first to react and headed the ball home. The noise from the Rangers end got even louder!

After half-time, when everyone drew breath, the game restarted at whirlwind pace again and Rangers took the lead within seventeen seconds of kick-off. Quintin "Cutty" Young played to Derek Parlane, and Alfie Conn pounced on his flick to race in on goal and slot the ball beyond Ally Hunter who had come off his line to close down the angle, with his centre half and Captain Billy McNeill stranded in no-man's-land.

Celtic dug deep into their reserves of character, and remember, this was a team in a winning habit with eight successive league titles behind them and it looked like a Dixie Deans piledriver had drawn them level, but Rangers skipper John Greig appeared out of the ether to fist the ball away on the goal line with his keeper beaten. Experienced referee John Gordon from Newport on Tay had no hesitation in awarding the penalty and unlike today, John Greig was allowed to stay on the field to play out the game!

George Connelly stepped up and slotted the spot-kick away in his usual calm cool style.

Ian Archer again in his *Herald* report captures the moment: "So an hour had proved nothing. The tension had partly abated and the 1973 final was there to be won by the team with the most skill. That was Rangers."

Alex MacDonald hit the post with a header then Derek Johnstone also had the same fate from an angled Tommy McLean delivery but this time the ball wasn't cleared, it trickled across the line and came off the inside of the other post and Tom Forsyth was on hand to force it over the line. Forsyth, who was not noted for his goalscoring prowess, was later quoted as saying, "I was so excited, I nearly missed it!"

A crowd of 122,714 had witnessed a thriller. Archer described it perfectly when he said Rangers had been "reawakened".

Sandy Jardine was a key member of that Rangers side on the day that the die was cast for an incredible period of Rangers success, although a further year in the wilderness was ahead.

In season 1973/74, Celtic won the Scottish Cup and claimed the double with their ninth league title in a row.

For season 1974/75, Wallace made subtle changes to his playing squad with Stewart Kennedy now first choice goalkeeper and Colin Jackson a cornerstone of his defence. It was the last of the old League One and the campaign started with a 1-1 draw away at Ayr United with Sandy Jardine on target from the penalty spot. Rangers then found their rhythm and went eleven games undefeated with Jardine adding to his goal tally, converting another three penalties against Kilmarnock, Clyde and Hearts. Goals were being shared throughout the side but Derek Parlane stole the show helping himself to five in a 6-1 demolition of Dunfermline Athletic on their own East End Park.

The fans sang "Parlane, Parlane... born is the king of Ibrox Park" but Sandy Jardine was king of the penalty takers, scoring again from the spot against Dundee United, Airdrie and Ayr United (again) before the turn of the year.

Celtic were thumped at Ibrox 3-0 in the New Year derby with Derek Johnstone, Tommy McLean and Derek Parlane the marksmen and perhaps proving that the 2-1 win at Parkhead earlier in the season against the reigning champs was no fluke.

The 29th of March is a day that should be remembered for ever in Rangers history.

That was the day that Rangers clinched the league title, the club's first in eleven years, stopped Celtic making it ten in a row and laid the foundations for the treble winning season of 1975/76.

Rangers travelled to Easter Road needing only a point against Hibernian to claim the league flag.

Ally McLeod opened the scoring for the home side and Sandy Jardine, uncharacteristically, failed to convert a penalty, striking the ball well enough but watching on in agony as it cannoned back off the post. He atoned for passing up that chance with a fine delivery to set Bobby McKean scampering away before delivering an inch perfect delivery for Colin Stein to claim his first goal since returning to Rangers from Coventry City – against the team who had sold him to the Light Blues the first time round.

Sandy Jardine captained Rangers that day with John Greig only fit enough to take a place on the bench. In the dying embers of the game with Rangers' destiny assured, Sandy took the decision to substitute himself and let Greig, the greatest ever Ranger, take to the field and be part of the celebrations.

It was a particularly poignant moment and gave a extra dimension to a special day for Rangers' senior players like Greig and Jardine who for too long had been in Celtic's shadow.

However, while Rangers celebrated and their fans partied in Scotland's capital, not many knew that a number of their league-winning heroes had almost left the club in the summer, before a ball had been kicked in the campaign.

There were issues on money within the Rangers dressing

room and Colin Jackson, Derek Johnstone and Sandy
Jardine were at the heart of the difficulties. Sandy was out
of contract and was effectively playing out his one-year
option. Jackson and Johnstone had said if an improvement
on wages wasn't evident they would be looking to continue
their careers away from Ibrox.

Sandy Jardine went to see then General Manager
Willie Waddell in the hope of negotiating a new contract
on improved terms but was dismissed with a flat "No".
Press reports suggested Tottenham Hotspur, Everton and
Manchester were all keen to sign the twenty-five-year-old
who had yet to hit the peak of his career.

Sandy was in his tenth season as a Ranger and was now
married with a family and it surely wasn't unreasonable to
expect long service, commitment and loyalty to be rewarded.
To make his point after the Waddell rebuff, these were the
key points Sandy made in a letter to the board. Sandy made
his point but at no time did he ask for a transfer and he
made it quite clear his preference was to stay at Rangers.

As usual at international squad gatherings, chat turns to
money between the players and Sandy had just come back
from performing better than very well at the 1974 World
Cup finals in Germany, and it was during this campaign it
became obvious that many of the Scotland squad who were
playing south of the border were earning double Sandy's
wages at Ibrox.

It wasn't quite a summer of discontent but it was close to it.

By the time Rangers entertained St. Johnstone in a League
Cup tie at Ibrox in early August, improved contracts had
been brokered and, before the game, Rangers announced
over the tannoy that Sandy Jardine, Colin Jackson and
Derek Johnstone would continue to be Rangers players.

The impact of this trio in that successful season should
not be understated.

Alfie Conn had been sold to Spurs, Dave Smith moved on
to Arbroath with Bobby McKean coming in from St. Mirren
and Colin Stein coming back for a second spell at the club.

The three "Js" trio of Jardine, Jackson and Johnstone were to be the most influential, with Jardine making forty-two competitive appearances and deputising as captain when John Greig wasn't available (Greig only played twenty-three games that season), and chipping in with an astonishing fourteen goals. Colin Jackson played in forty matches scoring three times while Derek Johnstone, who so often shuttled between centre forward and centre half, played thirty-five times and scored sixteen goals. Derek Parlane again finished top scorer for the third year running with eighteen.

Parlane holds special memories of that season and for one obvious reason in particular. "Winning the league that season was vital because if Celtic had, then they would have completed their ten in a row goal and we were all focused on ensuring they didn't do that, so when we beat Hibs 1-0 at Easter Road to take the title in what was the last ever old First Division before changing to the SPL, that sparked euphoria amongst the lads and the fans as something that I will never forget.

"Sandy had a great season scoring fourteen goals but I still finished top with eighteen."

Alex MacDonald is in no doubt about the pivotal game in the campaign. "We went head-to-head with Celtic in the New Year fixture on the January 4th at Ibrox and gave them a 3-0 doing. Should have been four but referee John Paterson chalked off my close-range effort that beat Ally Hunter in the Celtic goal. As I wheeled away to celebrate, I was pulled up for showing my studs as I lunged to turn the ball into the net. I was furious but goals from the two Dereks (Johnstone and Parlane) and wee Tommy McLean sent us to the top of the league that day!

"We never looked back and in that run-in to the Easter Road showdown we dropped only two points with draws against Morton away and Kilmarnock at home. Celtic, meanwhile, seemed to lose their way and took only six points in their next nine matches. They never got over that loss at New Year."

Rangers had wrapped up the title with four games of the campaign still to be played. It was a case of hard work paying off with the Wallace dedication and physical fitness key components, but probably more influential was the team spirit in the squad which was another factor that Wallace made happen.

It was also a triumph for players who weren't always in the starting side, but when called upon, guys like Jim Denny, Johnny Hamilton, Graham Fyfe, Ally Scott and youngsters Alex O'Hara and Ricky Sharp played their part and never let their teammates or the expectant Rangers support down.

The cup competitions that season weren't kind to Rangers, crashing out of the Scottish in the third round to Aberdeen in an Ibrox replay after a 1-1 draw between the sides, while the Light Blues didn't progress from the sectional round of the League Cup, losing twice to Hibernian. However, with the league secured at the home of the Leith club, revenge was sweet.

It had been eleven long years since Rangers' last title and now plans were being made to ensure Rangers would build on this success and go all out to be the first name on the shiny new Scottish Premier League trophy up for grabs in the next season.

16

MAKE MINE A TREBLE

With the First Division championship trophy now taking pride of place again in the Ibrox trophy room from the campaign of 1974/75, and with Celtic's monopoly of Scotland's top flight broken, Jock Wallace and his squad made winning the brand new trophy under the revised Premier League structure their main aim for season 1975/76.

There was no major surgery to the squad but youngsters like Derek Parlane and Bobby McKean, who had been recruited from St. Mirren, cemented their places as key men in the group, while the bedrock of the side was still there in the form of Euro winners Greig, Derek Johnstone, Jardine, McLean and MacDonald.

In the previous season, deposed champions Celtic could only finish eleven points behind winners Rangers, four points behind runners up Hibernian and in fact were tied with Dundee United on forty-five points, but took third spot with a better goal difference.

It was a traumatic time for Rangers' biggest rivals as Celtic had lost the services of the man who had delivered the European Cup and masterminded nine in a row. Jock Stein had been seriously injured in a car accident on the

A74 in July and as teams prepared for the new season, Stein was fighting for his life in Dumfries and Galloway Royal infirmary. Stein would recover from his life-threatening injuries but it ruled him out of influencing almost all of Celtic's season in 1975/76 and the campaign was managed by his long-term assistant Sean Fallon. Many felt Jock Stein was never quite the same after the accident and despite so many years of success, Celtic were looking at a potentially difficult period of transition.

As luck would have it, Glasgow's great rivals were paired together on the opening day of the league season. Ibrox was the venue and the Light Blues took the honours in a 2-1 win with Derek Johnstone and Cutty Young the goalscorers.

The new league had only ten teams and it meant they faced each other four times in the campaign.

The opening-day win set Rangers off on a fine run of six games undefeated before back-to-back defeats, both on their travels, crashing to a 3-0 loss at Ayr United then going down 2-1 to Motherwell at Fir Park.

Was confidence fragile? Apparently not. Rangers' next fixture took them into the lion's den of Celtic Park and a crowd of 60,000, the majority of which were home fans, saw Jock Wallace's men head back across the city with a share of the points. Derek Parlane broke the deadlock after a mix-up in the Celtic rear guard between Lynch and Callaghan but within three minutes, the home side hit back through a close-range finish from Paul Wilson after teenage debutant George McCluskey's pace had taken him clear of Rangers' defence. The game finished 1-1 but it was enough to position Celtic at the top of the league on twelve points from eight games with Rangers down to fourth place with eleven points, but having played one game more. Hibs and Motherwell in second and third were sandwiched between both halves of the Old Firm.

Despite that draw at Parkhead, as winter set in, the early season expectations were evaporating.

Hopes for the season had been heightened as Rangers

had already claimed the first silverware of the season with the League Cup being won by the end of October when, again, Celtic provided the opposition in another thrilling Hampden Final. The game had been scheduled for a lunch-time kick-off in an experiment to limit crowd troubles. Alex MacDonald's goal, an exquisite diving header from a Quinton Young or Cutty as his team mates called him, delivery, ensured the League Cup was inscribed with the name of Rangers FC for the eighth time in their history and the first leg of a potential domestic treble was secured.

Alex MacDonald recalls the memorable occasion and his goal in particular. "It doesn't get any better than that to score the winning goal in a cup final against your biggest rivals. I remember thinking, 'Just blow the whistle for full time!' I didn't want anybody else to score."

The League Cup campaign yielded twenty-seven goals for Rangers in ten games, starting with a 6-1 thrashing of Airdrieonians at Ibrox. Sandy Jardine claimed a hat-trick, which included converting two penalties, and his third coming from a sweetly-struck left-foot drive. Colin Stein and Derek Parlane also scored and another penalty was tucked away by Alex Miller. Airdrie's consolation also came from the spot with Paul Jonquin doing the needful for the Diamonds.

It was the only hat-trick of Sandy's senior career although he had previously gone one better in October 1968 by scoring four goals in a 7-1 Rangers rout of Queen's Park at Ibrox in a Glasgow Cup tie.

Next up it was a narrow win against Clyde with Derek Johnstone's goal the difference in the sides. Motherwell and Rangers settled for 1-1 after ninety minutes at Ibrox with skipper John Greig scoring, and when the sides met again one week later at Fir Park, it was another draw but 2-2 this time with another strike from Sandy Jardine and a penalty from the reliable Alex Miller. In between the Motherwell fixtures, Clyde were despatched at Ibrox with Rangers racking up another six goals. Parlane claimed a double which was added to by singles from Jackson, Miller with another spot kick, Young and Johnstone. The league section came to a close at Airdrie's quaint Broomfield stadium but Rangers were again too strong in every department and left with a 2-0 victory, with goals from Johnstone and Young ensuring Rangers progressed to the quarter finals of the tournament where Queen of the South would provide the opposition over a two-leg affair played home and away. Derek Johnstone was again on target in both legs with the only goal of the game at Ibrox and the opener at Palmerston, but it took a goal in extra time from Alex MacDonald after the game ended 2-1 in favour of Queens after ninety minutes.

After the match, Rangers schemer Tommy McLean took off his shirt in the tunnel and handed it to Queens' legendary defender Iain McChesney (he played for the club for twenty-one years!) saying you might as well have this as you have been pulling at it all night! Ten minutes later Rangers boss Jock Wallace went to the home dressing room and demanded the return of the shirt but McChesney claimed he had already given it away. In fact he hadn't, but he wasn't ready to relinquish his souvenir from a thrilling night for the Doonhamers.

Next up was a visit to Hampden for the semi-final to take on Montrose in a game played on a Monday night. It was Montrose's first ever national semi-final and despite operating in a lower league, manager Alex Stuart had assembled a useful side with a mix of youth and experience that had beaten Raith Rovers, St. Mirren, East Fife and Hibernian to book their place against Rangers.

Incredibly, Montrose showed no signs of nerves on the occasion and took the game to Rangers. After forty-five minutes, Rangers were chasing the game with The Gable Endies going in at half-time with a one-goal lead. Les Barr converted a penalty just short of the half-time whistle.

Into the second period and still Montrose were relent-less. Rangers rode their luck when a driven effort from Bob

Livingstone cannoned back off the base of Peter McCloy's post and into the path of Derek Parlane. The "King of Ibrox" made himself the King of Hampden as he ran the length of the national stadium to score a stunning solo goal to put his side back on level terms. That Rangers goal turned the game on its head and they never looked back, scoring another four goals from Johnstone, another Miller penalty and late strikes from Ally Scott and Sandy Jardine to put some gloss on the scoreline which saw Rangers through 5-1, but it was a much tougher tie than the final score suggests.

So it was on to the final against Celtic seventeen days later.

To get to the final, Celtic won their section that contained Heart of Midlothian, Aberdeen and Dumbarton. They beat Stenhousemuir home and away in the quarter finals and a 1-0 goal win against Partick Thistle in their semi-final was enough to put them in the final to defend their trophy, having thumped Hibernian 6-3 in the previous season's final.

Celtic were missing last season's final hat-trick hero Dixie Deans through injury while Kenny Dalglish shook off an ankle knock and was fit to play. However, Jock Wallace designated Tam Forsyth to do a man-marking job on Dalglish and he had little influence on the game because of the attentions of big Tam. The close attention paid to his man by the Rangers iron man greatly frustrated the Celtic support, as had recent events at their club that included Davie Hay being sold to Chelsea, Billy McNeill retiring, and the bizarre situation of George Connelly turning his back on the game to become a bus driver!

So the goal in sixty-seven minutes from MacDonald crafted by the guile of Parlane and Young settled the tie and Rangers claimed the cup for the first time since the sixteen–year-old sensation Derek Johnstone's winning goal of 1970.

Only one team could win the treble now.

Back to Premier League business and the cup final success was not quite the inspiration for Rangers as their fans had hoped for with results being inconsistent. Losses were recorded to Hearts, Hibs and Aberdeen but the 1-0 defeat at Pittodrie on the 6th December 1975 was a watershed fixture of the season as Rangers then went on an unbeaten run of nineteen games that took them through to 24 April 1976, when the title was won with a 1-0 victory at Tannadice. Derek Johnstone was again on target for his twenty-ninth goal of the season against the team he supported as a boy, Dundee United.

The other Derek, Parlane, had to concede top dog status on the goalscoring chart but recalls that the title wasn't won by eleven players, but by a squad of nearer twenty. "Winning the treble was awesome and I have fantastic memories of that team. League reconstruction meant a ten team set up so we had to play each other four times – it took a bit of getting used to, but I think we maybe adapted better than the rest. It was a real squad effort and I hit a spell of not firing on all cylinders around November time. One Friday I was called into manager Jock Wallace's office to be told I wouldn't be playing the next day. I was shocked and quite emotional about someone else wearing my number nine jersey but if I was being honest, I knew I hadn't been playing well. Martin Henderson came in as my replacement and grabbed his chance while I had to settle for a place on the bench. I remember Martin getting both goals in a 2-1 win away at Tynecastle. He scored a few and was a decent player."

That season, Parlane made forty appearances in all competitions and contributed ten goals while Henderson, who was later to join up with Jock Wallace again when he took charge at Leicester, contributed thirteen goals from thirty-three appearances.

Rangers started 1976 with a single goal win in the New Year's day Old Firm derby and it was another goal from Derek Johnstone that sealed the points.

It was the first Rangers-Celtic derby to be played on the first day of the year since 1969.

The only goal of the game came on the half hour mark,

and it was the accuracy of delivery from Tommy McLean and the timing of the jump from Johnstone that outwitted the Celtic defence as DJ powered his header out of the reach of Peter Latchford in the Celtic goal and into the net.

However, despite starting the year with a huge morale-boosting win, it wasn't enough to go top of the table. Both Rangers and Celtic had played nineteen games but Celtic had won eleven to Rangers' ten, and that was enough to keep them top of the new Premier League by a single point. However, Rangers were snapping at their heels and setting themselves up for a sensational 1976 and a season where Celtic failed to beat Rangers in five attempts.

While domestically Rangers were doing well, in Europe in 1975 it was another disappointment.

Their return to the European Cup started with a home game against Bohemians of Dublin and a comfortable 4-1 win followed up with a 1-1 draw in Ireland. Next up it was French champions St. Etienne who showed real quality to defend their 2-0 home leg victory and win 2-1 at Ibrox to eliminate Rangers three weeks before Christmas.

Perhaps the relatively early Euro exit was a blessing in disguise with the way things evolved on the home front.

The Scottish Cup campaign started just after Rangers had hit a winning run of form with a home tie against East Fife, and a 30,000 crowd saw Rangers ease into the fourth round where they would meet Aberdeen.

The side from Methil were despatched 3-0 with Alex MacDonald, Martin Henderson and Johnny or "Dingy" Hamilton as he was known to his teammates, claiming the second of the two goals he would score all season. Rangers again had the benefit of a home draw, and double the crowd that attended the East Fife third round match witnessed Rangers effect a demolition job on the Dons with a 4-1 victory. Alex MacDonald and Martin Henderson were again on target as were the two Dereks, Johnstone and Parlane.

We were now well into March and Rangers remained

on an unbeaten run when the quarter final draw paired them with Queen of the South just as it had done in the League Cup back in September, but unlike Scotland's other cup competition which was played on a two-leg home and away basis, the premier cup competition was a straight knockout tournament. When Rangers last visited Queens at Palmerston Park the game finished 2-2 but on this visit, Rangers were invincible and never gave the Doonhamers any opportunities of note, and ran out 5-0 winners to book their place in the semi-finals. The goals in Dumfries came from Martin Henderson, again showing his value to the squad, and doubles from Derek Johnstone and Bobby McKean.

Rangers were then paired with Motherwell in the semi-final and that would be a stern test as the Steelmen had knocked Celtic out in the third round, winning a 3-2 thriller at Fir Park. They had a really capable in form goal threat provided by the strong running Willie Pettigrew and the guile of former Liverpool man Bobby Graham.

That result and Rangers' good run in the league effectively meant Celtic were looking at a barren season for trophies.

Hampden Park hosted the semi-final and just like the Celtic-Motherwell tie, the game ended 3-2, although this time it was in Rangers' favour with the crucial goals coming from an Alex Miller penalty and a double for Derek Johnstone who just couldn't stop scoring. The result said a lot about Rangers' character, which was a word often used by then manager Jock Wallace, as they had been two down to goals from Stewart McLaren and Pettigrew, but Miller's early second-half penalty proved the inspiration for the fightback.

In the other semi-final it took Heart of Midlothian two games against Dumbarton to join Rangers in the final, prevailing 3-0 in a replay after the first match ended in a drab goalless draw.

The final was scheduled for Hampden on the 1st of May 1976, which was just over one month after the semis.

In the intervening period in April, Rangers clinched the league with that victory at Tannadice and with two games of the campaign remaining, Derek Johnstone and his teammates' thoughts were drifting to the potential of a sensational clean sweep of honours in the Scottish game. "The league was our priority but winning is habit forming and we took that into the cup run too, and after we won at Queen of the South, we just started to think, just maybe, that our name was on the cup."

Johnstone's goalscoring form was to continue and despite missing the opening tie in the cup against East Fife, Derek had scored five goals in three ties as Rangers booked their place in the final. At Hampden against Hearts Johnstone scored a brace, making it thirty-one in total and would round off a special season for the Dundonian who was still just twenty-two years of age.

Rangers were on the verge of completing the treble of the new SPL League title, the League Cup and the Scottish Cup.

This had only previously been achieved twice in the history of the club. The first in the 1948/49 season with the iron curtain defence side featuring legends Cox, Shaw, Woodburn, Young and current General Manager Willie Waddell and the last and most recent being under Scot Symon's management and the legendary team of Richie, Shearer, Caldow, Baxter, etc, in season 1963/64. Incredibly, Rangers skipper John Greig, who was part of the last treble winning squad twelve years before, was about to do it again.

For Sandy Jardine, his season had been interrupted by a serious Achilles tendon injury that limited his ability to play a full ninety minutes and would indeed require corrective surgery in the summer close season. However, ahead of the final, Sandy had made thirty-six appearances in all tournaments and chipped in with seven goals.

So on the first day of May 1976, Rangers were set to make history and started the match in the best possible fashion.

Sandy Jardine was only fit enough to be named as a

substitute with Alex Miller lining up in the right back berth. The game was scheduled for a three o'clock kick-off but despite crowds still streaming into Hampden, Referee Bobby Davidson started the match early and with only forty-five seconds on the clock, Derek Johnstone had given Rangers the lead. It was officially confirmed that the goal was scored before 3:00 pm!

That goal settled any nerves in the Rangers ranks and almost ended the Hearts challenge before it began. Alex MacDonald notched the vital second goal just short of half-time and Johnstone claimed his second and Rangers' third on the day before Graham Shaw scored a consolation goal for Hearts.

Sandy Jardine played his part coming off the bench for Dingy Hamilton in the second half.

The summer surgery was to prove successful for Jardine and he would go on to play in every competitive fixture the following season.

17

DOUBLE TREBLE TIME

If season 1975/76 was to be one that went down as one of the best in Rangers' history – winning all three domestic prizes – the following season proved to be the polar opposite with the Ibrox club failing to defend any of their trophies.

Arguably, the most significant influence on why Rangers failed to hit the heights of the previous season was the return of Jock Stein to the Celtic manager's office, having made a full recovery from the life threatening car accident of 1975. Stein's return saw Celtic recruit wisely, with the vastly experienced Pat Stanton coming in from Hibs to strengthen the defence and Joe Craig joined from Partick Thistle to increase their goal threat and take some pressure off Kenny Dalglish. His Thistle manager Davie McParland, who had been in charge when Partick shocked Celtic and Scottish football by beating them in the League Cup final of 1971, joined as assistant manager and later in the season, Stein made the extremely controversial decision to capture the services of Alfie Conn from Tottenham under Rangers' noses when the Light Blues had been favourites to re-sign their Barcelona hero.

Celtic had tooled up well to wrestle the title back from

Rangers who were looking to make it three league successes in a row. Jock Wallace had also supplemented his squad with Iain Munro swapping Easter Road for Ibrox while Colin Stein had returned to the club towards the end of the previous season. Youngsters Kenny Watson and Chris Robertson would enjoy more game time and giant defender Jim Steele came in on loan from Southampton, but he failed to make an impression.

Rangers played fifty-four competitive matches in season 1976/77 but could only finish second in the table, nine points behind champions Celtic, while cup competitions offered no success either. They were roundly trounced 5-1 in the semi-final of the League Cup by Aberdeen, exited Europe in the first round to F.C. Zürich with a tame 1-1 draw at Ibrox, and a 1-0 defeat in the second leg in the Swiss capital.

It left the Scottish Cup as Rangers' best bet for silverware.

That campaign started well enough with a 3-1 win at Ibrox over Falkirk with Sandy Jardine converting a penalty, and Johnstone and MacDonald also on target. Elgin were next to visit and again Rangers scored three through Jackson, McLean and another from MacDonald, this time without reply to set up a quarter-final clash with old foes Motherwell. Again, Rangers had home advantage and progressed with another clean sheet and goals from McKean and Kenny Watson.

It was Heart of Midlothian in the semi-final in a repeat of the previous year's final. Hearts failed to find their form however and Rangers were back in the final through goals from Colin Jackson and a Sandy Jardine penalty, having yet to play a tie in this campaign outside Glasgow.

It was an Old Firm final, the first since 1971.

The game was to be the first Scottish Cup final shown live on television since 1955. On the day, a combination of poor weather and the lure of TV saw the teams contest the match in front of the lowest post-war crowd for the final of only 54,252 inside the national stadium.

The match was settled by a penalty goal from Celtic full

back Andy Lynch after Derek Johnstone had been judged by Dundee whistler Bob Valentine to have handled the ball on the goal line.

The win gave Jock Stein his twenty-fifth and last trophy as Celtic manager.

It had been a season of major disappointment for the Rangers fans and changes for the next campaign were essential.

Rangers spent heavily in the summer of 1977.

Gordon Smith was signed from Kilmarnock for a fee of £65,000, while Clydebank banked a Rangers cheque for £100,000 for self-confessed Rangers fan Davie Cooper who had given the Light Blue defence a torrid time over the four games it took Rangers to progress against Clydebank in the League Cup the previous season.

Another signing was to prove an incredible piece of business by manager Jock Wallace. Wallace saw something in Bobby Russell, who was playing for Shettleston Juniors, to give the twenty-year-old a shot at the big time and what a visionary decision it was. Russell became a fixture in Rangers' midfield, playing forty-eight games in his debut season and scoring on his first competitive start for the club, albeit a consolation goal as Rangers lost their opening day league encounter 3-1 away to Aberdeen. If Russell was a shock, Gordon Smith proved a revelation with his free running from deep to support the strikers, and scored twenty-seven goals in that first season. Like Smith, Cooper made the most appearances in the squad with fifty-two and apart from his eight goals, his promptings, probing and precision passes reignited Derek Johnstone's scoring prowess, and DJ claimed an incredible thirty-eight goals from forty-seven appearances throughout the season. Derek Johnstone recalls a side that was extremely inventive. "We had loads of pace, particularly in the final third and remember, we didn't play to a conventional system. Often I was left to lead the attack on my own and it was about getting midfield runners beyond me."

"Smudger" (Gordon Smith) was ideal for that role. An injury free Sandy Jardine was also back to his best and contributed six goals as Rangers mounted a challenge on all fronts. Derek also credited Sandy with the development of Davie Cooper. "Coop was mostly all left foot but he was comfortable operating on the right. So often, Davie held it up for Sandy to go past him then Coop would clip inside on his left to exploit the space created by Sandy's movement, and of course, if it broke down, nobody was better at getting back to recover than Sandy Jardine.

"You very rarely, if ever, saw Sandy sell himself cheaply or go to ground. He wasn't a great tackler mind you. He didn't need to be – he just ushered his opponent into an area where he wanted him then would cutely lift the ball off his toe if he hesitated or pushed it any more than a half yard ahead of himself. That's all Sandy needed to win the ball back. His game was all about timing.

"For Coop though, Sandy communicated with him all the time and going forward it was some partnership, although Davie didn't maybe always return the compliment when we had some defending to do."

It could have been much different though as Sandy's former Rangers teammate from the 1967 European final in Nuremberg, Roger Hynd, was by then managing Motherwell and had a bid to buy Sandy and midfield fringe man Kenny Watson turned down by the Rangers board.

It wasn't the best of starts as the week after the opening-day defeat to Aberdeen, Rangers lost again, this time going down 2-0 at home to Hibernian. It was hardly the platform you would expect for Rangers to deliver the fourth domestic treble in their history.

The pivotal match was the first Old Firm meeting of the season. Ibrox was the venue, and after forty-five minutes Rangers were two down. Gordon Smith, who had claimed his first Rangers goals with a double in the league match previously in a 4-0 landslide victory over Partick Thistle, again scored twice, and Derek Johnstone got the other to overturn the half-time deficit and claim the bragging rights in the first pairing of Rangers and Celtic of the season. The Light Blues then went on a run of thirteen league games without defeat, but thirteen being the unlucky number as they were brought crashing back to earth on Christmas Eve 1977 with a 4-0 reversal against Aberdeen at Pittodrie.

Gordon Smith remembers reporting to Ibrox on his first day after putting pen to paper on a deal from Kilmarnock. "As I was walking toward the front door of Ibrox, a taxi drew up and John Greig and Sandy Jardine got out, both dressed immaculately and setting fine examples as the senior players of the side. Sandy immediately shook my hand and welcomed me to Rangers but Greigy just said, 'Don't know what we've signed you for – we've already got Davie Cooper!' Welcome to Ibrox? Maybe that comment was typical of the humour that would permeate the Rangers dressing room that season."

For Smith's first game as a Ranger, he was on the bench. It was against Swiss side BSC Young Boys and he looked on in awe as Bobby Russell ran the show. "I couldn't believe it. I had to ask, 'Are you sure he has just come out the Juniors with Shettleston?' He was so composed and comfortable on the ball. It was a great Rangers team that was being shaped by Jock Wallace and he told me when he brought me in he had a specific role in mind for me. That role was to be the man that got from midfield with pace to support the main striker. We really played a 4-3-3 with Tommy McLean and Davie Cooper wide, and I was effectively the second striker. Experience was in the back four, they knew exactly what they were doing. John Greig was captain and left back Colin Jackson teamed up with big Tam Forsyth at the heart of the defence with Sandy Jardine at right back.

"I had so much admiration for Sandy having played against him many times when I was used as a left winger with Kilmarnock, and now playing with him, I got to see just how good he was in all aspects of his game. It was a great spirit in that dressing room and giving out and taking stick was part and parcel of a day at Rangers. Sandy could give it out too, although he had a gentle and quirky sense of fun. Some people could take offence, and one of them was Davie Cooper. I had to take Coop aside and tell him that it was all just a kid-on and not to take it personally. That came about when in our early days at the club, as the kit man was laying out our strips, Sandy said, 'Is that Coop's pyjamas you are putting out there?' (in reference to his sleepy laid back style) I saw Davie's face fall, but full time football banter was different to his previous experiences when at Clydebank, he would see teammates only for a few hours' training twice a week and on match days. I knew from being at Kilmarnock that this was a different environment. It was only a bit of fun! Coop soon got the message and ended up being one of the most wicked wits in the squad!"

Another example of Sandy's wit again involved Smith and it was in reference to the hit TV show of the day *The Big Time* where someone would be taken out of their regular position at work and be given responsibilities or a job far greater than they were trained or experienced for. Effectively being put in the limelight for a day. The show was hosted by Esther Rantzen. One example was an amateur musician who was given the opportunity to conduct an orchestra at the Fairfield Hall, while in another, a cookery competition winner was given the opportunity to act as head chef and prepare a banquet at the Royal Albert Hall for former Prime Minister Edward Heath. Gordon recalls Sandy's barbed comment about three weeks after he signed: "Sandy quipped 'how long is Esther Rantzen leaving you here for?' and I joked back 'I signed here to save you getting four doings a year' (in reference to Old Firm games) and he just laughed. Sandy could dish it out but he loved it if you came back with a good retort.

"It was a hard dressing room to be in with a lot of strong characters. Big Peter McCloy and Alex MacDonald were still there, and big Derek Johnstone had a sharp tongue too. Even the manager Big Jock could give it out. The secret was being able to know when he was being serious and when he was just having a laugh.

"There is another story that indicates the kind of humour Sandy had. One day in the changing room he pinned up a newspaper cutting that reported on a giraffe collapsing in Glasgow Zoo, and he changed its name to Big Peter, but it was all about fun, nothing serious, even though big Peter produced two sets of boxing gloves and challenged Sandy to a few rounds, which I have to say Sandy flatly refused to entertain."

On the field, Rangers were deadly serious in their pursuit of trophies. Europe was a frustration but with hindsight, maybe it avoided distraction. Rangers progressed from the qualifying round 3-2 on aggregate over Young Boys of Bern, but failed in the next round against FC Twente, drawing 0-0 at home and losing 3-0 away. In the League Cup, St. Johnstone, Aberdeen and Dunfermline were all beaten over two legged home and away ties to set up a semi-final against Forfar. Forfar were beaten at Hampden and it would be Celtic that Rangers would face in the final scheduled for the 18th March 1978. On the way to the final, Derek Johnstone had scored five goals and Gordon Smith had delivered four from his advanced midfield position.

The Scottish Cup campaign started with a visit to Berwick Rangers and the ghost of 1967 was laid to rest. The big Rangers won 4-2 with Derek Johnstone and Colin Jackson both on target with two apiece. Next it was a narrow 1-0 home victory over Stirling Albion and the week before the League Cup final, Rangers scored four again in the Scottish Cup quarter final against Kilmarnock. The goals were shared by Johnstone, Hamilton, MacDonald and a penalty from Cooper.

In the league, Rangers had recovered from the defeat at Aberdeen and went seven games undefeated before losing again to Aberdeen, this time 3-0, but this time it was at Ibrox.

However, tragedy was just around the corner.

Bobby McKean, who had featured in fifteen matches that season and had been signed from St. Mirren in 1974, died in an horrific incident at his home in Barrhead outside Glasgow. McKean was only twenty-five when he died. He had been found dead in his car from carbon monoxide poisoning.

It was later confirmed that, after telling his wife he wouldn't be home that night, Bobby McKean had a change of mind and left the function he was attending in East Kilbride to drive home. Road conditions were terrible as the West of Scotland was gripped in a blizzard. Without a key and unable to rouse his wife to let him into the house, he garaged his car, closed the doors and made to spend the night there. Sometime during the night and in an effort to get warm, Bobby started the car and put the heater on. He was found the next day by a family friend.

Just three days after the death of teammate McKean, Rangers were to contest the League Cup final. Gordon Smith used to travel with McKean regularly as did Derek Johnstone. Both were devastated. Derek Johnstone was in fact waiting for McKean to pick him up on the morning before he was found, and eventually took a taxi to training. "I got into Ibrox and the boss gave me what for as I was late. I told him I had been waiting on wee Bobby McKean and big Jock told me that he hadn't turned up either. I couldn't believe it when the news broke that he had died."

On the way to the final Rangers had beaten Aberdeen, who were the holders. Gordon Smith was on tremendous form that October night with Rangers enjoying home advantage. "Jock Wallace said that was our most complete and best performance of the season. I scored a hat-trick, big Derek got one, Alex Miller converted a penalty and Alex MacDonald also chipped in for our 6-1 win.

"The final itself was difficult having just lost Bobby, but winning the match and the first silverware of the season helped, and of course, it was Celtic in the final."

Smith was again on target in that final as was another

summer recruit Davie Cooper as the game finished 2-1 after extra time. Smith's goal did cause controversy as Celtic goalkeeper Peter Latchford claimed he was impeded by Alex MacDonald as he went for an Alex Miller cross. Gordon Smith wasted no time in passing the ball into the unguarded net. The third of the new faces in the Rangers ranks was missing that day. Bobby Russell had played in every round up to the final but took ill on the morning of the match. Johnny Hamilton stepped in to fill the midfield berth. If there was to be disappointment for Russell, it soon disappeared when he was approached by Sandy Jardine. Bobby couldn't believe what was happening. "I wasn't well enough to play but I was there and trying my best to celebrate with the boys, but when you haven't played you don't quite feel part of it. Then Sandy came over to me and handed me his winners' medal. He said, 'You have it – you deserve it – you've played in every round and did as much as any of us to win the cup.'

"He wouldn't take no for an answer and even now I look back and remember that was my first ever senior medal, and thank Sandy Jardine for an incredible act of friendship. I'll never forget that gesture."

That match at Hampden was Jock Stein's last major final as Celtic boss, and his after-the-game comment to match referee David Syme, that "Your father would have been proud of you" saw him hit with a £200 fine from the SFA. It may have been a tongue in cheek line from Stein suggesting that the referee's dad had an allegiance to Rangers and that on the balance of play on the day Stein believed Celtic weren't given any favours by Syme.

Back on league business, Aberdeen, under manager Billy McNeill who would later that year succeed Jock Stein as boss of Celtic, were mounting a serious challenge.

The run-in for Rangers was challenging especially after Celtic got revenge for that cup defeat with a 2-0 win only seven days later at Parkhead in the league. Then two draws in a row against Hibernian and St. Mirren handed

Aberdeen the initiative with the Dons having beaten
Rangers in three of the four clashes in the championship.
Other than a frustrating home draw with Ayr United,
Rangers took full points in the run-in against Ayr United
again, Dundee United twice home and away as postponed
fixtures were finally played, then Clydebank, and capped
it all with a last day triumph and a 2-0 win at Motherwell
with Smith again on the score sheet as was Colin Jackson.
The treble was on!

Gordon Smith was never in any doubt about the quality
in that Rangers team. "Winning the first trophy of the
season laid down a marker and gave us a confidence boost
and in the run-in, nerves were never an issue, not with the
experience we had in that side including Sandy and the
others who had previously won trebles."

The Scottish Cup meant a lot to Smith. "That was the
trophy I wanted more than any other. My grandfather
had won it twice with Kilmarnock and on the day of the
final as I sat in the Hampden dressing room, I knew the
cup was ours. I looked round and my teammates were
relaxed and comfortable but fully focused and having
clinched the title the week before, two things stuck out
for me. The demeanour and the quality of the players.
We also had no nerves at all and that was down to Jock
Wallace."

Over the ninety minutes, Aberdeen never really threatened, even after getting a late consolation goal through
Steve Ritchie with five minutes remaining. Rangers
were in cruise control through Alex MacDonald's diving
header after thirty-five minutes and Derek Johnstone's
thirty-eighth goal of the season. Gordon Smith had a
sensational first season scoring twenty-seven times. (In
that second treble winning season under Wallace, Jardine
made forty-eight appearances and scored six goals.) This
time Bobby Russell didn't need charity from a colleague.
He played the whole match and ended the season with
three winners' medals for his efforts. What a difference a

year makes. Bobby Russell still has to check that it wasn't just a dream. "From Shettleston to Rangers was massive for me, but never in a million years when I signed did I think I would play forty-eight games and score three goals in my first season, never mind win the three major medals that I did."

Derek Johnstone sums up just how less than worldly-wise his teammate Bobby Russell, fresh out of the juniors, was. "We were on a flight to Sweden I think, the stewardess came up and said the manager had said it was OK for the boys to have a couple of drinks. When she asked Bobby what he fancied, he asked for 'a pint of sweet black and tan' (a mixture of stout and dark beer), which clearly bemused the stewardess but had the rest of the team in stitches. Even more so when the girl came back and said 'sorry sir we don't have any black and tans left!' Bobby settled for a beer like the rest of us!"

With Rangers' record now showing two trebles in three seasons, Smith remains unconvinced that it will ever be done again. "It's so difficult to do just once, but twice, as big Jock did in such close proximity, is an incredible statistic."

Rangers' season may have been over but the fans were in for a major shock. Jock Wallace's reign as Rangers manager was also over seventeen days after that Scottish Cup final win. Gordon Smith knew Wallace had been a major influence in further developing him as a player. "How could the board let big Jock walk away? He was a sensational man manager and delivered unparalleled success. My mother phoned me to say it had been on the news that Jock Wallace had left Rangers. I was devastated. He knew how to get the best out of me as a player but it wasn't just me, he got the best out of a rookie like Bobby Russell just coming into the game, and he also knew how to handle experienced guys like John Greig, Colin Jackson and of course, Sandy."

The precise cause of Wallace resigning has never fully

been explained as he chose to keep silent on the subject right up until his death in 1996. Speculation was rife that disputes on budgets and transfer targets were cited, as was a suggestion that Wallace's own salary was not being reviewed to his satisfaction, despite the haul of trophies he had just delivered.

18

ANOTHER WORLD CUP CAMPAIGN

After an unbeaten World Cup finals campaign in Germany 1974, four years on, with Argentina the venue, Scotland were again competing in the most elite tournament finals of the beautiful game.

Euphoria was evident as new Scotland manager Ally MacLeod whipped the nation into a frenzy with the promise of coming home with at least a medal.

MacLeod had replaced Willie Ormond in the middle of the qualifying rounds and was not short on confidence. In fact, the charismatic new man was probably the absolute opposite of quiet man Ormond who resigned his SFA position in May 1977 then took over at Hearts, with MacLeod coming in from Aberdeen where he had won the League Cup, beating Celtic in the final.

MacLeod introduced himself to his first Scotland squad with the opening gambit: "My name is Ally MacLeod, and I am a winner!" It's fair to say his bold statement raised a few eyebrows within the squad and raised hopes of a nation that believed him.

Five hundred days and seventeen games later MacLeod's claim was to be disproven in dramatic fashion.

The qualifying campaign had Scotland positioned in a section of only three teams including Wales and again by another quirk of fate, just like 1973, Czechoslovakia, who by now were the reigning European Champions.

Scotland lost the Group Seven opening game 2-0 in Prague with Willie Ormond still in charge and Sandy Jardine didn't feature. In the next match against Wales at Hampden, Scotland edged it, with an own goal from Crystal Palace defender Ian Evans enough to take the points. For this one, Ormond went with the McGrain and Willie Donachie full back pairing. For the next crucial fixture in September 1977 and MacLeod having replaced Ormond, the full backs voted the best in the world at the 1974 finals were back in business. On a memorable night for Scottish football, Jardine and McGrain were part of the side that lit up the national stadium with a 3-1 win over the Czechs with goals coming from Jordan, Hartford and Dalglish who were by then all playing their football south of the border.

The stage was set for the final showdown with Wales, and a Scotland win would secure qualification and a trip to South America. The game was hosted at the neutral venue of Anfield, home to Liverpool FC, as crowd trouble the year before in a Euro Championship match between Wales and Yugoslavia ruled out Ninian Park in Cardiff, and the Welsh Football Association decided that the other option of Wrexham's Racecourse ground wouldn't maximise the revenue from the fixture with the clamour for tickets enormous. It was a capacity crowd with massive numbers travelling in the Tartan Army again encouraged by manager MacLeod's optimism.

It was a pulsating match on a damp cold October night but neither side could get the important breakthrough until Joe Jordan took matters into his own hands. The goal came in seventy-eight minutes, but that was twenty minutes after Sandy Jardine had left the field with injury and Manchester United's Martin Buchan came off the bench as his replacement. Scotland had a throw-in in an advanced area and Asa Hartford wound up a long one that travelled in the air and straight to the heart of the Welsh rearguard. Jordan climbed to contest the ball with defender David Jones and the ball appeared to strike a hand as both players looked to use their arms for elevation. Was it Jordan or was it Jones that the ball struck? To this day Joe Jordan has never developed discussions beyond supporting the referee's decision which was to immediately award Scotland a penalty kick. Television evidence remains unconvincing but while Jordan was wearing a dark blue long sleeved shirt, Jones was wearing a short sleeved red one. French whistler Robert Wurtz had no doubts that it was Jones who handled the ball. The Welsh players protested but the penalty stood. Under huge pressure, Don Masson stepped up and despatched the ball behind Welsh keeper Dai Davies to give Scotland the lead. Ten minutes later, Scotland scored again and the Argentinian dream was on. For the second goal, Jardine's replacement Martin Buchan swung in a curling delivery from the right and Kenny Dalglish rose to flick a header into the net.

At least Jordan maintained a dignified silence on this controversial penalty incident, unlike Diego Maradona and his dubious "hand of god" goal against England in the 1986 finals.

Alan Rough had an outstanding match between the sticks for Scotland that night including denying John Toshack what looked a certain goal by arcing backwards to flick the net-bound shot onto the crossbar and behind for a corner. It was a breathtaking save and Rough is in no doubt the referee got the decision right. "I was at the other end of the pitch of course and the referee was much closer than me to the incident. I just saw them go up to challenge so I am sure the referee got it absolutely right. The fans were different class and Liverpool had been taken over for the day by the Tartan Army."

Scotland had qualified for the World Cup finals for the second tournament in a row, and also making it two in a row were England who had again failed to qualify.

After the obvious off field issues and lack of planning, including the failure to anticipate the quality of opponents of the 1974 campaign such as Zaire, Scotland would surely get it right this time.

Hopes of a more professional build up were lifted as Scotland, in anticipation of making Argentina 1978, had embarked on a summer tour of South America. However, controversy was again evident with questions being asked about the venue for the match against Chile where the Santiago stadium had previously been used as a concentra-tion camp. One year later, and despite the dress rehearsal visit, Scotland set up base camp in Córdoba. Off the field things were not good. All the usual problems were again all too evident. Meals where anything other than steak on the menu was a rarity, bonuses that had been promised but never materialised, the poor standard of accommodation and a particular annoyance for the players was the limited options available to them to relieve boredom between games.

Of the twenty-two-man squad, Sandy Jardine was joined by Martin Buchan, Kenny Dalglish, Joe Jordan, Willie Donachie and Gordon McQueen who had all experienced the finals in Germany four years previously. Also in the squad were Rangers teammates Tam Forsyth and Derek Johnstone, who with Jardine, had swept the boards of domestic honours in the season just finished. Former Ibrox favourite Willie Johnston was also in the party but he was by then playing with West Bromwich Albion. A twenty-five-year-old Graeme Souness was also part of the squad while Alan Rough was now considered number one goalkeeper. Rough remembers: "We had a good mix in the squad but maybe – with hindsight – the manager may have been too loyal to some of the guys who had done so well to get us there. We had a few that were getting towards the twilight of their careers."

Before jetting off to South America Scotland had to compete in the usual end of season British championships. All the games were played over a seven day period and Scotland played all three at home at Hampden. Games against Northern Ireland and Wales both finished 1-1, with Derek Johnstone scoring in both to keep up his stunning club form, but a single goal defeat to England with a strike from Steve Coppell enough to win the match saw England win the tournament.

In the match against Wales, Gordon McQueen picked up an injury and made him a serious doubt for Argentina. In the home internationals, Sandy Jardine started only one match against Northern Ireland while Derek started against Northern Ireland and Wales with both missing the England clash. Danny McGrain didn't feature at all and didn't make the squad for Argentina because of a continuously mysterious ankle injury.

It would be a similar story in Argentina with Jardine only featuring once and, incredibly, Derek Johnstone got no game time at all!

Derek looks back on perhaps why he didn't get a chance in Argentina. "After the Wales game, big Gordon McQueen had a bad one and it was quite obvious he would be struggling to be fit enough to be involved in the games ahead. We were staying at the Dunblane Hydro hotel and we were allowed a couple of beers to relax us after that game. Ally MacLeod and his back-room staff were sitting in the lounge when I came back in with a few of the lads, and I thought I was doing the right thing by approaching him to tell him that I could play at centre half. Now, whether he thought I was trying to pick the team for him I don't know and I was far from worse the wear with drink, but he clearly wasn't happy, and with hindsight, I wish I hadn't done it. Maybe he thought I wanted to play in defence but whatever it was, and despite being Scottish football Player of the Year and Players' Player of the Year, I never got a look in after that night."

Despite Johnstone's goal threat, Ally MacLeod chose to overlook him while Sandy Jardine was equally frustrated with the manager appearing to favour Stuart Kennedy, whom he had worked with at Aberdeen, for the right back role.

In the opening match against Peru it was almost like Zaire all over again, with nobody fully aware of the qualities or strength of the opposition and Scotland were sunk 3-1 with two spectacular strikes from Teófilo Cubillas catching Alan Rough cold after Don Masson had missed a penalty at 3-0. Sandy Jardine was an unused substitute but was restored to the side for the second match against Iran but again, Scotland failed to deliver and had to settle for a 1-1 draw with an own goal from Eskandarian giving MacLeod's side a share of the points. The campaign that had been hyped to the hilt and full of promise was now a real calamity and back home fans took their frustrations out by smashing the windows of Ally MacLeod's home in Scotland.

After this result, MacLeod was also a broken man.

Before that game against Iran though, controversy was again all too evident in the Scotland camp.

There had been previous security concerns not long after the squad had arrived at their Alta Gracia base with suggestions of players breaking curfews and climbing fences to head into town. All the claims had been greatly exaggerated as Alan Rough confirms. "Myself, Lou Macari, Asa Hartford and Sandy Jardine decided we would take a stroll into town and see what was what. We took a short cut by climbing a small fence rather than go through the main gate and after having a coffee and a wander round, we came back to the hotel the same way. Next day it was being reported that we had been apprehended by armed guards. It just wasn't the case!"

This time, Willie Johnston failed a random drugs test and

Balgreen Primary School, 1960. Billy Jardine – back row, second from left. His twin brother Jamie – back row, third from right. Headmaster Mr Stevens (far right) was a great football man and mentor to the boys.

Tynecastle High School, 1963. Billy is back row, third from right – he was confident of a (V for) victory that day!

Sandy and Shona tie the knot, 1969.

The Rangers squad under Jock Wallace.
Sandy is left of centre, next to John Grieg.

© SNS GROUP

Sandy Jardine
(left) of Rangers
in action against
Celtic's Johnny
Doyle.

19/04/72: European Cup Winners Cup Semi-final Second Leg – Rangers v Bayern Munich (2-0) – Ibrox. Rangers players Peter McCloy (left), Derek Johnstone (centre), Alex MacDonald (2nd right) and Sandy Jardine celebrate after the final whistle.

The Sandy Jardine Testimonial match programme – sold for 50p at Rangers v Southampton, 09/05/82.

25/08/84: Premier Division Hibs v Hearts (1-2) Easter Road – Hibs' Paul Kane (left) is shadowed by Sandy Jardine.

1985/86 Hearts team – *Back row* (l to r): Sandy Clark, Malcolm Murray, Roddy McDonald, Brian Whittaker, Craig Levein, Neil Barry, Ian Jardine. *Middle row* (l to r): John Binnie (coach), Andy Watson, Jim Sandison, Henry Smith, Brian McNaughton, George Cowie, Walter Borthwick (coach). Front row (l to r): Alex MacDonald (manager), John Colquhoun, Gary MacKay, Walter Kidd, Kenny Black, John Robertson, Sandy Jardine (Assistant Manager).

03/05/86: Dundee v Hearts (2-0) Dens Park – The Hearts fans look on stunned as Albert Kidd celebrates his strike for Dundee.

May 1984: Hearts squad, including guest Kevin Keegan, who lost
3-2 to Rangers in Alex MacDonald's Testimonial.

The Management: Doddie and Sandy as joint managers at Hearts.
Their contribution to the club was recognised in September 2016
when they were inducted into the Hearts Hall of Fame.

Sandy on the steps of Hampden park with 8000 Rangers fans protesting about SFA sanctions on their club in 2012.

San Francisco NARSA Convention 2013. "Does my bum look big in this?"

The Masters of Augusta. Sandy and pals celebrate David Ross's birthday in style.

08/12/12 IRN-BRU SFL DIV 3 – Rangers v Stirling Albion (2-0) – Ibrox: Rangers fans show their support for former player Sandy Jardine.

Jim Hannah with the bronze bust of Sandy before its unveiling ceremony.

26/04/14: Scottish League One – Rangers v Stranraer (3-0), Ibrox: Tributes continue to be laid in respect for club legend Sandy Jardine.

was sent home in disgrace. Wee Bud had taken a banned substance, "fenkamfamine", which contained reactivan which was on the FIFA banned list. It was naive in the extreme on Johnston's part. He thought he was taking harmless medication for his hay fever complaint. The drug was widely used by players in England and it was suggested Willie wasn't the only one in the Scots playing party that had used the same tablets to alleviate the symptoms of hay fever and other allergy issues.

It was portrayed as a scandal and did nothing for squad morale. It also ended Willie Johnston's international career.

However, despite all that, Scotland still had a chance to qualify.

All they had to do was beat the Netherlands by three goals to have a chance. For this final group game, Scotland had moved from Córdoba to Mendoza. Stewart Kennedy took Sandy Jardine's starting jersey and Graeme Souness made his first start in the finals. Things looked bleak when Holland took an early lead through Rensenbrink but Scotland fought back through Kenny Dalglish and a double from Archie Gemmill, including his iconic second goal where he beat three defenders before lifting the ball over Dutch keeper Jongbloed and into the net. Scotland had hope and for a fleeting four-minute spell, a place in the next round looked a real possibility, but hope was ended when Johnny Rep latched onto a Rudi Krol pass to pull a goal back for Holland. Scotland did win the match but it wasn't enough. For the second successive tournament finals Scotland were eliminated on goal difference.

Derek Johnstone still carries frustration from that campaign. "No doubt about it we reserved our best performance for the last game, but the damage was done in the defeat by Peru in the opener. It was pretty obvious as soon as the game got underway that we had totally underestimated them. From a personal perspective, I was at the top of my game as was Sandy having just won everything there was to win on the domestic front that season, but Ally had his own ways and neither of us really got the chance to make the contribution that I don't doubt we could have."

The experiences of Argentina took a long time for the Scotland squad to get out of their system and the tournament was effectively a disaster in every way. It is perhaps best highlighted by the fact that the team flew to Argentina on first-class tickets but travelled back economy!

For Sandy Jardine, Argentina signalled the curtain coming down on his international career as he played for his country only three times thereafter including his final appearance against Belgium when he again captained the side.

19

MOVING ON AND MOVING DOWN
A GORGIE SOS

Sandy Jardine had been a Ranger for seventeen years and worked under Scot Symon, Davie White, Willie Waddell, Jock Wallace. Now his former teammate John Greig was in charge and the Ibrox side were again in a period of transition.

Greig had replaced Jock Wallace who for no obvious reason had resigned in May 1978 after winning the treble, and the club moved quickly to install retiring Captain John Greig as his replacement.

He had a huge shadow to walk in when he replaced Wallace. Two trebles in three years was an almost impossible act to follow. In more recent years under similar terms you only have to look at how difficult it has been for the managers of Manchester United to replicate the success of Sir Alex Ferguson. The added pressure is enormous.

However, in his first season, he almost replicated the 1978 treble by winning the Scottish Cup, beating Hibernian in the final, albeit it took three games to do so. Rangers also retained the League Cup beating a rapidly emerging Aberdeen side 2-1 with goals from Colin Jackson and Alex MacDonald. But in the league, Rangers could only finish second to eventual winners Celtic with the pivotal match being a 4-2 Old Firm defeat at Parkhead leaving only two games still to be played, and their biggest rivals in an unassailable position to take the title. In Europe, however, Rangers did deliver when the chips were down. Italian champions Juventus travelled to Ibrox with a slender one goal win from the first leg and it wasn't enough. Alex MacDonald and Gordon Smith scored to put Rangers through. Next it was PSV Eindhoven away and despite being held to a 0-0 draw at Ibrox, over in Holland Rangers won in thrilling style with Bobby Russell scoring a sensational winner to see the scoreline finish 3-2 in Rangers' favour. Rangers' good run was ended by German title holders Cologne, winning 1-0 at home and completing the job with a credible 1-1 draw in Glasgow.

Sandy Jardine made sixty appearances in all competitions and scored two goals.

John Greig needed to make changes to an ageing Rangers playing squad. Ally Dawson had come in to offer options in the full back berths, John MacDonald had also come through the youth ranks and scored nine goals in his first season while other youngsters, including Billy MacKay and Gordon Dalziel, looked capable when they were given a chance. Rangers had also spent big in the summer with the capture of Gregor Stevens from Leicester and Ian Redford from Dundee.

It was in Greig's second season in charge that things dipped dramatically with Rangers finishing a distant fifth behind champions Aberdeen, and analysis shows that picking up only ten points from eighteen away matches in the league influenced the inability to really mount a challenge. Aberdeen also knocked Rangers out of the League Cup and while John Greig managed to take some satisfaction by beating his old teammate Alex Ferguson's Dons side in the Scottish Cup semi-final, Rangers lost in the final to Celtic by a deflected goal by George McCluskey in extra time. The final will be better remembered as rioting fans of both sides invaded the pitch at full time and as a result, the sale of alcohol was banned at sporting events in Scotland.

It was a season that did not yield a trophy for Rangers, and while domestically it was a disaster, again they showed they were well equipped for the European arena. As Scottish Cup holders, Rangers entered the European Cup Winners' cup and started well by eliminating Lillestrom of Norway and Fortuna Düsseldorf of Germany before going out to Spanish cracks Valencia who would go on and win the tournament.

Sandy Jardine again was the model of consistency with fifty-one appearances and five goals.

For the 1980/81 season John Greig had the backing of the Rangers board. Jim Bett came from Lokeren in Belgium and Willie Johnstone returned for a second spell having been playing in Canada with Vancouver Whitecaps. Jim Stewart joined from Middlesbrough to offer competition to long serving goalkeeper Peter McCloy. Colin McAdam was a controversial signing from Partick Thistle.

Rangers got off to a good start and went on a run of fifteen matches without defeat including two wins against great rivals Celtic. Bett and Miller were on target when the sides met at Parkhead late in August and it was all Rangers as they won convincingly when Celtic came to Ibrox on the 1st of November, with a double from McAdam and one from John MacDonald. John's namesake Alex had moved on to Hearts in the close season.

However, after the fine start, Rangers lost their way and a disastrous run through November and December all but ended their title challenge. Celtic went on to wrestle the title back from Aberdeen, and Rangers could only finish third, fully fourteen points behind Celtic who had former Lisbon Lion defender and Captain Billy McNeill at the helm having replaced Jock Stein as manager in August 1978.

Rangers got some consolation with success in the Scottish cup. Airdrie, St. Johnstone, Hibernian and Morton were all beaten on the way to the Hampden final against Dundee United who had already won the League Cup, beating city rivals Dundee 3-0 in the final played at Dens Park.

Rangers were held to a drab no scoring draw at Hampden on the Saturday but Rangers lifted the cup with a convincing 4-1 win in the replay three days later. John MacDonald was again on target with a double, and Davie Cooper and Bobby Russell were also on the score sheet.

Sandy Jardine was still pretty much a fixture in the side with forty-two appearances and three goals.

Rangers were still chasing the holy grail of the title but it wasn't just Celtic they had to contend with, now the "new firm" from north-east Scotland in the shape of Dundee United and Aberdeen had the credentials to compete with the best of them. These four would make up the top four places in the season ahead.

1981/82 saw Scotland's three major honours shared three ways. Celtic were Premier Division champions, Aberdeen lifted the Scottish Cup and Rangers' only reward was lifting the League Cup. In a rerun of the previous season's Scottish Cup final, Dundee United provided the Hampden opposition in November 1981 with Rangers winning 2-1 through goals from Cooper and Redford. It would be Sandy Jardine's last medal as a Rangers player. Sandy was involved in fifty-two matches during the season and scored four goals.

Rangers had again come up short on league business as Aberdeen ran Celtic closest to the title, finishing only two points behind the Parkhead club with Rangers a distant third, ten points behind the Dons.

Elsewhere in Scotland, Heart of Midlothian had finished third in the old Scottish League Division One and were consigned to another season in Scotland's second tier. Sandy Jardine's closest friend in football Alex MacDonald was now player-manager at Hearts and whispers in the game were that Sandy Jardine would be joining him to try and win promotion in season 1982/83.

Before then, however, Sandy Jardine's seventeen years at Rangers were to be rewarded by a testimonial. This was quite a rare event down Ibrox way as since World War Two, only two other players had been recognised in this way.

John Greig had his service to the club acknowledged with a testimonial match in April 1978 against a Scotland X1 as part of their preparations for the Argentinian World Cup finals, while Everton sent a team to Ibrox to play a benefit for Colin Jackson in 1981.

Southampton were to provide the opposition in Sandy's match on the 9th May 1982. At the time, they were one of England's top sides. The Saints had Lawrie McMenemy in charge and he believed his team were capable of winning the English championship and showed his commitment to the cause by turning down the chance to manage Manchester United in the summer of 1981. He had built a strong and experienced squad including Kevin Keegan who had returned after a spell with Hamburg. World Cup winner Alan Ball was there along with other England inter-nationalists Steve Williams and Mick Channon. Ivan Golac, who would later manage Dundee United to cup glory, was Sandy's opposite number at right back in McMenemy's side.

As part of the arrangement, Rangers would travel to the Dell seven days after the Ibrox meeting to play another testimonial, this time for Saints stalwart George Horsfall.

This honour bestowed on Jardine after Greig and Jackson was surely fitting reward for a career that spanned nearly two decades at Rangers. Before Greig's testimonial, the last previous similar match was in 1925 when Davie Meiklejohn's Light Blue career was recognised in a game against Huddersfield Town.

The day before the Sunday fixture, Rangers played their penultimate league game of the season winning 4-0 at Dens Park with twenty-year-old striker Gordon Dalziel scoring a hat-trick and former Dundee favourite claiming the other.

Against Southampton, Dalziel again showed why he was rated so highly, scoring the only goal of the game. Dalziel, now a radio football pundit who was sold by Rangers to

Manchester City the following season, remembers Sandy's day. "The talk of the dressing room for a few weeks was that Sandy would be leaving. He and Doddie were best friends and Sandy always had a hankering for Hearts so it made sense that he would join him and maybe cut his teeth in coaching too. Against Southampton my goal came with a ball over the top from Jimmy Bett I think, and it sat up nicely for me to volley it into the top corner.

"After the game, Sandy gifted every player involved a beautiful gold chain with a gold football pendant. I gave mine to my mother and she wore it until the day she died. My daughter now has it and she cherishes it too."

From the match programme for the Southampton testimonial, top Scottish football writer Hugh Taylor, then of the *Evening Times*, wrote: "Princely pairs of backs have graced the Scottish football scene almost since the game began and ancient eyes glint as the great partnerships are recalled. Few, however, can have surpassed that of Sandy Jardine of Rangers and Danny McGrain of Celtic, perhaps the best Old Firm double act since the attacking duo of Bob McPhail and Jimmy McGrory when they played in Scotland shirts. So when we talk of Sandy Jardine, we should remember his splendid performances for his country and recall too how well the Old Firm stalwarts combined in internationals. But then cooperation is perhaps the name of Sandy Jardine's game. He's a player who knows so much about the football ins-and-outs that he would have been a star in any position and indeed, when he arrived at Ibrox, it was a toss-up whether he would develop into a lively striker or reliable defender. In the end Sandy Jardine decided that defence was his position. And how well he has done, how many magnificent, intelligent matches has he played for Rangers. A prince of defenders indeed. An inspiration to all aspiring players, a man of many parts, intelligent, sporting, affable, Sandy Jardine epitomises the modern professional footballer. He will go down in history as one of the great Rangers players, a splendid exponent of his craft who relied on brain in preference to brawn."

What a fantastic tribute to Sandy Jardine which confirms the esteem he was held in as time was ticking on his Rangers career.

It really was with reluctance that John Greig approached this board of directors and asked Sandy to be released to allow him to take up a coaching role at Hearts. Greig and Jardine were both from Edinburgh and travelled to Ibrox to training together, and had a genuine bond that was evident right up until Sandy's death in 2014. In his position as Rangers manager, John Greig wrote in Sandy's testimonial match programme: "No Rangers player ever had a harder baptism than Sandy Jardine, coming into the side as he did just one week after we had been knocked out of the Scottish Cup at Berwick. But that was fifteen years ago. The fact that Sandy is still playing tells you something about his dedication and consistency – his strong points throughout his career. In a way Sandy's career was built on the same lines as my own. When I was a kid I used to travel through by train from Edinburgh each day with Jimmy Millar and Ralph Brand. They helped to educate me. I'd like to think that Sandy derived some benefit when a few years on, he did all his travelling through to Glasgow in my company. Looking back, I can recall that Sandy always had ability, but while he filled several positions for us, it wasn't until Willie Waddell moved him to right back that he really found himself. Of course the World Cup in 1974 really made him. It gave him all the confidence he needed. If ever Sandy has been criticised for performances since then it is only because they may have slipped just a little from his own very high standard. Sandy always helped himself by being a first-class trainer, and in more recent years, he's taken a leaf out of my book and trained during the close season. I did this because I'd schooled myself to play until I was thirty-six. Sandy saw how this policy benefitted me and now it's working for him as well. Mind you he's still a kid at thirty-three. His ambition I know is to stay in the game in some capacity or other when he stops playing. If he feels that I can help him in any way, he only has to ask. I'm happy for him that he's made such a success of his career. What with freedom of contract nowadays, Sandy may well prove to be one of the last of the long serving players. Good quality players like him will be all the harder for clubs to hold on to in future."

But Rangers were not ready to hold on to Sandy Jardine in the summer of 1982.

John Greig resigned his position as Rangers manager in October 1983 when another campaign to win the Scottish title was doomed to failure.

Alex MacDonald had replaced Tony Ford in the Hearts managerial hot seat but was still playing regularly at the time. His first choice as his assistant manager was another Barcelona legend, Tommy McLean, but he elected to stay at Ibrox and take up the position of number two to John Greig. Sandy had been at Ibrox for the full duration of Alex MacDonald's time at Rangers and had roomed together for away games and trips to Europe. They were on the same wavelength and Jardine was just nine months younger than MacDonald. Then Hearts Chairman Wallace Mercer took advice from his manager and did a deal to make Sandy a Jambo. Alex MacDonald recalls: "Sandy was thirty-three at the time but a really fit thirty-three–year-old. Training under Jock Wallace had underpinned his condition for the challenges over the years. It wasn't a difficult sell even though we were in the old first division. Sandy had supported Hearts as a kid when he was growing up in Edinburgh."

MacDonald was still learning on the job himself and in the match programme for the first home game of the season, Jardine in his column noted: "Hearts are a club I have dreamed of playing for. I was born only a few miles from the ground and from the age of seven I was a regular at Tynecastle. So taking on the role of assistant manager and helping out Alex MacDonald is something I'm looking forward to. My duties will obviously include playing and coaching but I am here to help the manager in all aspects of the job and I'll be learning all the time. The set-up at Tynecastle is excellent and everything is geared for Premier Division football by the end of the season."

So time was up on Sandy Jardine's playing career at Rangers but he was far from finished and a new chapter unfolded in the maroon of Hearts.

It wasn't long before MacDonald and Jardine were joined by another ex-Rangers favourite when Willie Johnstone arrived after another spell in Canada with Vancouver Whitecaps.

The Tynecastle side may have had a *Dad's Army* look about it but Alex MacDonald had recruited players who had been winners throughout their careers and he wanted that winning habit to continue now they were all together at Hearts.

20

HEARTS IN GOOD HEALTH

When Hearts finally got back to the top tier in Scottish football, Chairman Wallace Mercer was determined to have them challenging and he was prepared to back his management team in the transfer market if need be, but with the club having been hit with a signing embargo, that may have been easier said than done.

Hearts had struggled to maintain payments to Dundee United following the signings of Willie Pettigrew and Derek Addison and suffered the sanctions from the hierarchy of the Scottish game.

So with the 1983/84 season pending and with the prodigious striker John Robertson still just eighteen years of age but having proven himself in the previous promotion-winning campaign, Alex MacDonald had every confidence that Robbo could deliver again – even allowing for going up a level – but he needed help to take some of the weight off his young shoulders. Further experience was recruited with Donald Park returning for a second spell at Tynecastle, and he would prove to be a terrier in the engine room and provide the service to Robertson and his experienced front partner Jimmy Bone. He had been signed despite it looking like he would join Hearts' rivals Hibernian after his release by St. Mirren. George Cowie also joined from West Ham and at twenty-two he brought the average of the side down a notch or two and it wasn't going to break the bank to sign him.

Hearts started life back in the top division with five consecutive wins. Opening up with a 1-0 victory at St. Johnstone then taking the honours in a 3-2 thriller Edinburgh derby against Hibs at Tynecastle, they followed that with another very satisfying home win for Messers MacDonald and Jardine as they beat John Greig's Rangers 3-1. Next up it was back to back away wins at Dens Park and St. Mirren. The sensational run was ended by two goals from Peter Weir in a 2-0 win for Aberdeen at Pittodrie on the 1st of October. That good start gave Hearts a real platform for the campaign that saw them finish fifth in the table and qualify for Europe.

Along the way and with winter approaching, Alex MacDonald and Sandy Jardine approached Chairman Mercer to try and have the flamboyant businessman open the purse strings for a young player that the management team felt would be a real star in the future. How right they were.

Craig Levein was a talented young footballer playing part time with Cowdenbeath while learning his trade as an electrician. Craig vividly remembers the first words Sandy Jardine ever said to him. "I couldn't believe it …Sandy said 'how would you like to play for Hearts big lad?' Nothing too strange in that you might think except it was in the middle of a cup tie at a corner kick for Cowdenbeath with me going forward to support the attack and with Sandy Jardine marking me as part of Hearts' defence!

"I wasn't sure he if he was just trying to put me off my game or if he was being serious!"

Clearly Jardine's unusual method of "tapping up" his opponent was genuine and not a rouse to gain an advantage during that League Cup tie in August 1983. The Blue Brazil, with Levein at the heart of their defence, had held Hearts to a goalless draw in the opening round of the League Cup at Central Park and set up a replay at Gorgie. It was in these meetings that Jardine was convinced Levein had what it took to make the grade. As it was, it took penalty kicks to determine a winner and for Hearts to progress to the next round which was then changed to a sectional mini league format. Levein duly joined Hearts but it took a hefty fee in the region of £35,000 going to Cowdenbeath for his services.

It was originally suggested that Craig Levein had been recruited as a replacement for assistant manager Jardine, but it was in midfield rather than centre back that Levein would be predominately used in that first season.

Sandy Jardine would sign a new two-year contract at the end of that season that would see him operate as assistant to MacDonald but also continue to play as required.

And why not? On that first season back with a European campaign to look forward to, Sandy Jardine could reflect on his Hearts contribution of forty-five games played which was more than anyone else in the squad. Old warrior Jimmy Bone had played forty-one and scored nine goals while the promise of John Robertson was now a reality with twenty goals scored from forty-three appearances. Craig Levein made twenty-one appearances after signing, nineteen of which were in the league.

Levein recalls his first season at Tynecastle with genuine fondness. "That night when Sandy asked if I wanted to sign, I met my girlfriend, now my wife, Carol, after the game for something to eat and I couldn't get Sandy's words out my head. In fact I couldn't get them out my head for weeks so when I finally did sign, I was just delighted. It meant full-time football and it was a great dressing room to join.

"The chemistry in the squad was fantastic. Experienced campaigners Donald Park, wee Bud Johnston, Walter Kidd and Jimmy Bone did a great job on the park but they also made sure guys like myself, Gary Mackay, Dave Bowman and Wee Robbo learned the game properly. The team were maybe full of "odd couples" but it worked. Sandy and manager Alex MacDonald or Doddie as Sandy called him were opposites really. Doddie to Sandy maybe, but Gaffer to us players was aggressive but committed and fair while Sandy was much more analytical and approachable. He was the level-headed one of two firebrand redheads!

"Alex MacDonald used to single out one of the experienced players and give him a torrid time if things weren't going well at half-time in matches. What we didn't know was that it was all pre-planned and Donald Park or Jimmy Bone knew what was coming and were happy to play along for the effect. For us younger players, all we could think was, if the manager can speak like that and give a senior player such criticism, what could he say or do to us? You better believe we kept our heads down and couldn't wait to escape the heat of the dressing room to get back on to the park to put things right!"

Hearts had secured European football at the first time of asking on their return as they finished the season with real resilience in their last eleven games. They lost to Dundee United 3-1 at Tannadice in mid March with their record showing only one reversal, and went down down 1-0 to Aberdeen who would go on and win the title. There was a last day loss at Motherwell, but in between, they claimed draws against Rangers, Celtic and Hibs in an exciting end to a satisfactory campaign.

For season 1984/85 further changes were evident in the playing squad. Andy Watson, who had been a league and European Cup Winners' Cup winner with Aberdeen, came in from Leeds United. Kenny Black, who had broken through at Rangers when Sandy Jardine was there, joined from Motherwell, but Hearts couldn't replicate the sensational start of the previous season, and struggled to get into a rhythm wining only two games from their opening eight matches, although the fans did enjoy another derby success at the home of their rivals Hibs with a 2-1 win in late August.

By this time, Craig Levein was the regular centre back partner of Sandy Jardine, with former Celtic defender Roddie McDonald also featuring in a side that regularly shaped up with a back three.

Again, despite his age, Sandy Jardine played in forty-five matches across all tournaments while Craig Levein – fifteen years his junior – managed only two more!

Craig said it was a huge benefit to play alongside Jardine. "I was nineteen going on twenty around that time and I was enthralled by the way Sandy just got everything right. He would talk constantly and his anticipation was uncanny. He would tell me to take a half yard left as my opponent was about to peel off to receive a pass, or he'd give me the nod to step up or come back a yard in anticipation of a ball over the top. He was always right. Sandy had incredible levels of concentration and his experience of the game including in Europe and at international level really paid dividends. He really had seen it all and done it all. I was learning from a master of his trade, and he taught me a lot – even down to details not just in a match environment that I took into coaching and management myself many years later.

"In fact the partnerships thing is one prime example. When I was in charge of Hearts, I signed big Andy Webster from Arbroath and paired him with Steven Pressley at the heart of our defence. I encouraged Elvis, as was his nickname, to take on the Sandy role while I saw big Andy as a lot like myself, and I have no doubt both players benefited from the decision. Elvis relished the responsibility and Andy was his young apprentice."

The seventh place in the league was a disappointment but it took Aberdeen to stop Hearts in the Scottish Cup as the Dons marched on to the double. They saw off Alex MacDonald's side in a quarter final replay 1-0 at Pittodrie in front of a crowd of over 23,000 after a 1-1 draw at Tynecastle. The League Cup was also to offer only disappointment, Hearts losing both home and away to Dundee United at the crucial semi-final stage. Europe was a harsh school for the side from Gorgie. The first round paired them with French giants Paris Saint-Germain. Going down 4-0 in the Parc des Princes in Paris made the return leg at Tynecastle an almost impossible task, although John Robertson claimed a double and Hearts banked a respectable 2-2 home draw.

Kenny Black knew something special was happening at Hearts as soon as he joined up from Motherwell. "I had experienced great facilities and was well looked after when I was at Rangers, but I was still only twenty when I joined Hearts and it was obvious things were changing. At Motherwell I had played fairly regularly, but it was at Hearts I kicked on and that was down to the quality of guys in the dressing room. Wee Doddie knew how to put a team together and with the previous financial issues just about a thing of the past, it was a good time to join. In their first season back they had done well, but that was all about the way the senior guys went about their business and they ensured the younger contingent didn't slack either.

"Sandy Jardine was a great trainer. He led from the front and when it came to building your confidence and motivating you he excelled, even when he and the manager rolled back the years and took us to Gullane to train on 'murder hill' just as they had done under Big Jock. It certainly paid off and if Sandy could cope with the rigours of the sand, the rest of us would get through it too, although I think the seagulls may have looked forward to our visits and the extra feed they maybe enjoyed as a few of the boys recycled their breakfast after another gruelling vertical climb in what was for all the world like running in glue."

Kenny, who had an extended career himself by still playing with Airdrie beyond his fortieth birthday, is in no doubt. "Those five years for me at Hearts made me as a player and taught me all the good habits. Wee things also were put in place, like having a players' lounge and dining room which saw players getting together after training and talking about experiences. The young guys were willing students to the more mature of the squad, and that helped it all come together on a Saturday. Sandy Jardine was an integral part of all that was good about Hearts then. I know I have a special relationship with Alex MacDonald and worked with him again at Airdrie for many years when I came back from Portsmouth, but Sandy Jardine was the model professional that had the total admiration of everyone in the dressing room, and that wasn't easy to win while he was still playing and doubling up with his responsibilities as assistant manager. Often in those circumstances, players are cautious on what they say or do for fear of it being carried back to the boss. Sandy's integrity meant that situation was never likely to happen. He was one of the best."

That season, Sandy Jardine brought the curtain down on his twentieth season in senior football in the most bizarre fashion. We all knew about Sandy's versatility having served club and country as a full back or central defender and, even with Rangers, he had spells as a centre forward, wing half and winger – but goalkeeper? Surely not? Well it happened. The records will show that Hearts went down 5-2 at Love Street against St. Mirren on the 11th May 1985, but you have to dig a bit deeper to find that Hearts lost goalkeeper Henry Smith to injury with the score 3-1 in favour of the Paisley side. It was in the days before substitute goalkeepers were stripped and on the bench. Smith had slipped on the dressing room floor and was quite distressed before a ball had been kicked that day, but he was patched up to take his place between the sticks. Kenny Black actually gave Hearts the lead but it was obvious Smith was struggling and would have to be replaced. Sandy Jardine was first to volunteer to take over and pulled on the goalkeeper's jersey and gloves, but there was to be no *Roy of the Rovers* style fairy tale. Saints ran out comfortable winners but Sandy did produce one diving save to deny the Buddies striker Frank McAvennie, but Peter Mackie was quick to follow up to slot the ball into the net from Sandy's parried stop.

So on to season three, back in the top flight for Heart of Midlothian FC, and the season when the Gorgie boys became the nearly men.

21

DEVASTATED AT DENS
LAST DAY ANGUISH FOR HEARTS

In season 1985/86, Rangers had again underperformed and it signalled the end of the road for manager Jock Wallace who was in his second spell in charge of the Ibrox club. A bright new radical development was pending by the appointment of Graeme Souness as Wallace's successor. It was an appointment that would change the face of Scottish football as we knew it.

Before then though, the Premier Division was there to be won and Celtic were determined to wrestle the title from Aberdeen who along with Dundee United, were definitely Scotland's "New Firm" under ambitious and streetwise young tracksuit managers in Alex Ferguson and Jim McLean. Rangers hadn't won the league since their treble season of 1977/78. Celtic had won it three times since then but Aberdeen claimed back-to-back successes in 1984 and 1985 with Dundee United taking the honours in 1983.

It was a chance for Sandy to team up with his Barcelona Bears team mate Alex MacDonald who was player manager of the Edinburgh side.

In their first season back in the top ten Hearts finished a credible fifth in the table and even claimed a UEFA Cup spot but the following season they found the going to be tougher and ended in seventh place but perhaps more importantly, things were improving off the field at Tynecastle under Chairman Wallace Mercer. Debts were being reduced and good foundations were being laid to benefit the club in the longer term.

Those benefits and the longer term plan were soon paying dividends. The following season Hearts came within seven minutes of being crowned champions of the Scottish Premier Division.

A draw or better in the last day fixture against mid-table Dundee at Dens Park was all that was required.

On the same day, 3rd of May 1986, Celtic had to travel to St. Mirren needing to win and win well and hope that Hearts failed in Dundee.

The Tynecastle side were two points clear at the top of the table and had a four goal superior goal advantage but on an epic day of drama, Hearts lost 2-0 at Dens Park and Celtic won 5-0 at Love Street.

Celtic were champions. Hearts were broken.

Alex MacDonald's side had only to avoid defeat to Dundee to be crowned Kings of Scotland and claim the league flag for the fifth time in their history and their first since season 1959/60.

Going into the game Hearts had been in scintillating form with a run of thirty-one games without defeat and a cup final place already booked to give added incentive to a group of players who were on the verge of making history.

It was a remarkable turnaround from the previous season when Hearts won only thirteen of their thirty-six league games. They did take some consolation from that campaign in the knowledge that great rivals Hibernian had still contrived to finish one place below them.

The league had almost been won the week before that titanic first Saturday in May with Hearts scraping a narrow 1-0 win at home to take the points against Clydebank, but Celtic dug deep to prevail with a 2-0 win at Fir Park the following midweek to take the race to the final day.

Hearts travelled to the city of discovery in good shape having already drawn there 1-1 back in December and the expectation of the fans was understandable. Even a defeat could still see Hearts crowned champions as long as Celtic did not win by four or more goals against the mid-table Buddies who had little to play for, and it was only in April that Celtic struggled to win 2-1 against the same opponents at the same venue.

Celtic had some sensational players in that side though, concedes Hearts legend Sandy Clark: "Danny McGrain, Brian McClair and Mo Johnston were all capable of winning any game." Clark, who later went on to manage Hearts, recalling the obvious disappointment said: "We pushed them all the way and in the end it just wasn't to be.

"We had one final game at Dens Park. We needed to win or even just avoid defeat then we knew we would be champions."

As the game in Dundee swung towards half-time with a blank scoreline, news filtered through that Celtic were four goals up in Paisley!

The next forty-five minutes were going to define Hearts' season and perhaps even the whole future of the club.

With the clock ticking and the draw that Hearts wanted looking ever likely, disaster struck and it came from an unlikely source. Dundee boss Archie Knox had introduced Albert Kidd for only his twelfth appearance of the season, eight of which were as a substitute and, with seven minutes of the match remaining, Kidd fired Dundee in front latching on to a flick-on from John Brown who was later to star for Rangers during their nine–in-a-row period. It was a scrappy, instantly forgettable strike but the consequences of the goal were massive. Hearts were now in a desperate position and Celtic fans at Love Street were ecstatic. The exuberance of expectation prior to three o'clock on Tayside had moved rapidly south and it was the Celtic fans who now believed the title was theirs.

Meanwhile, Rangers were ending their campaign with

Motherwell the visitors to Ibrox. The home fans were jubilant when they heard that Kidd had scored at Dens but their joy was short-lived when they realised it had been Albert for Dundee that was on target and not Jambo's skipper Walter with the same surname. At Easter Road, the Hibernian players were equally confused when the home support started celebrating before the game was finished, considering the team were playing out a nothing-at-stake end of season match against Dundee United. Like the Rangers faithful, Hibs fans did not want to see their city rivals win the title.

Six minutes after the opener and with one minute of regular time remaining, Hearts' title hopes were fully extinguished when Albert Kidd struck again. This time the journeyman midfielder, who had previously played for Brechin, Arbroath and Motherwell, produced a cracker with a stunning finish after a surging solo run down the right-hand side.

Hearts were done for and headline writers everywhere were not struggling for inspiration.

The massive Hearts travelling support were dumbstruck and looked on in disbelief. Their team had led the table from the 21st of December but relinquished the spot when it mattered in a seven-minute spell in Dundee.

However, during the match that fateful day, Hearts had chances and also had a very strong penalty claim rejected when Sandy Clark appeared to be tripped in the box by a very raw Colin Hendry who was later to have a stellar career for club and country after his move to Blackburn Rovers. He carried the nickname "Braveheart" with distinction as testimony to his winning mentality in the style of Sir William Wallace himself. But perhaps bravery on such a season defining season decision was not evident from Edinburgh referee Bill Crombie who was widely known to have a soft spot for the team from Tynecastle. It had been a controversial appointment for such a high-stakes game and could certainly have been considered a conflict of interests and undoubtedly heaped pressure on the whistler, which could have been avoided with the game being given to a more neutral man in the middle. Sandy Clark is still in doubt despite the passage of time. "I believe the football authorities made an absolute mess of things by appointing Bill to our game. Everyone knew Bill was a Hearts fan and I for one think he was uncomfortable refereeing that Dens Park clash.

"The last thing Bill would have wanted was to be viewed to have any bias in our favour but with the penalty call, I think he went too far the other way."

Clark continued: "It's fine margins but I still believe had we got the penalty in that first half with the score 0-0 and scored, we would have been champions and the rest would be history. It was a momentous decision that Bill and every Hearts fan will have to live with for the rest of our lives."

While Hearts had gone into the game at Dundee in good form on the park, they had serious problems in their preparation leading up to that title showdown. In a season that had been kind to them on the injury front, a virus struck the squad in the week of the biggest game of their season. Kenny Black was first to show signs as did John Colquhoun and Neil Berry. All three were banished from the training ground and didn't join the group until Wednesday. As Black, Colquhoun and Berry showed signs of recovery, Brian Whittaker and George Cowie were next to be laid low. It was hardly the best preparation but the biggest blow was still to come when Craig Levein was confined to bed and called off on the morning of the match. Kenny Black remembers that week well. "It was just a nightmare but we all wanted to play. Losing Craig was a massive blow but big Roddie McDonald came in and was outstanding. I came off the bench for big Roger (Brian Whittaker) and being honest, between the two of us, we weren't fit enough for one person."

In a post-match interview Sandy Jardine described his feelings as just "emptiness" as he struggled to put into words just how he felt that day at Dens.

For the record, Celtic went on to win 5-0 against St. Mirren with goals from Paul McStay and a double each from Brian McClair and Mo Johnston giving Parkhead boss David Hay his one and only league championship as manager of Celtic.

Hearts gaffer Alex MacDonald was distraught at full time and candidly admitted: "When the full-time whistle went I could have wept. In fact when I got back to the dressing room I did weep – along with everyone else." After all these years, Alex still hurts. "I've never really quite come to terms with how the title was snatched from us in such unbelievable and dire circumstances."

It was a day of anguish for everyone associated with Heart of Midlothian Football Club but somehow Alex MacDonald, Sandy Jardine and the players had to lift themselves for another huge game that was just seven days away.

It was the 10th of May 1986 and Aberdeen were to provide Hearts' opposition at Hampden Park as they would contest the 111th Scottish Cup final.

On the way to that final, Hearts had beaten Rangers 3-2 in Round Three, Hamilton Academical in Round Four then St. Mirren were demolished 4-1 at the quarter final stage. Their Hampden place was booked with a single goal victory over Dundee United. Nine goals had been scored in four games on the Hampden journey but did they have anything left in that tank after the trauma of Dens Park?

A season that promised so much was on the verge of ending in tatters.

It was Hearts' first Scottish Cup final in ten years, and on that occasion the Edinburgh side lost 3-1 with now Hearts boss Alex MacDonald on target to add to a double from Rangers frontman Derek Johnstone. Incredibly, Sandy Jardine was listed as a Light Blue substitute that day.

Hearts made Seamill Hydro their base to prepare for the final, a facility that Celtic used regularly as a hideaway, but while MacDonald and Jardine's task was aided by the squad having a clean bill of health from the virus that struck in the lead up to the game at Dundee, and the physical condition of the players wasn't a problem, their mental state was a serious concern. Jardine and MacDonald were veterans of cup finals from their Rangers days and knew the benefits of being relaxed and confident going into big games, and both also knew that had Hearts won the league, the demeanour of the squad would have been quite different.

This time, Sandy Jardine was in the starting line-up but in the maroon of Hearts, and a fit again Craig Levein joined him in defence. Hearts started well but fell behind to a goal from John Hewitt in five minutes and their fragile confidence was further dented. However, they showed spirit to battle back, coming close through John Robertson. It was Aberdeen who went in at half-time with the advantage. Four minutes after the restart, the Dons doubled their lead when the mercurial Hewitt struck again. Neil Berry darted forward from midfield and crashed an effort off the bar but there was no way back for Hearts when Billy Stark gave Aberdeen a three goal lead with fifteen minutes of the match remaining.

A week of frustration perhaps boiled over in those closing stages as Walter Kidd was red carded for petulantly throwing the ball at an opponent. It was now a case of damage limitation for Hearts but what a damaging seven days it had been for the Tynecastle troops.

Manager MacDonald said: "Wattie (Kidd) throwing the ball wasn't malice, it was frustration and summed up how we all pretty much felt after a horrid eight days that left us on our knees."

After that final Sandy Jardine was quoted as saying: "I've won quite a few medals and honours in my time. During the last two weeks, Lady Luck deserted Hearts and we were cruelly deprived of the reward I think we deserved. For all that, it was a season any one with an interest in Hearts will never forget."

Sandy Jardine did secure some consolation that weekend when he was named Player of the Year by the Scottish

Football Writers Association while Alex MacDonald's efforts were also recognised with the Manager of the Year award.

Reflecting on the season that ended in double defeat for Hearts at Dens Park and then in the Scottish Cup Final at Hampden, former Heart of Midlothian manager Craig Levein, who later returned to the club as Director of Football just short of thirty years on from a season that promised so much but failed to deliver, remembers: "That really was our best chance ever to win the league. We had a really good side with Alex and Sandy making some terrific sign-ings and although I didn't play that day because of illness, I can vividly remember listening to the game unfold on the wireless and I can only describe it as surreal. I felt helpless being stuck at home in Fife while our dreams disappeared in Dundee. I was in a daze. Would winning the league have taken Hearts to another level or changed the club for the better? I honestly don't think so.

"The complete dynamic of the Scottish game changed the following season when Souness took over at Ibrox. Prior to that there wasn't much between the top teams by way of quality of players while wages were very similar at Aberdeen, Dundee United and even Rangers and Celtic, but when Souness came in, it became a case of who had the most cash could take the trophies. I think the fact that nobody other than Rangers or Celtic have won Scotland's top league since puts it all into perspective.

"Maybe now that the pain has healed a bit – although it will never go away – we should look back with pride on just how close we came and in retrospect, it wasn't that bad a season all things considered."

22

THE MANAGEMENT

It's fair to say Alex MacDonald was shocked when Hearts Chairman Wallace Mercer decided he was the man to replace Tony Ford in the Tynecastle hot seat. Ford had come to the club as part of former Newcastle United and Scotland defender Bobby Moncur's back-room team and had gone on to replace Moncur. However, Tony Ford's tenure as Hearts manager lasted only five months with a defeat to lowly East Stirlingshire along the way not helping his credibility. After Moncur had resigned in June 1981 following Wallace Mercer gaining control at the club, the new board had approached Jock Wallace, then at Leicester City and Jim McLean at Dundee United was also on the Hearts Directors wish list to succeed Moncur but when those moves proved fruitless, his assistant Ford was handed the reins. Ford had an unremarkable playing career with both Bristol clubs City and Rovers and had briefly managed Hereford United before teaming up with Moncur at Hearts. But with Christmas approaching in 1981, it was MacDonald that Mercer and his board of directors turned to to take the club forward and Ford's short spell in charge was ended.

Alex MacDonald was taken aback by the proposal.

"I never saw myself as a manager. I didn't really think about anything than just playing. I really thought Hearts would have gone for somebody with experience." It was a major consideration for MacDonald as he was just thirty-three and still saw himself first and foremost as a player. However, after chatting through the opportunity with his wife Christine the next day, he went back to Mercer and accepted his offer. The die was cast for MacDonald for the next nine years.

Sandy Jardine was still playing for Rangers at the time but wheels were soon set in motion for MacDonald to bring in his long term friend and confidante from the Ibrox dressing room as his assistant, but both would continue to play as well. It was quite a revolutionary plan from Wallace Mercer but there again, Mercer didn't really do convention!

When MacDonald, and later with Jardine as his lieutenant, realised the scale of the task they faced, they went about their business with gusto and determination. After relegation, Hearts had trimmed their playing squad dramatically and didn't have a proper reserve structure either.

Gary Mackay, who would go on to become a Hearts legend, was a seventeen-year-old trainee on the ground staff when the MacDonald and Jardine partnership made its presence felt. "What we ultimately achieved even without winning the league or the cup for me was up there and on a par with what Aberdeen and Dundee United achieved in the '80s. They had a structure already in place and a platform to develop and improve from. We didn't. We had no infrastructure and what we did achieve was all down to the unbelievable efforts of 'the gaffer' (Alex MacDonald) and Sandy."

Mackay started at Hearts in 1980 and left in 1997 to again work with Alex MacDonald after he had moved on to Airdrieonians. He still holds the record for the most competitive appearances for the Gorgie club with 640 games in his time at the club he supported as a boy when he attended Tynecastle High School, only a throw-in away from the Hearts stadium. In fact, that was also the high school where Sandy Jardine studied. Mackay remembers: "Sandy used to come to my school, not just Tynecastle High but Balgreen Primary and present medals and things as these were his two schools as well but I didn't think an awful lot about that at the time. He was from Rangers and I was a Jambo! Although later when I was playing alongside him, I think he used to give me extra stick and was quick to give me the proverbial boot up the backside because of that school relationship, while the gaffer was much more about an arm round the shoulder towards me."

Gary is first to admit that Sandy and Alex had a special bond. "They had an uncanny inbuilt knowledge about each other and about whatever the other was about to do. That must have been honed over their long time together at Rangers. They were naturals, nothing was stage managed and the balance between them was just right." Former teammate of Gary Mackay, Craig Levein, agrees: "They both knew the game inside out and had won a sack full of medals. They commanded and deserved all the respect they got. Together they just blended."

That blend and bond between MacDonald and Jardine was further strengthened in November 1986 when again in a radical move, Wallace Mercer chose to give Alex and Sandy parity with a change that saw them titled joint managers!

The driver for this change can really only be speculated upon but it's no coincidence that on the 6th November 1986, Alex Ferguson, long before he was a knight of the realm, took over at Manchester United after Ron Atkinson had been shown the door and rumours were rife at the time that Sandy Jardine was the man the Pittodrie side's board of directors had identified as a replacement. Ferguson had delivered unparalleled success at Aberdeen, not just by breaking the Old Firm stranglehold on domestic competitions, but delivering the European Cup Winners' Cup in 1983 and even beating Real Madrid in the final to do so. It was suggested that Ferguson himself had recommended to his board that Jardine should be his successor. Top sports-writer Ray Hepburn is in no doubt why Mercer took the gamble on the co-management decision. "Sandy was made joint manager because Wallace thought that Aberdeen were after him, but in truth I don't think that was the case, although there is no doubt there was a stage when he would have been on a candidate list for any job that became vacant. It made no real difference to how they functioned as a management team and the Hearts players would be happy to tell you that they always regarded Doddy as the gaffer no matter what titles they had."

That can be confirmed in the words of Gary Mackay. "The relationship between the gaffer and Sandy didn't change when they were given equal status – in fact the way they went about their jobs didn't change either. I guess previously the financial package, salary and bonuses were probably weighted in favour of the manager but this move if anything brought them further together although Alex remained 'the gaffer' and Sandy was still 'Sandy'. I don't think that bothered him at all."

Hepburn recalls: "Alex was happier using his great talent as a motivator, using the best of what he had learned from Jock Wallace, while Sandy, given that by then he was the only one of the partnership still playing, spent most of his time organising the players on and off the pitch. Not only were they two compatible working men, they were great pals and it was more important that they were able to work together. What they were called made little difference."

Gary Mackay believes togetherness was the key to that Hearts side. "It was a case of parallel relationships and while the dressing room was tight which is so important to foster team spirit, Sandy and Alex's relationship was possibly even tighter. In any working environment relationships are important and that was, for me, something that the management at Hearts back then made their priority." Mackay also respects the way MacDonald and Jardine built teams by identifying players that would fit the system they wanted to play, and were prepared to take a chance on players from lower divisions. "Look at Mike Galloway, he was spotted playing with Halifax Town and the season after we pushed Celtic all the way in 1987/88, he got his move to Parkhead. John Colquhoun had come from Celtic a couple of seasons before and was transformed into a top performer by the gaffer and Sandy and all the while other real quality youngsters were coming through and were being given their chance. Alan McLaren and Scott Crabbe to name just two. Wayne Foster and Neil Berry came in on free transfers from south of the border and had great Hearts careers. No doubt in my mind these players didn't just prove to be lucky signings as all the diligence had been done by the management with many long hours spent travelling the length and width of Britain in search of the right quality of player and person, and maybe more importantly, at the right price! For that, and having experienced the demands of managing a football club myself, they both have my total admiration."

Gary confirmed: "Sandy holding down two roles spoke massive positives about his ability to organise and balance the demands of the football job and his family life. I can't understand yet, to be honest, how he did it. I saw a recent article from Barry Robson who retired from playing in 2016 with Aberdeen to take up a coaching role at Pittodrie, and he admitted he found the demands of his new position to be much more tiring than he had experienced in his playing career! Sandy somehow managed to make it look easy!" Robson's career spanned two decades with a number of top clubs including Dundee United, Celtic, Middlesborough Sheffield United and even for a period in Canada with Vancouver, picking up seventeen Scotland caps along the way.

Mackay added: "I have no doubt in my mind that had Alex MacDonald and Sandy Jardine delivered the holy grail of the league title at Heart of Midlothian, a club I have the deepest affection for, I have no doubt they would have gone on to manage the club they had the deepest affection for – Rangers."

It may have been considered a controversial decision by Hearts Chairman Mercer to go down the joint manager route but it wasn't exclusive to Hearts at the time. Earlier in 1986, Aberdeen tried to ensure Alex Ferguson would stay at the club after they had fended off interest for their manager from Rangers, Tottenham and even Liverpool over the years by elevating his right-hand man Archie Knox to co-manager status but as it was, that partnership would head to Manchester together. Dunfermline also trialled it by hooking up coach Iain Munro and boss Jim Leishman as joint managers in 1990, but it was doomed to failure with both men having quite different ideas on how the club should be run, how the game should be played and they couldn't even agree on the players they were looking to sign. It didn't work and Jim Leishman – who was Dunfermline through and through – left the club embittered by the co-manager experience. Aberdeen did try it again when Jocky Scott, who had previously done well while managing Dundee, was given shared manger status with Alex Smith after Ian Porterfield had resigned his position at Pittodrie. Smith had been recruited from St. Mirren where he had won the Scottish Cup and he was to go on and repeat that feat at Aberdeen with Scott standing shoulder to shoulder with him. In fact during that three year period under Scott and Smith, Aberdeen ran Rangers closest, finishing second behind them in each of the three seasons. The double of the Scottish and League Cups were also secured by that management pairing in 1990.

Jocky Scott moved on during 1991 to take over at Dunfermline with Alex Smith left in solo charge. Smith himself left Aberdeen in February 1992 after a run of bad results despite almost winning the title the season before by losing to Rangers on the last day of the campaign when a draw would have seen them crowned champions. Shades of Heart of Midlothian at Dens Park five years previously.

So joint managers can work, some much more success-fully than others. Perhaps one to consider is the way the

Icelandic national team lit up the Euro Championships in France in the summer of 2016. Iceland were unfancied but had a togetherness that saw them beat England in Nice – the shock of the tournament. Ultimately, they were despatched from the tournament, losing 5-2 to hosts France to end their fairy tale. It was Iceland's first ever major international tournament. The Vikings were also the smallest nation to ever compete in the finals of the Euros.

In charge of Iceland were joint managers: Heimer Hallgrimsson who, when not coaching football remains a dentist by profession, and Swedish born co-manager Lars Lagerback. The partnership was dissolved after France, and Hallgrimsson will be left to plot a route to the 2018 World Cup finals, which are scheduled to be hosted in Russia.

Alex MacDonald and Sandy Jardine worked tirelessly together and Alex remembers when he was told that Sandy was being rewarded for his contribution to the partnership. "I had no problem with the decision and Sandy stepping up. We had been colleagues for so long at both Rangers and Hearts but maybe more importantly we were friends first and foremost."

The joint manager arrangement ended in November 1988, two years after it had been forged. Mercer, who put the partnership together, jettisoned Jardine after Hearts lost 3-0 to Rangers in the league. Rangers had also knocked Hearts out of the Skol Cup and with Hearts sitting in eighth place in a ten-team league, the chairman felt change was necessary. Sandy Jardine had begun to ease himself out of the playing responsibilities but his commitment to his management position was never in question. It was Hearts' sixth consecutive season in the top flight and the club had progressed dramatically since firstly Alex MacDonald, before being joined by Jardine, took control.

Jardine and MacDonald were called individually to a meeting with the chairman and his directors, with Jardine first to meet the Tynecastle board. In a matter of minutes with MacDonald waiting to be called, Sandy appeared in a state of shock to advise his friend that he had been sacked. MacDonald's first reaction was that if Sandy was going he was too – it was a pact that had been arranged previously.

MacDonald still carries the pain of that day. "It was almost like a death in the family and it still doesn't sit right with me. After Sandy told me what had happened I went in to face the music half expecting the same treatment, but Mercer in a cold and calculating way just told me that they had sacked "Mr. Jardine" and that he would be looked after financially and that I was to revert to being my own man as manager, but should I decide to walk away with Sandy, I would need to resign and there would be no similar package for me. I was stunned. I went outside and caught up with Sandy and he told me to soldier on. In fact, he was insistent." Alex MacDonald admits he drove home that day in a bit of a daze, still undecided on what he should do, but a long discussion with his wife Christine put a plan in place to stay but on his terms. Alex was a man on a mission. "I went back to see Mercer the next day and put a case to him that I should be looked after and if he could pay off my mortgage as part of a new contract they could take the money back each month from my wages and I would stay. I was equally surprised when he agreed to it and that was pretty much it."

There is no doubt the integrity of Sandy Jardine would not be compromised even in the most challenging of situations and he clearly put his friendship with Alex MacDonald ahead of anything else. So Jardine walked but MacDonald would continue at the helm of Hearts for another couple of years.

For Sandy Jardine, he was at a crossroads and nobody really understands why Mercer split the partnership. Certainly it was a period when results weren't at their best but there may still have been a bit of a hangover from the disappointment of failing to win the title eighteen months previously, while some suggest the chairman was frustrated by Jardine's popularity in and around the club and throughout the Scottish game. Interestingly, just days before Jardine was dismissed, Hearts Director Douglas Park of Parks of Hamilton motor trade fame, resigned his position. Was there a split in the board? Later, Park would take up a director's role at Rangers.

So what next for William Pullar Jardine?

Football writer Ray Hepburn looked back on those dramatic events at Hearts that saw Sandy Jardine effectively walk away from coaching and management for a life away from football. "I'm not so sure that Sandy walked away. As time went on, I did feel that people within the game, potential employers among them, began to realise that despite the confusion that Wallace's promotion created, it was always wee Alex that had made the telling contribution. So after Hearts and being introduced to the commercial and later the administrative sides on his return to Rangers, I think he was happy to concentrate on that to continue working and leave the more precarious world of coaching and management to others. So he probably didn't so much walk away, as cross the road."

Hepburn continues: "It's hard to know what football would make of Sandy Jardine now, such was the ease with which he did everything. He would probably be regarded as a genuine superstar. When you reflect that throughout his playing career his thirty-eight Scotland caps were gained despite opposition from Danny McGrain, John Brownlie and Davie Hay. Kinda puts today into perspective."

So the end of an era. What was next on the Jardine agenda?

23

WRITERS' FAVOURITE

When Sandy was told that his next appearance in a Hearts jersey against Celtic at Tynecastle on April 6, 1985 would be his 1,000th competitive match, and thus he would become the first player (and almost certainly the last) in the history of the Scottish game to reach this figure, he smiled and said: "At my age (thirty-six) I just take every game one at a time." A predictable response from one of the game's gentlemen.

Right there, or maybe the evening before he made his historic appearance before a crowd of 14,883, he might well have looked back on a career that earned him every reward in the beautiful game.

Scotland's top sportswriter of the period, Allan Herron, was captivated by the qualities of Sandy Jardine the player then, while he retains total respect for Sandy Jardine the man even after his death. "Sandy's record was incredible … I recall that astonishing run of 171 successive games in a Rangers jersey from April 29th, 1971 to August 30th, 1975. A run that ended because of an injury. He had played in 105 league games, thirty-nine Scottish League Cup ties, thirteen European Cup Winners' Cup ties and eleven Scottish Cup ties. A quite remarkable spell in the modern game, proof of his dedication to his craft, his conditioning and fitness while his ability was never in doubt, and he did it while performing in any role he was asked to play.

"His sheer consistency was rewarded with two League Championships, two Scottish Cups, one Scottish League Cup and the European Cup Winners' Cup in that memorable night in Barcelona. While he was proving his world class on the domestic and European fronts he also managed to fit in three under-23 appearances for Scotland and twenty-six full caps (including twenty-three in a row at right back) and by then he had been given the captaincy five times – against East Germany, Sweden, Wales, Northern Ireland and England.

"While playing for Scotland's World Cup team in Germany in 1974 he formed a full-back partnership with Danny McGrain of Celtic in the unbeaten three matches against Zaire, Brazil and Yugoslavia. This 'Old Firm' defensive combination was officially voted by the press as the outstanding duo of the Tournament. A decision which did not come as any surprise to the suits of the FIFA organising committee members."

Given the odd extra game here and there, Sandy had played in over 200 competitive quality games without a break during his peak period of four years and four months. In all, he made 674 appearances for Rangers and scored 77 goals before moving to another career with Hearts in 1982 at the age of thirty-three.

Allan Herron was part of the group of Scottish football writers that recognised Sandy Jardine's qualities to make him their player of the season not just once, but twice, and he was also, of course, part of the Scotland International squad that took the award in 1974.

Sandy first won the prestigious Scottish Football Writers' Association award in 1975, the year after the German World Cup adventure, becoming only the third ever Rangers player to receive the award, joining John Greig (1966) and Dave Smith (1972) in the history books. Also recognised by the writers before Sandy were Celtic Captain Billy McNeill in 1965, who was the first recipient of the award, Lisbon Lion goalkeeper Ronnie Simpson in the year of Celtic's greatest ever triumph, Gordon Wallace of Raith Rovers, Bobby Murdoch of Celtic, Pat Stanton of Hibernian, Martin Buchan at Aberdeen before his move to Manchester United, and another winning Celt was George Connolly. However, Connolly proved to be a real enigma, turning his back on the game in 1977 just four years after his Writers' success and after a series of "walkouts" on Celtic.

So Sandy Jardine took the coveted prize in 1975 and Herron recalls the decision was pretty much unanimous from the members. "We can be a difficult bunch to satisfy at the SFWA, but Sandy Jardine had the majority of the votes as he wasn't just a genuine model of consistency, he was a role model for any young player making their way in the game and all in all, Sandy was just a great advert for our game in everything he did!"

Incredibly, eleven years after taking the award in 1975 and at the age of thirty-seven, Sandy Jardine became only the second player ever to take the Writers' prize for a second time. John Greig was a worthy winner in 1976 having skippered Rangers to the treble.

In the intervening years, heroes of the domestic game from a host of different clubs have enjoyed taking centre stage at the end of each season when those who earn their living writing about the game in Scotland get their heads together to recognise those who have been excellent on the park through that particular period. Winners between Sandy's first and second successes were Danny McGrain, Derek Johnstone, Andy Ritchie, Gordon Strachan, Alan Rough, Paul Sturrock, Charlie Nicholas, Willie Miller and Hamish McAlpine. The names truly reflect the changing face of Scottish football at the time with the emergence of young talent in the form of Charlie Nicholas, but perhaps more importantly, it also reflects on the inspirational characters from the 'New Firm', Aberdeen and Dundee

United, who had been determined and indeed successful in breaking the 'Old Firm' dominance on their stranglehold of domestic silverware.

Ray Hepburn was the football writer who had his finger on the pulse for all things east of Scotland at that time, and recalls: "In 1986 it would have been pretty close to a unanimous choice as Sandy Jardine for our player of the year at the Scottish Football Writers' Association. Not only was there the added factor of his age and the fact that he was still performing so well, but Sandy was a tremendously gifted player at any stage of his career. As he grew older, Sandy used his brain more and his legs less but his contribution to the team was never diminished because of the dexterous way he used his assets. The buzz phrase in football now is economy of effort. The big clubs in Europe have specialist coaches, tutoring players on how to autopilot through periods of a match so that they are fully energized in the closing quarter. Sandy had that perfected before they were born. Without doubt, Sandy was a very worthy winner second time round."

A host of other top players who have made their mark and left a lasting impression on Scottish football following Sandy's award in 1986 include Ally McCoist, Paul McStay, Richard Gough and teammates Goram, Hateley and Laudrup, John Hartson, Craig Burley, Nakamura and Lambert from Celtic and, of course, Paul Gascoigne. But only a handful of other players can boast of convincing the Scottish Football Writers' Association to award them the Player of the Year gong twice. Other double winners are John Greig of course, the man who lit up Celtic Park, Henrik Larsson, and Rangers' home-grown cultured midfielder who could hold his own in any company, Barry Ferguson. In recent years, possibly reflecting the decline in our game, Leigh Griffiths is also now a double winner but fair play to Griffiths who has real talent. His recognition firstly in the colours of Hibernian in season 2013 then repeated as a Celtic player in 2016 tells us more about his desire and determination to learn and continue to improve his game but to be classed in the same league as a Jardine, Greig or in more recent years Brian Laudrup and genuine Celtic legends like Larsson, Bobby Murdoch or McStay is also surely testimony to how different the game in Scotland is now.

Mark Guidi who was President of The Scottish Football Writers' Association for the three year period 2013 to 2016, and has been a member for more than twenty years, confirmed: "Traditionally it's an open vote to determine the winner. That is, no shortlist is created and voted on so with a membership of around 100 writers, the nominations can be quite diverse and varied, it's all about personal choice.

"I wasn't involved when Sandy Jardine won it for a second time but it's a huge accolade to have won it on so many counts ... only the second ever second-time winner ... winning at the age of thirty-seven ... and winning it with a provincial club."

Mark continued: "Normally the votes are cast and the results concluded about three weeks before the season ends, so even then you can only imagine that the members back in 1986 were pretty convinced that Hearts were looking likely champions, and if you analyse the winners over the years with the exception of the period when Aberdeen and Dundee United were to the fore of the Scottish game, it's a rarity to see a winner from outside of the Old Firm.

"We have had the odd landslide vote over the years and Henrik Larsson and Brian Laudrup immediately spring to mind as being in that category. Halcyon days!"

Gordon Smith is in no doubt why his former Rangers teammate was still playing at forty years of age. "Sandy taught me good habits. Apart from natural fitness in the days before sports science, you were conditioned at the start of the season then it was up to yourself after that. Sandy got me into sprinting and I can recall him telling me about the professional sprint days with George McNeill and Bert Logan at Powderhall when he competed with the best. He also gave me my first pair of spikes and we regularly used to stay behind at Ibrox for extra training round the track and in the warm-up area under the main stand. It certainly made me much pacier and Sandy was the inspiration.

"I am sure the way he lived his life prolonged his career and while I was never fortunate enough to win the Scottish Football Writers' Award, for Sandy to win it twice tells you everything about what he brought to the Scottish game."

Alan Rough took the award in 1981 when with Partick Thistle and said: "It was a real feather in the cap to win the Football Writers' Player of the Year. Every year we give them stick and moan about the man-by-man marking results they give us but deep down, everybody that plays the game wants to win it. Other than the PFA Player of the Year that is voted on by your playing opponents and teammates, it's a wonderful accolade to receive. The names that have been awarded the prize are all legends and when you see that Sandy Jardine won it twice – and to do it with an eleven-year gap – is unbelievable, but that was Sandy. Consistency was what his game was all about and that consistency clearly was recognised by the Football Writers' Association. I am proud to be up there with him as a recipient of that award."

Veteran journalist Roger Baillie added: "It's always harder for defenders to win the prize as strikers are usually the glory boys and their goals are good vote gatherers. I was the secretary of the Scottish Football Writers' Association when Sandy won Player of the Year the first time, and to win it again eleven years later is truly a remarkable feat.

"I had the pleasure of reporting on Sandy's career from his first game for Rangers against Hearts after the defeat to Berwick and I was also on duty on the day of the cup final of 1986 against Aberdeen. It says so much about Sandy's dedication and incredible consistency in a wonderful career spanning two decades, and when you recall who else has won the Writers' Player of the Year award twice, and Sandy has a case to claim he won it three times if you factor in his part of the 1974 World Cup squad that took the honour too, he is not only in elite company, but in a pretty unique position too."

24

RETURN TO RANGERS

John Gilligan watched Billy Jardine make his Rangers debut playing up front and wearing number nine, so when the chance came to work with him around twenty-three years later, Gilligan, who was appointed to the Rangers board in 2015, admitted to being a little bit star-struck. Of course by then Billy was now universally known as Sandy from his days as a player at Ibrox and had just left his joint manager position at Heart of Midlothian FC, and now Sandy Jardine was about to embark on a major career change.

Sandy wasted no time after his dismissal at Tynecastle to get straight back into employment. After all, he had a family to support and while Jardine had been well rewarded for his time in the game, footballers' earnings during his playing days were not so dramatically different to those of a regular working man as they are today.

Alistair Wilson, Sales Director of Scottish Brewers, was the man who gave Sandy Jardine the responsibility of promoting his company's products including finding ways to promote McEwan's Lager. The brand was struggling to gain share from the market leading Tennent's product and aligning the product to football was the strategy established and that saw John Gilligan, then Development Investment Manager, team up with Sandy Jardine in the drinks industry. The job was totally different to anything Jardine had experienced before but he met the challenge with relish and soon made a major impact on the business. John Gilligan rolls back the years. "It was fantastic to work closely with Sandy and the first thing that I recall about him was his humility and energy and a real desire to succeed. In that regard, maybe the skills required in his new marketing position weren't that different to those that had made him such a success as a footballer.

"Using footballers or former footballers to raise the brand profile was popular in the day with Kevin Keegan the face of Newcastle Brown Ale, while up here we also had Jim McSherry who previously played with Kilmarnock also joining our team. McEwan's Lager became shirt sponsors of Rangers from 1987 to 1999, so it must have worked well for both parties."

As part of his responsibilities Sandy, accompanied by his wife Shona, also made regular visits to Ibrox to meet and greet the corporate guests of Scottish Brewers in the McPhail suite. John Gilligan recalls Sandy's early days in his new position: "Sandy had time for everybody and blended in straight away, joining in with the banter too as we had a few Celtic fans in our department, as was the Edinburgh–Glasgow thing, but Sandy just clicked and it wasn't long before he moved into a senior marketing role with the business and despite not having been given any formal training, he was a natural. We were spending the guts of £1 million per year at that point and relations with Rangers weren't great but Sandy got things back on track. He was a really clever boy with genuine intelligence and I think Sandy would have succeeded in any job in any industry. We were lucky to have him and in fact when he left us, it was to go back to Rangers in a similar role and it still worked well for us as we now had a friend in the Rangers camp that understood the needs and aspirations of both businesses."

It was Bob Reilly, then Commercial Director at Rangers, that recruited Sandy as he set about putting a team together to promote the club and maximise revenue streams including the growing market for corporate hospitality. The same day Sandy Jardine rejoined the Ibrox payroll, Martin Bain also started his employment at the club. Bain would later become Chief Executive at Rangers under David Murray but in 1994 he had been headhunted by Reilly to pair up with Jardine to develop brand Rangers.

Bain had previous experience of both the club and Sandy Jardine as he had been involved in a consultancy capacity while in the employment of a Glasgow PR company. Martin remembers: "It was exciting times! It really was so helpful for me because Sandy knew the club and the people so well and we were effectively given a free rein to make things happen. To learn more, I was despatched to Manchester United for a week to study their methods, while Sandy was sent to Nike to try and tap into their ideas and methods. There is no doubt that Sandy himself was a great ideas man and was never frightened to present them no matter how off the wall or otherwise. He was very astute and a real creative thinker, which was allied to his man management skills honed over his playing and management days in the game. He was also a quick learner; he was able to bring it all together and would have taken on any task for the good of the club no matter how demeaning others may have considered it. That could include handing out magazines and match programmes at brand-building events or meeting guests from all walks of life when they came to the club. Sandy took it all in his stride. There was never anything Sandy refused to do and in fact he did it all invariably with a smile on his face."

Sandy's qualities were soon recognised and his role at the club was broadened beyond Commercial, PR and Marketing to take on Ambassadorial duties and that included taking over the maintenance and archiving of Rangers' history records, artefacts including those still on display in the Blue Room and the Trophy Room at the top of the Ibrox marble staircase. Martin Bain remains convinced Sandy was the best man for the job. "Sandy's passion came through constantly and I remember one day Jim Baxter came into the office and wanted a Rangers coat. We didn't have any spare but by the time Jim had sat down with a cup of tea and a biscuit, Sandy had jumped into his car, driven into Glasgow and bought one. He was back to present Jimmy with the coat and Jim had no idea that Sandy hadn't just gone to a cupboard to find him one. That was typical Sandy." Martin continues: "John Greig may carry the accolade of the "Greatest ever Ranger" but I think Sandy is worthy of equal status!"

Sandy also proved to be a great ally to the football department and was always on hand to chauffeur potential new signings to and from the airport or their hotel, and took great delight in showing prospective signings round Ibrox and the training complex. Sandy's involvement was often the trump card played by Chief Scout Ewan Chester. Chester left Rangers after seventeen years in the job in 2004 but was brought back by Walter Smith in 2007. Ewan recalls: "Sandy had taken over from Greigy on player liaison and he was a sensation at introducing players and their families to the club. When I came back in 2007, Walter told me we have to get things right and we did of course. Madjid Bougherra, Pedro Mendes and Steven Davis were all recruited fairly quickly in Walter's second spell in charge and Sandy was influential in selling the club to them all. How could players not be influenced?

"Here was a man that had done it all in a distinguished playing career and in his time at Hearts with Alex MacDonald, was considered one of the hot tickets of the period as the management team with the most potential in Scotland. Funnily enough, I remember sitting with Graeme Souness when news came through that Hearts had sacked Sandy Jardine and Graeme said, 'Who do they think they can get that can do better than what they have now

– incredible!' But of all the signings I brought to Rangers, the most recent one that Sandy liked the best from memory was Steven Davis. I think Sandy saw a bit of himself in Steve and the way he conducted himself was so important to Sandy. Walter told me he felt the side needed legs and energy in midfield and I immediately proposed Steven Davis as I knew his game well, having been involved in his transfer from Aston Villa to Fulham during my time at Craven Cottage. Walter said he knew of Davis but hadn't seen enough of him but I was prepared to put my reputation on the line for this one and said to Walter 'If it doesn't work out sack me', so I was given the OK to make the deal happen and when Steven arrived in Glasgow, it was Sandy who gave him the tour and convinced Steve his future lay at Ibrox."

Not long before that Steven Davis deal was done, Sandy Jardine was the man who smoothed the move and relocation of David Weir to his home in the south to Glasgow when he signed for the club in 2007. David is still grateful for the help he enjoyed from Sandy when he moved up from Everton. "Sandy did it all. Nothing was too much trouble for him. He sorted me out with a car, a flat and even managed to have my SKY TV installed for me. It was great to have help but to have it from a real legend in Sandy Jardine was extra special. I was in awe as I had been a fan and although it was a roundabout route for me to take to become a Ranger, it allowed me to just focus on my football without distractions, and Sandy knew how important that is to a player. Nothing was ever a hassle for Sandy and he did so many jobs about the club. I take pride in seeing my international cap framed and displayed on the wall and that was down to Sandy. I know recent internationalists like Lee Wallace and Lee McCulloch haven't had theirs put up yet and that is only down to the fact that Sandy is no longer with us.

"Sandy knew what the club was all about and he made sure new faces were aware of the heritage, and that's something Mark Warburton and I have taken on as we make new signings. Sandy was never one to seek attention and was happy to have a low-key position, and while he was proud of what he achieved in the game, he never burdened you with it or was boastful about it at any time. He was a real role model and if Sandy said he would do something – he did it and he did it properly, the Rangers way."

Sandy Jardine with Colin Jackson were the inspiration behind the Former Players Club. Rangers fan Bobby Roddy, who is Chief Executive of SCS Construction, worked tirelessly with them both to raise funds for the club which was established to assist former players in need. Bobby recalls the first meeting with Sandy and Colin to arrange a dinner to commemorate the fortieth anniversary of the European success in Barcelona. Bobby had built a strong bond with Sandy, sharing a love of golf and having travelled together on numerous trips watching Rangers playing abroad. "The Former Players fund had a total of £7,000 in its account but with the right people involved, including Rangers men like Billy Montgomery and Andrew McCormack, we raised £70,000 and Sandy and Colin were over the moon with the success. We went on and had another number of successful fundraisers and Sandy acknowledged my contribution by gifting me a replica of the medal the players won in Barcelona, and on the reverse it's inscribed 'To Bobby – It's a real privilege to call you a friend. Sandy.' I have never taken it off since he gave me it.

"Sandy was so committed to Rangers, much more than anyone could ever imagine. In February 2012 he phoned me and asked me to meet him at the stadium. When I got there he was sitting with Rangers Supporters Liaison Manager Jim Hannah and they were both ashen-faced. Sandy said 'Bobby – the club is in trouble. Serious trouble. We have no money and things are looking very grim indeed.' Sandy then went on to say that the security company were withdrawing their services as they hadn't been paid. I made a few phone calls and had everything in place to cover things using some of my own staff and recruiting a few other

Rangers fans that we knew we could trust. However, it wasn't required. Sandy appealed to the security company and they agreed to continue to carry out their duties. That was agreed because they trusted Sandy Jardine."

Bobby Roddie was also involved in the Rangers fighting fund that Sandy and Jim Hannah were active in and remembers being on holiday in Dubai and being approached by some ex-pat Rangers fans. "I went along to the Desert Bears club to watch the game and I was asked to say a few words about what was happening at Rangers at the time. Before I left I had been handed £10,000 in donations to the fund and asked to hand it personally to Sandy because they knew the money would be in good hands! It was some gesture and perhaps tells you just how high the esteem Sandy was held in by the fans despite them being so far away from Glasgow.

"Sandy Jardine did so much for Rangers and I doubt if the club made a better signing when they brought him back after his time at Hearts."

Perhaps Sandy Jardine's contribution to Rangers from a non-playing perspective is best summed up by Club Director John Gilligan. "It must have been awful what guys like Andrew Dickson, Ally McCoist and Sandy went through. These guys tried to work with all that came through the Rangers boardroom over recent years and they policed them as best they could during those terrible, terrible years – when I came in with Dave King and Paul Murray, we were left to pick up the pieces – there could easily have been nothing left at all had it not been for Sandy Jardine."

25

HALL OF FAME

In the year 2000, Rangers Chairman David Murray came up with the idea of a Rangers Hall of Fame. The inspiration for the initiative was Sandy Jardine who was now actively working behind the scenes with another Light Blue legend, Colin Jackson, to establish a former players club that would ultimately secure charitable status and be on hand to assist any ex Ger who had perhaps fallen on hard times, or just needed some support from the Rangers family at any difficult period.

Sandy drove the Hall of Fame project and was surprised when he himself was named as one of the inaugural inductees. He was joined by some illustrious company from players across all the eras including Laudrup and Goram from the most recent nine in a row squad, Greig and Baxter from the all-conquering swashbuckling side of the '60s, Waddell and Thornton who excelled post World War Two and later managed the club with distinction. Founding Father Moses McNeil was recognised at the same time as was Wee Blue Devil Alan Morton whose portrait adorns the marble staircase. Jardine was not out of place in that company though.

The strict criteria for inclusion included consideration to length of service to the club, talent and international recognition while a Ranger, and ambassadorship for all things Rangers.

Sandy Jardine passed all aspects of membership with flying colours. A key man in treble-winning teams of 1976 and 1978 and major honours that are confirmed as three Championships, five Scottish Cups, five League Cups and of course, success in Europe in 1972. With 674 Rangers appearances and thirty-eight caps for Scotland, Jardine's inclusion in the Rangers Hall of Fame was more than merited.

The Rangers Hall of Fame has gone from strength to strength since the early days of its inception when it was the first of its kind for any football club in Britain. Even in bad times, special service has been acknowledged with Lee McCulloch joining the elite club in 2014 and you just know that, as Rangers force themselves back to the top of the game, a host of future heroes will be privileged to join Sandy Jardine on that imposing board half way up the iconic Ibrox stairway from the Edmiston Drive reception.

Club historian David Mason worked closely with Sandy on a number of projects and confirms: "Sandy had strict beliefs about what constituted nominations for the Hall of Fame. When potential candidates were discussed, Sandy always looked beyond the obvious and woe betide anyone prepared to suggest a former player who Sandy may have believed hadn't always behaved himself on the park and away from the game with the decorum and dignity Sandy considered Rangers were all about.

"Dignity was something he talked about all the time and standards instilled in him as a youngster never left him, and he encouraged everyone associated with the club to conduct themselves with dignity and to never forget that 'you' were representing Rangers Football Club. When you look at that Hall of Fame board, which will be there to tell the story of great Rangers for generations to come, you can understand why Sandy put such great importance on why only those and such as those would or should be recognised."

Sandy was also assured of his place in football folklore when he was honoured by The Scottish Football Association in 2006 by being given a place in the Hampden Hall of Fame too as recognition of his exceptional contribution to the game in general, and his commitment to the dark blue of his country.

However, despite Sandy cherishing his SFA award, he threatened to hand it back during those difficult days of 2012 when Rangers and the power lords of the Scottish game were at loggerheads.

Interestingly in 2016, twenty years after his death, twice treble-winning Rangers manager Jock Wallace remains overlooked by the SFA for a place in their hall of fame despite making a huge contribution to the Scottish game. Wallace won eight major honours in a five year period, most notably the two clean sweeps of domestic honours in 1975/76 and 1977/78. Rangers legend John Greig, who was honoured to be included in the SFA hall of fame in 2004, two years before his great friend and former teammate Sandy Jardine, called for the situation to be remedied. "When you analyse Big Jock's contribution to the game and what he achieved, it's amazing that he has been overlooked. Twenty years after his passing it is surely appropriate to put matters right and give Jock Wallace his rightful place in the game."

At Rangers' annual Hall of Fame Dinner in 2014, the club launched a Special Recognition award.

Hosting the event that night was Sky Sports presenter Jim White who laid out the criteria for this extra-special prize. "It has to be someone who has the class, dignity and upholds the standards, traditions and history of this football club." It was tailor-made for William Pullar "Sandy" Jardine.

Sandy wasn't in attendance that night but in his absence, then manager Ally McCoist showed real emotion as he collected the award on Sandy's behalf. McCoist said to the enthralled black-tie audience: "No one is more deserving of this award. Sandy is a legend in every sense of the word. A remarkable man and I am honoured to call him a good friend. No one has done more for this club in times of difficulty and no one has been more supportive of my position when I needed someone to talk to."

Ally then produced an acceptance speech from Sandy which read, "It was a great honour and privilege to be involved at the start of the Hall of Fame project and I am truly humbled to receive this award. It's a true honour and one my family and I will cherish forever. I was extremely fortunate to enjoy a successful career and again to return to Rangers when my playing days were over. I have to say, seeing my name on the Hall of Fame board in Ibrox stadium is the greatest honour any Ranger could receive and having spoken to others who feature too, they all agree. To have my name permanently etched there means more than the world to me and my family.

"Rangers are more than a football club, they are a 142 year old institution and events like the Hall of Fame dinner confirms what a special club we are. It's always an honour to be a Ranger, it meant everything to men like Woodburn, Meiklejohn, Greig, Baxter and Cooper. Being in the Hall of Fame is a fantastic honour and something to be proud of. Once a Ranger, you are always a Ranger and I want to be remembered as a Ranger forever.

"I hope you are all enjoying your evening and I thank you all for your kindness."

The assembled guests then enjoyed a video tribute to Sandy to the tune of the Rangers anthem 'Simply the Best'.

It almost brought the house down.

The dinner was hosted on Sunday, 30th March 2014 and within a month Sandy was no longer with us.

But the Rangers fans were not finished acknowledging their hero yet, and a bronze bust of Sandy was commissioned by the supporters with renowned artist Helen

Runciman given the responsibility of capturing Sandy's smile, and a fine job she made of it too.

It was fitting that on a home game in April 2015 against Heart of Midlothian, one year after Sandy's death, his wife Shona in the company of Rangers legends John Grieg and Alex MacDonald unveiled the magnificent bust which now sits proudly halfway up the marble staircase and under that Hall of Fame board that Sandy was so delighted to just be part of.

Less than one year before the statue was organised, the club themselves honoured Sandy's memory with a fitting tribute by renaming the Govan Stand the Sandy Jardine Stand. It is a permanent and fantastic way to pass on the legend of a great Ranger to generations to come.

Rangers goalkeeping coach Jim Stewart says walking into the Ibrox reception and up the marble staircase is still special no matter how many times he does it. "Mr Struth is there, and the board with men through the generations that shaped this great club, and now the bust of Sandy is there too. It's special."

In 2010, another of Jardine's teammates was inducted into the Hall of Fame. Derek Parlane had been Rangers' top marksman in four out of five of the league seasons after the Barcelona triumph. Parlane was brought up a Rangers supporter and to find himself recognised in this way took his breath away. "I am delighted to have been part of Rangers. If someone had said to me at sixteen when I joined this great club that one day I would be part of their Hall of Fame, I would have thought they were having a laugh." With 111 goals in 300 club appearances, Parlane played in a hugely successful period for the Rangers. He was always a worthy candidate for inclusion.

Only two players received a Hall of Fame place while still playing with Rangers. David Weir, who made such a massive impact when Walter Smith brought him to Ibrox despite being in the twilight of his career, and Lee McCulloch, share that honour, but in 2014 then manager

Ally McCoist tipped Lee Wallace to join that elite club with his loyalty being a key factor in his favour.

McCulloch who was joined by Fernando Ricksen and Nacho Novo when he was inducted in 2014 confirms: "Of all the medals and honours I have won in my career, this is up there. To be acknowledged as a Ranger and have my name on the same board as the magical players at this club like Baxter, Henderson, Greig and of course Sandy Jardine is humbling. I never expected it and from the team I watched as a boy, Super Ally, Durranty and Terry Butcher are all there too. I am just so grateful."

For David Weir, when he was signed by Walter Smith in 2007, it could have been construed as a stopgap short-term solution to plug a leaky defence. Weir himself actually thought that was the case having turned thirty-seven and having been at Everton almost eight years. David says: "It's an incredible story as I look back. 231 appearances, five goals and three League titles, two Scottish Cups and three League Cups, it was more than I had ever won in all my years in the game elsewhere. It really was some five years. Being inducted into the Hall of Fame is a very special memory too, and I remember chatting to Sandy Jardine about it and he told me how he had started the ball rolling on the Hall of Fame project with previous chairman David Murray, but never at any time when I joined did I think I would ever be included."

Now in his role as Assistant Manager to Mark Warburton, David Weir knows that the culture, heritage and history of Rangers is paramount and he is in no doubt that the Hall of Fame board facing you as you climb the famous marble stairs is part of the fabric of the club. "It's awesome and so imposing that you can't miss it when you come through the doors. It's there and it just reconfirms for everybody what a great club with a great tradition Rangers is." Further confirmation is also offered from Rangers Captain Lee Wallace who was with club throughout the journey from the bottom of the Scottish game to their return to the Premiership, and their first league game back in the top flight against Hamilton Academical in August 2016. "Every time you walk up the stairs at Ibrox it's an inspiration. We have so many new players to help us compete back at Premiership level and they all talk about the Hall of Fame board and the great names that are on it.

"Would I like to appear there myself one day? Of course I would. It would be a huge honour to be in the company of the greats that are there including Sandy who was a fantastic help to me when I signed from Hearts, but I don't believe I have done enough at this club to justify it. Maybe one day!"

26

SANDY'S OTHER BATTLE
ILLNESS CONFIRMED

It was just another day at the office for Sandy Jardine as he made his way to Rangers' training complex at Murray Park in Milngavie outside Glasgow in late 2012. Or was it?

Jardine had steered Rangers through their darkest times of administration and through the ignominy of liquidation. He had fronted marches and fundraising campaigns, he had been the rock for so many of his colleagues in troubled times – including manager Ally McCoist. Sandy also displayed character and energy his former boss Jock Wallace would have been proud of, as whenever required, you could be assured Sandy had "the battle fever on". So when in November he suffered from a sore throat, and originally put it down to the change of weather and perhaps doing too much, including travelling west every day from his Edinburgh home to continue to champion the cause for Rangers, Sandy was sure it would pass.

As a precaution Sandy mentioned the sore throat to club doctor Paul Jackson whose early prognosis was swollen glands, but the doc also noticed another little lump and arranged for it to be checked further by specialists.

A biopsy followed and within a week the bad news was

confirmed to Sandy. He was diagnosed with throat cancer and to further complicate matters, a secondary cancer was also confirmed in his liver.

Because of the severity of Sandy's condition, the medics first operated on his liver, and around eighty per cent had to be taken away. Sandy was a non smoker and at sixty-four years of age, was physically fit and active prior to this bombshell. Now Sandy Jardine was fighting for his life.

After the first operation, Sandy picked up an infection and had to spend twelve days in the high dependency unit. It was a really fraught time and friends and family feared the worst. However, against the odds, Sandy made a recovery and called upon that spirit that had stood him in good stead throughout his career.

At the time Sandy was quoted as saying: "I don't think the added pressure from the Rangers situation had anything to do with it." He did take time to acknowledge the debt of gratitude to the medical staff who looked after him, saying: "I couldn't speak highly enough of the doctors and nurses who have been treating me."

Four weeks after moving from the high dependency facility to a ward, Sandy was able to go home to further recuperate but chemotherapy and radiotherapy on his throat was to be a weekly feature. It was Christmas Eve 2012.

Despite his own obvious pressures and condition, Sandy still found time to talk about Rangers with everyone he came into contact with, in typical Jardine unselfish fashion, and he was quoted at the time as saying: "I was maybe a figurehead for the club along with Ally McCoist during our troubles, but behind the scenes, the rest of the staff and the fans were absolutely brilliant. They all deserve a medal for everything they put up with. The players will get one for winning the league but the staff and the fans should get one as well.

"People have got to remember we have just started this journey and while we will get back to the SPL, we need to compete with Celtic when we do.

"That is a long way off and there is a long road to go, but I'm very positive with the supporters behind us we will get there."

Prophetic words from Sandy Jardine going back to 2013, despite more Ibrox boardroom troubles being only round the corner.

During his illness, Sandy was away from Rangers for a year but was encouraged and deeply touched by thousands of letters of support he received from all over the world. Those letters included a touching note from Celtic Chief Executive Peter Lawwell, an email from Rod Stewart and a card from sports broadcaster Hazel Irvine.

Every communication was an inspiration and a source of strength to Sandy on his road to recovery.

Another inspiration by this time was the way the Rangers support had developed the two minute Sandy Jardine applause. Every home game when the clock showed two minutes, in recognition of Sandy's long term Rangers number two shirt number, the fans stood as one and clapped for a full minute. It was a small and simple acknowledgement from the fans to let Sandy know he was one of their own and he was in their thoughts and it meant the world to Sandy.

Derek Johnston, a Rangers fan from Kirkintilloch, was named after a former Jardine teammate of the same name, but with an "e" on Johnston. But Sandy was his hero – not the alternative D.J. Derek had also been a key member of the supporters group who plotted the Hampden march of 2012 and had worked closely with Sandy in the planning of the event and the stewarding on the day. Derek admitted he struggled to hold back tears every time the two minute applause started, and said: "The support have never been more together than when we all held Sandy in our thoughts. I'm not afraid to admit it, I was usually in tears as was just about everyone else who sat near me in the Copland Road stand.

"Sandy got us through our really bad times. It was the

least the support could do to try and help Sandy through his."

To help his rehab, Sandy increased his exercise levels and walked as often and as far as he could each day with his goal being getting back to Ibrox one day.

On the 2nd March 2013, he achieved that goal when he declared he was fit enough to travel to Ibrox and take in the game against East Stirlingshire.

Jardine even found time and the energy to address the legions via the Ibrox PA system before the game, and when the applause kicked in on the second minute, it was even more emotional than before especially when Sandy stood from his seat in the directors box to wave to the fans in every corner of the ground.

After the game, Rangers manager Ally McCoist expressed his joy at seeing Sandy Jardine make a return to the club as Rangers edged closer to the Third Division title with a 3-1 win.

It was a momentous week for the Ibrox club with Lord Nimmo Smith's independent commission earlier ruling that despite having been found guilty of breaching registration rules of the Scottish Premier League, the club would not be stripped of any of it's fifty-four league titles.

Things were looking up and Sandy Jardine made a return to Ibrox in early August to unfurl the Third Division championship flag ahead of the League One opener against Brechin City. Within three weeks, Sandy was back behind his desk in Argyle House.

27

SANDY'S LAST INTERVIEW

Reproduced from *We are the People* magazine.

Robert Marshall is a lifelong Rangers fan and owns the Louden Tavern bar which is a short free kick away from Ibrox.

The Louden is famous for its question and answer nights hosted by Robert, and legends such as Colin Stein, Willie Johnston, Derek Parlane, Graeme Souness and others have all had the pub bursting at the seams with Bluenoses lapping up the intimate details of careers of players who have graced Ibrox in the famous Rangers jersey.

Robert counted Sandy Jardine as a friend and despite Sandy's failing condition he granted Robert a ninety-minute interview on his career. It is believed to be the last interview Sandy ever gave and it was published originally by WATP magazine.

It is with thanks to Robert and WATP magazine that we are privileged to reproduce that interview in its entirety.

Interview by Robert Marshall

Part One

RM: Sandy Jardine is one of the true legends of our proud club's illustrious 141-year history. He is without doubt Rangers' best right back in living memory and can be held up as one of the greatest players to have turned out in a blue jersey.

Born in Edinburgh with the Christian name of William, not far away from Hearts' Tynecastle Stadium, I first remember laying eyes on Willie Jardine (as he was then known) when we played Queen's Park in a Glasgow Cup match at Ibrox.

He scored four goals that day, something that as a twelve-year-old I would never forget! It's fair to say I was impressed. I think to put it in context, if I had to pick a greatest ever 'World XI' then Sandy would be my first choice, not Cafu, not Lahm, not even the great George Cohen – he was that good. Some people might disagree but I watched him all through his career at full back and I never witnessed him having a bad game.

I have been lucky enough to have known Sandy for a few years now and I was delighted when he accepted our invitation to do an interview with WATP Magazine. There is always something special about speaking with one of your heroes, that little thrill separates them from us mere mortals. Sandy is recovering from a life-threatening illness and it was really nice to be able to speak with him.

Sandy, first of all how is your health?
I'm coming along fine Robert, I'm looking to be back working full time next year.

I've always known you as a bit of a workaholic so how are you coping at home?
It's been a bit frustrating but I've been working away in the garden, taking things day by day and going on walks to build my strength up. Thankfully I have been able to get back to a few games now.

How did you feel when the fans were applauding you in the second minute?
It was both humbling and emotional. I'm really grateful for all the messages of support I have had from the fans. They have been excellent.

Let's start from the beginning, how and when did you join Rangers?
I went straight from schools football to Ibrox in 1965. I used to get on the train at Haymarket in Edinburgh through to Queen Street in Glasgow and jump on the subway over to Copland Road (as Ibrox underground was known back then). I even travelled with some of the greatest legends of that era: John Greig, Jimmy Millar, Ralph Brand, and later on we were joined by the Fife lads – including Billy Mathieson, Colin Stein, Willie Johnston. It was different then.

They would have been real legends to a young lad like yourself, how did you feel travelling with them?
Oh, they were great! They were always giving me advice and always had a good story to tell.

How did it feel going up the marble staircase for the first time?
You always remember your first time going up the marble staircase. It really epitomises everything about our club – class and dignity.

Moving to on-field matters, I remember you scoring four goals against Queen's Park in a Glasgow Cup tie as a youngster coming

through, what do you remember of that?
I was playing centre forward that night, and everything just clicked for me. It seemed that every time I touched the ball it went into the net.

I remember you as 'Willie Jardine' then, when did you become known as Sandy?
The players started calling me it around the time I made the first team, obviously because of the colour of my hair. I'm not really sure when it became my name publicly.

You seemed to play a few different positions before you settled down at full back, how did that come about?
Well, I made my debut in February 1967 against Hearts and played at right wing half. We won 5-1 and I kept my place for the rest of the season. When Willie Waddell came, he converted me to a right full-back. I felt I was suited to playing there, and was there for most of my career.

RM: Sandy is being humble when he said the position suited him. He was the first overlapping full-back I ever witnessed in Scotland and he was outstanding there. He had everything you could want – stamina, speed, superb at a standing tackle, a fantastic reader of the game who brought others into play, and he was fond of popping up with a goal. I'm not exaggerating when I say he was world-class.

You were well known for your fitness. How influential was Jock Wallace in that?
Big Jock was brilliant for the players. He introduced the notorious Gullane Sands, which set us up for the season. People might joke about it but there were about nine members of that team that played well into their mid-thirties, which was uncommon in those days. We attributed that to his physical conditioning methods. Jock Wallace used to be an Army PT instructor and was quite revolutionary in what he introduced in training. He even brought

in a professional sprint coach, which I felt I benefitted greatly from. We always seemed to score goals in the last ten minutes of games when other sides were tiring and that was due to Jock. The players all loved him, he was honest and upfront with you.

You played over 1,100 first-class games in your career. Which one was your favourite?
I wouldn't say I had favourite games. I loved playing in every one. As far as importance goes, then obviously the European Cup Winners' Cup Final victory in Barcelona in '72 was the pinnacle of my career. Being a member of the only Rangers side to win a European trophy is something special. I played in the 1967 European Cup Winners' Cup Final defeat to Bayern Munich, and I never really appreciated how big an achievement it was to get that far. It made me appreciate the victory against Moscow Dynamo even more.

Barcelona is one of my finest memories as a Rangers Supporter, what do you remember of the game?
It was a really good performance from the whole team. We were 2-0 up at half-time through Steiny and Bud. We came out for the second half and when Bud added a third we had the game completely in control. The Russians, who were a very good team, scored a goal near the end and added a second with about five minutes to go. It must have been the longest five minutes of my career! The only disappointment was not being able to show the fans the trophy on the night.

That was a magnificent achievement, the single greatest triumph in our history – I thought everyone was fantastic on the night, but Dave Smith in my opinion had the best game of his career. Would you pick out anyone for special praise?
Davie had a brilliant game, but the whole team was brilliant. Throughout my career I wouldn't like to pick out

individuals. We won as a team and we lost as a team. We had a great spirit about us.

Although the team was fantastic on the night, I actually thought the best single team performance in the European Cup Winners' Cup run was the semi-final at Ibrox against Bayern Munich. What are your memories of that game?
Well we were all-square from the first leg in Germany. Over there, we took an absolute battering that night! But we limited them to one goal. They were a great team, and went on to win three European Cups in a row with half the team being West German internationals. We got our equaliser through an own goal, but strangely in the last ten minutes of the game we were chasing the winner as Jock Wallace's training methods allowed us to keep going for the full ninety minutes. The second leg at Ibrox was completely different. We were always confident of beating anyone at home. That night there were 80,000 people crammed in to Ibrox and the atmosphere was amazing – probably the best I've ever played in. We started very brightly, and in the second minute I gathered the ball on the right-hand side, got myself forward and managed to hit the ball with my left foot and it sailed over Sepp Maier and into the top left-hand corner. You couldn't hear yourself think. We added a second through Derek Parlane, who had replaced John Greig after he failed a fitness test. I had never seen any German team lose self-control the way they did that night, they were even arguing on the pitch. We had really gotten to them.

You must have been so proud to have played in that team.
I was and am. It was an amazing time, playing with great players and great people.

RM: From a personal point of view, the 1972 Cup Winners' Cup campaign defined the Rangers team of that era for me. We took on the national cup winners of France, Italy, Portugal, West Germany and Russia – some of the biggest footballing nations in Europe. We played with a style that was suited to the European arena and Willie Waddell must take great credit for that. Players like Sandy, John Greig, Derek Johnstone, Tommy McLean, Peter McCloy, Colin Jackson, and Alex MacDonald went on to be the mainstay of the team for most of the next decade. We also had the very underrated Willie Mathieson and Alfie Conn, the sublime Dave Smith, and of course Willie Johnston and Colin Stein. Some of these players must be included amongst the greatest ever to wear a Rangers shirt.

And we will leave it here for part one. We have covered Sandy's arrival at Rangers up to Barcelona 1972. In the second part we will concentrate on his domestic successes, on leaving Rangers and all his subsequent work at the club. We will also cover the march to Hampden and his hopes for the future.

I'll reiterate, it was an absolute pleasure to interview Sandy Jardine. He's the quintessential Rangers man and everything you would expect from someone who has represented our great club both on and off the pitch for so many years. I was impressed with him as a player since I was twelve years old, and today, I am impressed with him as a man.

Part Two

Sandy what was the first domestic success you had with the club?
The first trophy I won with Rangers was the League Cup in
October 1970. There were over 100,000 people at Hampden
Park to see us take on Celtic. John Greig had failed a fitness
test and Ronnie McKinnon was captain. It was a really
good game which we won by a single goal. It was scored
by a young lad playing only his second game for the first
team by the name of Derek Johnstone. It was obvious even
then that Derek was a special talent. If I remember correctly
Steiny hit the woodwork in the last few minutes and that
would have confirmed that we were well deserved winners.

*I remember it well! It was the first trophy I had personally
witnessed Rangers winning. How did it feel to be part of that?*
It was a great feeling. We'd lost the final the year before
so it was a real indication that the team was making
progress. You know, it is great standing with the trophy
and looking to the crowd knowing that you have helped
them go into work on Monday morning with a smile on
their face.

*The next domestic trophy you got your hands on was a special
one, the Scottish Cup Centenary final in May 1973. What can
you recall from that day?*
Well firstly, every trophy is special. But this one had royalty
presenting the trophy, HRH Princess Alexandra, which
added to the occasion. We were playing Celtic again and it
was generally accepted to be one of the greatest cup finals
of its era. Derek Parlane and Alfie Conn got the first two
goals for us and no one who was there will ever forget the
look on big Tam Forsyth's face running towards the dugout
after knocking the winner in from about three yards with

the sole of his boot. A big quiet lad off the park, but once he put his boots on he would have run through a brick wall for Rangers. As I say, it was a fantastic game and a great occasion.

In 1975, you finally got your hands on the league title. John Greig was out injured for most of the season, which meant you were captain. How did it feel to lift the trophy?
It was brilliant. We needed one point from our game at Easter Road and a headed goal from Colin Stein ensured we got it. Big Jock had said to me before the game that he was going to bring John on for the last couple of minutes if the result was going in our favour. I was happy to agree to this and the rest of the lads were the same. John was a massive influence on the club and all the players looked up to him.

You've done it again Sandy, you haven't mentioned you won the Player of The Season award that year.
Yes, I was fortunate enough to be considered for it. Although, I am very proud to have won it, the credit must go to my teammates as well. We were all in it together.

Right Sandy, now we are on to the era that shaped the 1970s for me, the 1975/76 treble team, the 1977/78 treble team and the Drybrough Cup match of 1979. Winning a treble is the highest domestic honour a Rangers player can attain. How do you feel to have been part of two teams that have achieved this?
There is no doubt that it is a great honour to be associated with these players. We had great unity and worked tirelessly for each other. And what a lot of people don't remember is that the second treble team was quite different from the first. To be part of both is something I am very proud of.

RM: Sandy, as usual plays down his part in these occasions. In 1975/76 we entered into a new league set-up. For the first time the league was ten full-time professional clubs facing off against each other for four matches. In my opinion, this vastly increased the difficulty level and for Rangers to come out of it with a treble was borderline miraculous. We finished the league with a winning margin of six points ahead of our rivals across the city (at a time when it was two points for a win) and had remained undefeated against them. We beat Celtic in the League Cup by a goal to nil, courtesy of Alex MacDonald, and saw off Hearts 3-1 in the Scottish Cup (with goals from Derek Johnstone and another final goal from MacDonald). At the time I didn't know how the players felt, but as a young fan it was my first treble. It was magnificent.

Sandy refers to the second treble team as 'quite different' from the first. The team of 1977/78 is, in my opinion the better side. The goalkeeping position was shared by two players, Peter McCloy and Stewart Kennedy. Our back four consisted of Jardine, Jackson, Forsyth, and Greig. In midfield we had Tommy McLean, Bobby Russell, Alex MacDonald, and Davie Cooper. And upfront we had Derek Johnstone with Gordon Smith playing off him. That is a superb team. We had a slightly shaky start but after Smith came in, he showed he was the missing link needed to gel the team together. Sandy only missed five games in total that season, participating in both the Scottish Cup and League Cup victories over Aberdeen and Celtic, respectively.

Sandy won a further two Scottish Cups (1978/79, 1980/81) and two League Cups (1978/79, 1981/82).

Before moving on to your departure from Rangers, we must talk about the Drybrough Cup final of 1979. How does it feel to score such a fantastic goal and have so little discussion about it today?

To be fair to Coop, his goal was sensational. His goal was that good that I sometimes even forget I scored. Players do things like that in training but rarely in a game and never in a final. Only Davie had the skill and audacity to even attempt such a goal. It is as good a goal as anyone will ever see.

Well I remember your goal so well Sandy, you intercepted a pass on our eighteen-yard line, you beat seven or eight players and calmly stroked the ball into the back of the net. If it wasn't for your goal against Bayern Munich I would say it was your greatest ever goal.

That's very kind of you, but I feel for John McDonald. He scored the opener that day and no one (except for John himself) talks about him scoring!

Yes, I have been in John's company and he is very proud of it – quite rightly! Now to move on, how did it feel to leave Rangers for Hearts? Was there any animosity?

No none at all. I had a great career at Rangers, and will always be grateful for my time at Ibrox. I played with some fantastic players and made friends with some fantastic characters. Obviously, I was sad to leave but I knew John [Greig] had difficult decisions to make. Some would work out for him and others wouldn't but he always had Rangers' best interests at heart.

You went to Hearts with your old teammate Alex MacDonald who was Hearts manager at the time. How did you find it there?

Yeah I really enjoyed myself. It was a fresh challenge and to be honest it was probably what I needed at that time. Alex discussed it with me and we decided I would play at sweeper. Later on I would go on to become co-manager. We were proud of what we achieved at Hearts. We qualified for Europe three times, were very close to winning the league and Scottish Cup, and, with a bit of luck, we could have been double winners. However, we just came up a bit short.

And not to forget your Player of the Year award at the age of thirty-seven in 1986. You are the only player to have won that award with two different clubs and of course you were a member

of the 1974 World Cup Squad that was awarded it as well. How does it feel to have that honour?
I played with great teams and great players throughout my career. You only really ever get individual rewards for being part of a good team and that was the case with me.

We haven't even really covered your games with Scotland. Can you give me a few words to sum up your international career?
What can I say? I played thirty-eight times for my country and enjoyed every minute of it. I went to two World Cups and played in big games. What more could you ask for? I've always been very proud to have represented Scotland.

Sandy, you led the Rangers Support on the march to Hampden where over 8,000 marched with you. How did that come about and how did you feel?
And the same number on the street supporting us! The idea came from a group of young Rangers fans. We also got a lot of help from influential supporters, but I wouldn't like to single anyone out. Everyone played their part that day. To lead that march was a tremendous feeling and I was honoured and privileged. To be honest it's one of my proudest moments during my time at Ibrox and I have been here a long time.

Finally, do you have a message for the Rangers support reading this?
We have had an unsettling time in the last two years, but our fans have been magnificent and if we stick together we will be all right.

RM: I'd like to reiterate that it has been an immense honour and privilege for myself to do this interview. It is no secret that Sandy is one of my all-time heroes. I would just like to finish this by wishing him the best of health and I look forward to the day where he is back full-time at Rangers. A true Rangers Legend.

28

A LEGEND LOST

On Thursday 24th April 2014, Rangers Football Club confirmed that Sandy Jardine had lost his eighteen-month battle against cancer.

Rangers confirmed their thoughts and condolences were with Sandy's wife Shona, children Steven and Nickolla, his seven grandchildren, family and friends.

Ally McCoist, then manager of the club, was quoted on the club website: "Everyone at Rangers is devastated at the loss of a legend and a great man. Sandy was respected not only by Rangers fans but also the wider football community, and he is a huge loss to the game. I had the privilege of watching Sandy playing for Rangers when I was a young boy, I had enjoyed the pleasure of working with him closely since I returned to the club in 2007, and he was a truly remarkable human being. His achievements both on and off the pitch are second to none and I was honoured to regard him as a friend.

"He gave everything for this great club and worked tirelessly in a number of roles because he wanted to ensure the traditions, history and standards at Rangers were maintained. He recently told me he was proud to be a Ranger and wanted to be remembered forever as a Ranger. Well Sandy, you will go down in history as one of the greatest of all time and we will miss you terribly."

During his time at Ibrox, Sir Alex Ferguson was a team-mate of Sandy's and on hearing of his passing, the former Manchester United manager Sir Alex and his wife Cathy paid their own tribute. "From Cathy and I, this is some of the worst news we have heard. Sandy was a noble and courageous man. The respect he is held in at Rangers is immense. He was one of the greatest players ever to wear the jersey. To Shona and family we express our sympathy and sadness."

Campbell Ogilvie, President of the Scottish Football Association, added his condolences. "I am extremely saddened by the news of Sandy's passing. I have known Sandy for more than forty years and found him to be as warm and courteous off the field as he was reliable and elegant on it. As well as being a talisman for both Rangers and Heart of Midlothian during an illustrious and enduring playing career, he was also a terrific servant to the Scotland national team."

Celtic Chief Executive Peter Lawell also paid tribute. "This is absolutely devastating news. Sandy Jardine was a very fine man and it was a privilege to know him. Sandy was widely respected across the game and he will be sadly missed by us all."

William Pullar Jardine's funeral was held at Mortonhall Crematorium in Edinburgh on Friday 2nd May 2014. He was sixty-five when he died. "Sandy" to the football community but just "Billy" to his family and friends.

29

GOVAN TRIBUTE
GOVAN STAND RENAMED

It became clear early in 2014 that Sandy's health was deteriorating, and one man at Ibrox with whom he had built a close bond since his appointment in October 2013 was Rangers Chief Executive Officer Graham Wallace. Graham and Sandy's relationship had originally been established during his time at Manchester City when Graham brought a Sky Blues team up to play the Light Blues in a pre season friendly at Ibrox in the summer of 2009. Graham recalls Sandy with genuine fondness. "I had actually met Sandy a couple of times before I was appointed CEO at Ibrox and had been impressed by his professionalism and clearly his affection for everything connected with Rangers.

"In my time at Manchester, Sandy had attended a game at the Etihad with then Rangers CEO Martin Bain and we enjoyed lunch together. In 2009 as the teams were meeting in Glasgow, Rangers was a long established top flight European team competing in the Champions League whilst at Manchester City, we were just embarking on the project to rebuild and refocus the club following its acquisition by an Abu Dhabi company in late 2008. Our vision was to build

Manchester City to be capable of challenging for consistent domestic and European success.

"On this visit to Ibrox in summer 2009, and knowing personally about the Ibrox trophy room and its history, I asked Sandy if he would show the City players the trophy room pre match and talk to the players about the success that Rangers had over many decades as is evident from everything in that room. I wanted to do this as a means to instil in the Sky Blue players at that time a sense of what long-term success looks like, and as a means of reinforcing the ambition and long-term success that we were seeking to build at our club. Sandy was of course delighted to be able to do this and absolutely captivated the City players and manager Mark Hughes with his commentary and knowledge of virtually every piece in the trophy room.

"I know the City players on that occasion, many of whom were young professionals, were left with a very positive view of Rangers and the success the club had delivered over many years from the strength of Sandy's presentation. Even the internationalists and experienced campaigners in the squad including Craig Bellamy, Shay Given, Kolo Toure, Gareth Barry and Emmanuel Adebayor were taken by Sandy's passion for his club."

Rangers won the match 3-2 that day with Nacho Novo and Kenny Miller on target before David Weir popped up with a last-minute winner.

Graham Wallace continues: "When I joined Rangers as CEO in the Autumn of 2013 in the midst of well documented turbulent times, one of the first people to request a meeting with me was Sandy Jardine. We met one afternoon within my first two weeks of joining the club and spent a couple of hours over several cups of tea where Sandy took great pride in telling me his perspective on all things Rangers past and present. His love for the club and his strongly-held belief about the conduct of the club and anyone who represented the club, was clearly evident. He had played such an important role during the darkest days post administration in 2012/2013 based on his belief that the club was too important to not stand by it, and shown leadership to help commence the rebuilding.

"At that point Sandy had an important role in helping players new to the club to understanding the history and the standards that Rangers had always been known for."

That can be confirmed by the words of Fraser Aird who left his family and home in Toronto to join Rangers at the tender age of sixteen. "On one of my first days at Murray Park, Sandy told me, 'This club is all about traditions son, on and off the park. Represent yourself with class and the rest will take care of itself. Always remember that now you are a Ranger ...' Sandy's words will stick with me for the rest of my life. He was a great man."

Fraser made his top-team debut against Montrose in September 2012, aged seventeen. During Mark Warburton's first season as Rangers manager, Fraser returned Canada on loan to Vancouver Whitecaps to further his development.

As Sandy and new CEO Graham Wallace continued to chat over another cup of tea, he took the opportunity to impart the same wise words to his new boss. Graham remembers: "I think our first meeting that afternoon was in many ways Sandy doing what he regarded as his job – to help those of us new to the club to understand at least some of what had come previously. Not in a lecturing or condescending manner but in a way that showed his passion for the club and wanting only the best for it. Anything he could do to help in this regard was what he wanted to do.

"Our time working together was all too short. I enjoyed a warm personal relationship with Sandy, meeting him regularly, and when his health deteriorated such that travel to Ibrox was too difficult, we would still speak regularly on the phone. I valued his council as someone who truly understood the club and who was well placed to offer an informed perspective on many matters. Sandy knew the magnitude of the task that I had taken on and was always helpful and thoughtful when I sought his input.

"As part of our conversations, we discussed a broader future remit for him at the club when he felt able to do so – sadly we never managed to put this into effect as his health deteriorated rapidly.

"It was with great sadness that in what transpired to be my final personal meeting with Sandy a few weeks before his death he told me face to face that he knew he only had a matter of weeks to live."

For some time before Sandy's death, a small team at the club had been engaged on looking at how the club could honour and mark the tremendous contribution he had made as a player and statesman for Rangers. Any acknowledgement or honour needed to truly reflect the standing Sandy Jardine enjoyed with everyone connected with the club. Graham Wallace took the initiative: "Irene Munro, Carol Patten and Stephen Kerr were tasked by me with identifying an appropriate way to honour Sandy. Many options were considered by this small group of Sandy's colleagues and it was agreed that renaming the Govan Stand would be the most appropriate gesture – significant, permanent and totally deserved."

In his role as CEO, Graham Wallace duly took the proposal to the board of directors with his recommendation that the Govan stand be renamed the Sandy Jardine Stand. It was voted through unanimously. Graham now had to put his plan in place. "I was delighted the board were united and supportive for my recommendation and we quickly went to work to make it happen. Originally our thinking was to have the renaming effected prior to the end of the 2013/14 season."

As part of the planning, Graham arranged to meet Sandy. "I met personally with Sandy to let him know that the club wished to commemorate his contribution by renaming the Govan Stand and wanted to ensure that he was comfortable with this proposal. Sandy was speechless at the gesture, overcome with pride and it took him a little while to compose himself and accept the offer I had made him.

After thinking about it for a few minutes he said it would be an honour that he would gratefully accept, however he asked me to do one thing for him. That request was to delay the name change until after his passing. He did not want to have a day in the spotlight given how ill he was. I duly accepted his wish and notified the board accordingly. We agreed to the renaming of the stand and commenced all the detailed logistics, sign manufacture etc., however we all knew that it would be some time before we would be able to announce to the Rangers family how the club wished to honour Sandy."

Sadly, Graham and the others involved in the project did not know how rapidly Sandy's condition would worsen and on the 24th April 2014, Sandy passed away.

During the summer, Graham Wallace liaised with Sandy's widow Shona and his son Steven to effect all the necessary arrangements for the unveiling of the Sandy Jardine Stand.

As the fixture list would have it the first home match of the 2014/15 season was against Sandy's "other" club Hearts – and the scene was set for the ceremonial unveiling.

It was a full house at Ibrox as many of Sandy's former teammates led by John Greig, formally confirmed that the previous Govan Stand would now be known as the Sandy Jardine Stand in perpetuity.

John Greig's attendance was a triumph for Graham Wallace, as the man who has the worthy title of "The Greatest ever Ranger" was making a rare return to Ibrox. John Greig had been on the board when Craig Whyte was in charge at Ibrox, but John resigned along with former club chairman John McClelland believing their positions as non executive directors were impossible to fulfil properly. Graham confirms: "I met with John personally in advance of the occasion and asked him if he would attend this particular match against Hearts to honour his friend and former teammate. John of course had decided some time previously to relinquish his position as a director at the club and that he would not attend matches for reasons of his own – however he agreed to attend on the day, and he accompanied Sandy's widow Shona in the directors box on the occasion and after the stand was unveiled."

A permanent and fitting tribute to Sandy. Graham Wallace fittingly finishes his memories of Sandy. "I was personally sad that Sandy left us as soon as he did – as I had no doubt that he would have had a large part to play in shaping Rangers' future – just as he had done so in the past."

Stewart Collins runs his third-generation family butchers business from Coatbridge, but has had three season tickets for the Govan Stand from the first season after Graeme Souness was appointed manager. He was fully behind the tribute, saying: "I can't think of a better way to honour a true Rangers legend in Sandy Jardine. I was in Barcelona in 1972 and Sandy was always one of my favourite players, but I originally had my ticket in the main stand but when Souness came I had to get my boys involved although they were only young at the time, but the vantage point from the Govan Stand front was ideal. They were probably fed up listening to me constantly going on about the great Rangers teams of the past, and the pace, flair and style of Sandy Jardine and my other favourite, Bud Johnston, but they saw for themselves what a great Ranger Sandy was in the horrific period from 2012 as he represented the club with dignity in everything he did. The boys may not have seen Sandy play but they were delighted that the board backed the decision from Sandy's colleagues to rename that part of Ibrox stadium which holds so many memories for us, and many like us, having taken in just about every game over the years and celebrated many championships together as a family in the same seats over such a long period of years. The decision was surely a no-brainer. The Sandy Jardine Stand was just the right thing to do. I am sure every Rangers fan would agree."

Jim Stewart was a teammate of Sandy Jardine at Rangers and with Scotland. Jim still coaches the Rangers and

Scotland goalkeepers, having been brought back to Rangers by Walter Smith in 2007 after he replaced Paul Le Guen, and he believes Sandy Jardine having the Govan stand named after him is a wonderful tribute to his former colleague. "It's perfect the name. Sandy Jardine will live long in the memory of Rangers fans for generations to come."

Stephen Kerr worked closely with Sandy at Rangers within the media department and built a very strong bond with the Rangers legend. Stephen, now a director with the successful Glasgow PR company LEVEL5PR, confirmed it was a privilege to work with Carol Patten and Irene Munro to establish a suitable manner of recognition for Sandy's commitment to the club, and was delighted that Graham Wallace and the board were fully behind the proposal to have the Govan Stand renamed The Sandy Jardine Stand. "Everyone agreed – it was the right decision and so sad that Sandy passed away a few months before it happened.

"His family and close friends from Edinburgh were in attendance the day the stand was officially unveiled – fittingly against Sandy's old club Hearts on the opening day of the season.

"I always regarded it as an honour to work at Rangers for the best part of fourteen years, and playing a small part in arranging that tribute to Sandy despite the sadness of the situation remains one of the highlights of my time at Ibrox."

30

BEST FRIENDS

On the 5th of April 2015, Rangers further recognised the contribution the late Sandy Jardine made to the football club by unveiling a bronze bust of their former player, and again on the day, it coincided with a match against Hearts. Hearts, Rangers and Sandy Jardine were intrinsically linked to each other. Jardine was brought up a Hearts fan. He was watching Hearts the day Rangers crashed out of the Scottish Cup to Berwick that accelerated his call up to the first team and it was of course Hearts who were in opposition for his debut! In August 2014, Hearts were again visitors to Ibrox on the day the Govan Stand was official retitled 'The Sandy Jardine Stand', and it was the Gorgie side who were the visitors just over a year after Sandy died when the bust, the commissioning of which was funded by the fans, designed and crafted by renowned Scottish artist Helen Runciman, was given its prime position on the iconic marble staircase.

On the day, Rangers won the match 2-1 with first-half goals from Kenny Miller and on-loan Newcastle midfielder Haris Vuckic, but the result was academic. Heart of Midlothian were already champions although Rangers were playing to secure the best possible play-off position.

It was an emotional day and the ceremony was conducted with wonderful dignity as Rangers Supporters Liaison Manager and great friend to Sandy, Jim Hannah, said a few heartfelt words as Sandy's widow Shona with Rangers legend John Greig unveiled the perfect likeness in bronze in front of a small gathering of family, friends and colleagues.

The man awarded the accolade as the greatest ever Ranger, John Greig, had a very special relationship with Sandy Jardine as they were travelling companions from Edinburgh together for their daily commute to and from training, and that relationship developed from just team-mates to being great friends. John Greig saw a lot of himself in the teenage Jardine when he joined Rangers in 1965. "Like me, Sandy was from Edinburgh and like me, Sandy was a Hearts fan when he was growing up.

"We definitely built a special bond and when he moved up beside me in Edinburgh and our houses were only about 600 yards apart, we were colleagues and neighbours and our wives and kids grew really close too. I tried to pass on to Sandy the same experience I had enjoyed from Jimmy Millar and Ralph Brand. In those days I was the youngster, and Jimmy and Ralph were the senior players scoring goals every week in the Rangers first team. Just listening and talking to these guys was invaluable and it helped shape me as a person, not just a footballer and perhaps even more importantly, I was being educated in the Rangers ways. I tried to relay that same solid advice to Sandy although he was probably still Billy in those early days. We would take turns at picking each other up, sometimes driving through to Ibrox, but usually we went for the 08:30 train to Queen Street.

"It was obvious Sandy was a player with huge potential, you only had to see him on the training ground to know that and I even won a £1 bet from him, but I'm sure looking back it was a £1 note that he would have been happy to part with. I had predicted that Billy, before his nickname Sandy had actually stuck, would play in the first team before

Christmas 1968. Billy said it was 'impossible' and dismissed the suggestion but I won the money when Scot Symon named him in the team to play Hearts in February 1967, ten months ahead of the deadline I had set. By the end of that year and still a teenager, Sandy had exchanged handshakes with the Prime Minister of Russia, Mr Alexei Kosygin, who had attended a game we played at Kilmarnock, made his European debut against Zaragoza of Spain, and played in the European Cup Winners' Cup final. That was some progress!"

John recalls that European final of 1967, saying: "I didn't notice it at the time but having watched the tape after the game, I think Sandy was one of the best players on the park against Bayern and that was with guys like Beckenbauer and Müller playing too." Those early days laid the foundations for a bond that lasted fifty years and even in the close season, John and Sandy were often together. "I tried to encourage Sandy to work on things that I believed would let us play on for as long as we could, and in the summer, Sandy would work with guys like Bert Logan and Tom Paterson on sprint work including competing with the professionals at Powderhall and other places. Wee Willie Johnston did the same and there weren't many quicker in their day than that pair. We used to do stamina work by running around Arthur's Seat which is the biggest hill in Edinburgh at Holyrood Park. No doubt those days helped us both play longer than many players of that era did. That dedication with desire and ability are the things that set great players apart from good players. Sandy was very much in the former category."

John highlights the importance of respect in any relationship. "I had total respect for Sandy Jardine as a player and a man and I know he had the greatest respect for me and for that I will always be grateful, but more importantly, Sandy was a Rangers man and he respected what Rangers stood for.

"He was a tremendous asset to this club in every role he

embraced. The bronze bust is a wonderful way to remember Sandy as is the stand and while he's sadly no longer with us, he will never be forgotten. Rangers Football Club is bigger than any individual and in the pantheon of who's who of great players and managers who have contributed to Rangers history over the years, Sandy Jardine is up there with anybody."

Also in attendance at Ibrox for the first public showing of Sandy's bronze bust was another former Ranger who, like John Greig, had a special friendship with Jardine. Alex MacDonald had joined Rangers in 1968 and immediately hit it off with Sandy although Alex, or Doddie as he's known to football fans everywhere, had his own nickname for his pal. He called Sandy "Tiger" in a bit of a parody of the former Rangers iron man, defender Jock "Tiger" Shaw who captained the club between 1938 and 1950. Shaw's nickname had been established because of his robust and physical tackling style, not quite strengths or qualities associated with Jardine. "Sandy couldn't tackle a fish supper,"said Doddie with an impish grin. "You appreciate that Sandy eventually had to stop playing because his arms were knackered after more than twenty-five years of squeezing and pulling them together like he was playing an accordion, trying to signal to the full-backs in the team to get more narrow to make it easier to defend!"

MacDonald remembers his first meeting with Sandy Jardine while he was still playing with St. Johnstone. "It was the Musselburgh five-a-side tournament and I was playing against Rangers. Sandy was in the Rangers team. I nutmegged big Davie Provan, who was just coming back from a broken leg and he punched me. I did it again and he punched me again so I just gave him a whack in the next tackle! It was bedlam. Sandy and wee Bud Johnston both wanted to batter me but big Davie didn't, he was being stretchered off at the time! Incredible to think that Bud, Sandy and me would be together at Rangers and Hearts and still be friends all these years later."

Alex MacDonald has that wicked sense of humour that he often displayed in his playing career and recalls when many years after his boots were hung up, he was driving for a living and looked into Ibrox to see Sandy for a cup of coffee. "I parked the van and went into reception looking for Sandy. The girl obviously didn't know who I was and even when she took my name, she then asked me if Mr Jardine would know who I was and why I was calling. I said, 'Of course he'll know me, I slept with him for twelve years!' The poor girl was a bit shocked and wasn't quite sure what I was meaning!" What Doddie was alluding to of course was the fact that he and Sandy had shared hotel rooms on all their trips with Rangers over the years both at home and abroad. Alex continues: "We were on the same wavelength, you had to be, spending so much time in each other's company but we were maybe a bit more like Jack and Victor of 'Still Game' fame in later years with Sandy liking to be early to bed while I was a bit more hyper, especially on the night before a game, and a bit of a telly addict. I don't know how many times I battered him with the pillow when his snoring was drowning out something I was trying to watch on TV! But whether we got a good sleep or not, we were still probably the two fittest boys at the club. So it must have worked alright."

Strangely, despite having such a strong bond in their football lives, Sandy and Alex didn't really socialise together, but from day one at Ibrox, Alex was aware of the big characters in the Rangers dressing room. "There is no doubt Sandy was a great help in settling me into life at Rangers. Yes, I was a Rangers fan but the dressing room was full of Rangers fans and big, big players of the period – Greigy, Willie Henderson, Dave Smith and Sandy. The banter would be on the go in the dressing room and you had to be able to handle yourself when the barbs were flying about. Sandy was quick with the one-liners and I was too, and I think that was what helped bond us early. We always went about together – me, Sandy and Alex Miller. It was a strong and united dressing room but you had your wee gangs within it in those days like Greigy, Smith and Willie Mathieson, they always hung about together but there was never any division between the boys. However, if any of the younger players were looking for advice, I used to tell them what I thought then tell them to go and speak to Sandy and he always gave them words of wisdom and it didn't matter how long it took.

"I think looking back to those days, that's probably when I decided that if I ever became a manager, Sandy would be the guy I would want to be with me. Although being honest, back then I didn't really have any genuine ambition to be a manager and I think when I did get the job at Hearts, it was by default as much as anything. I was probably cheap and in the right place at the right time.

"Not long after I was in the job, Sandy became my priority signing. I was a Glasgow boy and this was an Edinburgh club. I realised it needed an Edinburgh boy involved that the fans and the directors could relate to. There was nobody better placed or qualified for the job than Sandy Jardine. John Greig was manager of Rangers by then and didn't want to lose Sandy but they were pals as well, and knowing Sandy always had a soft spot for Hearts and recognising the great service he had given Rangers, he made a case to the directors to let Sandy leave. I know if things had worked out differently we may well have had the opportunity to team up again to manage at Ibrox but after Souness came in, that was that! Being honest with you though, looking back, I'm glad Souness came in because he took Rangers to another level and look at the big names he brought to the team as English clubs couldn't play in Europe at the time because of a ban, and Souness capitalised. We tried to up-trade everything we did at Hearts too and while we managed to improve things, Rangers were off the radar."

When Sandy was sacked by Hearts chairman Wallace Mercer, Alex remembers Sandy's reaction. "He wouldn't hear of me resigning meaning two of us would be out of work and that was typical Sandy, always thinking of others. But when I think back to Mercer's reasoning for putting Sandy down the road, it can only have been that he wasn't happy that Sandy was getting all the press and was in the limelight more than he was."

Alex believes a return to Rangers was always on the cards for Sandy. "When Sandy went to work for the brewers who were Rangers' sponsors then, it was inevitable that he would end up back at Ibrox, and the work Sandy did when he did go back was incredible. He wasn't happy with some of the songs that the fans sang and he was vocal about that, but Sandy knew the penalties and sanctions could be severe and eventually the penny dropped with them. But Sandy was the one who worked harder than anybody to make the supporters see why certain songs should not be in the fans' repertoire. When you think too that only three people in the history of Rangers have been honoured with a statue, Sandy is in some company. Only Sandy, John Greig and Bill Struth have that honour. He deserves it. He lived for the club and when I go into Ibrox for a match now, I have to stop on the stairs and have a word with him. I can hear him answering me and then telling me to 'Stay off the bevvy wee man!'

"That bust means Sandy will have his eyes on everybody coming and going at the club and I can't think of a better guardian of the club traditions than my best pal Sandy Jardine."

31

COLLEAGUES' COMMENTS
TRIBUTES AND MEMORIES

Fourteen years working alongside Sandy Jardine certainly made a huge impression on Stephen Kerr. "The word legend is certainly overused in football but the word is entirely fitting when applied to Sandy as he epitomised everything that is good about Rangers. He was a man of principle and class and his contribution to the club – both on and off the pitch – was truly remarkable. Sandy was a credit to Rangers for decades and his dignity, class and love for the club always shone through. A true gentleman who will never be forgotten by all who knew him. A world class footballer but more importantly a world class human being and we didn't know him as Sandy the former player – he was just Sandy our pal and work colleague.

"Carol (Patten) and I were fortunate enough to work with him closely every day and his boundless energy and enthusiasm for life was infectious.

"During the dark days of administration, he and Ally McCoist were giants and inspirational characters to the staff who were going through hell and concerned about their jobs. With no chief executive or chairman in situ, Sandy and Ally took it upon themselves to visit staff in the offices at Ibrox on a daily basis and my respect and admiration for both is difficult to measure. It truly was a family back then and Sandy was at the head of the table. He used to come in to the press office and have a cuppa – in his famous china mug and saucer – and provide us with unbelievable support.

"I remember Carol calling me when he was diagnosed with cancer to warn me that he was about to call me with the sad news as I wasn't in the office that day. I couldn't believe it. He called a few minutes later and it was difficult to hear this giant of a man – who was our hero – telling me he had the deadly disease.

"We nearly lost him during his operation but he survived against all the odds at that time, and we were all thrilled to see him back at Ibrox again and of course, he deserved the honour of unfurling the league flag. It was a privilege being part of the process that resulted in the Govan Stand being named in his honour.

"We immediately thought a stand in his honour – similar to the renaming of the Main Stand in Bill Struth's honour – and we mentioned to Jim Hannah and a few others at the club. Every person agreed so we took it to then Chief Exec Graham Wallace and it was ratified by the board.

"Sandy's family and close friends from Edinburgh were in attendance the day the stand was unveiled – fittingly against Sandy's old club Hearts on the opening day of the season. I always regarded it as an honour to work at Rangers for so many years and playing a small part in the tribute to Sandy was one of the highlights of my time at Ibrox. Another highlight – which again involves Sandy – was when we arranged for Ally McCoist to interview Sandy on his career. We set up the interview in the manager's office and it was such an intimate and enlightening discussion between two true blue legends.

"Sandy was ill at the time but he was gracious enough to discuss his career with Ally and it was a privilege being in the room for the interview. Both men are Rangers giants and watching them discuss their careers and bounce off each other was a privilege. It is difficult to watch knowing we have lost Sandy – but it is a fantastic interview and again I was delighted to play a part in making it happen.

"I would urge all supporters to watch this interview – it's on YouTube – Sandy's love for Rangers is clear. Sandy was loved and respected by all – not just Rangers fans but football fans around the UK – and his achievements are unique and unlikely to be seen again in the modern game. Sandy was based in the offices at the Govan Stand for many years when he returned to the club he served with such distinction as a player, so it is fitting this particular stand now carries his name.

"He was a credit to Rangers for decades and his dignity, class and love for the club shone through. We have lost a true gentleman but he will never be forgotten. It was an honour to know and work with Sandy so closely – he would have loved seeing Rangers clinch promotion back to the top flight. We will always miss him but he will never, ever be forgotten."

Another from the Ibrox back room who worked with Sandy for many years is Club Historian David Mason. David has served Rangers with real passion for his responsibilities since the early days of Graeme Souness but was a Rangers fan long before joining the club and remembers a young 'Billy' Jardine making his way in the game. "Sandy came from Edinburgh and travelled with players from the first team who regaled him about their successes of the early sixties. Even after Brand and Millar had moved on, Sandy travelled with John Greig and undoubtedly they plotted many tactics and game plans during their journeys, and it was even suggested by others that Sandy and John almost picked the team on occasion as they travelled the tracks. Sandy was thrown into the team at the deep end after Berwick and it was a case of sink or swim. Sandy proved he was made of stern stuff and I don't doubt those early challenges in his Rangers career stood him well and laid great foundations for a great career. Perhaps the Scot Symon influence comes into play here too. He was one of the most generous men I ever met and if any good cause needed a signed shirt to assist fundraising or similar, I've known him to even give away one of his own even if it was worn in a high-profile cup final or European clash. Sandy was the man so many turned to for advice and even when Rangers held a special ceremony in January 2011 to commemorate the fortieth anniversary of the Ibrox disaster, the Reverend Stuart MacQuarrie sought council from Sandy on the part he was to play. Sandy replied in typical style 'just make it tasteful'. That was just Sandy's way. Sandy used to get so frustrated by fans' forum websites and felt too often they didn't represent the true thoughts of the majority of the Rangers support, and Sandy held Rangers' principles and standing in such high regard he hated anything that threatened to undermine them. He regularly talked about 'the Rangers' but that wasn't just a line used cheaply by him, it was his way of life. Rangers fans owe Sandy Jardine a huge debt of gratitude for the way he represented the club on and off the park for nearly half a century.

"In my eyes Sandy Jardine is the closest we've had at Rangers to Bill Struth than many perhaps would admit or appreciate."

Robert Carmichael was another who worked closely with Sandy in his role as Rangers' Official Statistician. Sandy was determined that the phenomenal history of Rangers was to be captured for posterity and that the details had to be exact, ensuring generations to come could access them to truly understand and value the traditions and successes Rangers had recorded and indeed delivered. It meant working long hours but Sandy had the energy and dedication to the task in hand.

Robert recalls: "When Sandy first contacted me to research all the games that Rangers had ever played, with the objective of building a database of Rangers history, it was clear from the outset that he had already given this quite a lot of thought and knew more or less exactly what he wanted.

"As time went on and I got to know him better, it was clear that the history of the club meant a great deal to him, be it the attention he gave to the items in the trophy room or the consideration he gave to the Hall of Fame.

"He was always looking for ways to display the achievements of the club, either individually or as a team and another example of this was the plaques that he had made that are displayed in the tunnel area which list the honours that Rangers have won since they were formed. He was very keen to make sure that these plaques fitted in with the general look of Ibrox and had several designs mocked up before choosing the gold lettering on a blue background. They are certainly an impressive feature and are a helpful reminder to the current players of the standards that are required to be successful as a Rangers player.

"One of the first questions I asked him when we started on the database was did he want first team friendlies included as well as competitive games. He immediately said that he did because pulling on the blue jersey was a tremendous honour, no matter what was at stake. He then recalled playing in front of 100,000 fans in the Camp Nou in Barcelona in a pre-season tournament, technically a non-competitive game as far as the stats go, and reasoned that games of that nature could not be ignored and, as a result, all first team games including friendly matches were researched for the database.

"In addition to the match and player database that was created, Sandy was keen to create another database, but this time to basically collate an electronic archive of all the trophies and other precious artefacts that exist within the walls of Ibrox Stadium. To this effect he got Kirk O'Rourke, the Rangers photographer, to take high resolution photos of all the trophies and gifts that are displayed in the trophy room as well as the collection of medals and international caps that are on display around the stadium.

"Indeed, this work actually came in handy for a different purpose a year or so later. When Alex MacDonald had his Cup Winners' Cup medal stolen while on holiday in Spain, Sandy was able to send UEFA the high resolution photographs of his own Cup Winners' Cup medal that had been taken for the archive so that an exact replica could be made for Alex.

"Sandy was keen to promote all that was good about Rangers and being a Ranger. He was interested in learning how new technologies such as phone apps could be used to the benefit of the club and supporter alike, and was always thinking up new ideas on ways to show off the achievements of a club that he was evidently very proud to have represented for so many years, both on the pitch and behind the scenes.

"He always wanted success for the club, not only on the pitch but also off it. On the occasions through his illness when he couldn't come to the games, I would text him with updates on how the game was going. As the game was getting near the end, I would always get the same text from him – 'What size is the crowd?' He always wanted Ibrox to be full – obviously the club was going through its own problems at the time and I think he saw a good crowd as a sign of recovery within the club."

Andrew Dickson (Rangers Media, October 2007 to November 2014), added:
"Even in this era of five-star stadia, which helps to ensure the United Kingdom remains one of most enticing places to watch football in the world, there are few grounds which remain as alluring when they sit empty as when they are packed to capacity in the way Ibrox does. Breathing in the atmosphere, the history and tradition of the famous old place in Sandy Jardine's company during my first afternoon working for Rangers Football Club stands as one of my most memorable experiences in the seven years I spent with Scotland's most successful sporting institution. Ibrox has often been seen as a trump card when Rangers have

been making moves to sign new players. They would first take them to the training ground for a medical and impress with facilities which are still among the best in Europe almost two decades after the complex first broke ground. It was when they drove their prospective addition from Milngavie to Edmiston Drive, however, that they really upped the ante. Merely being led up the marble staircase into the trophy room would be enough to inspire many contract completions given the impact it has. And yet the real trump card in that part of the process was probably Sandy rather than the stadium itself. He put meat on the bones, gave the place meaning and made the new man relate both to what had been achieved there in the past and what it was hoped could be done in the future. His knowledge, passion and love of Rangers was infectious and I would hazard a guess Sandy's input has been a more decisive factor in the club signing some of their targets over the years than many appreciate.

"In the same way new playing recruits were given the tour before they put pen to paper, Rangers' commercial staff got that treatment too from Sandy after they had committed and it was one of the many ways he immersed himself in life at the club. I am unfortunately too young to have seen him play in person but I can assure those lucky enough to have watched him from the terraces my view of Sandy behind the scenes at Ibrox was also one of a man who performed with absolute dedication, flair and unbridled enthusiasm. He was usually someone you heard before you saw, the sound of Sandy whistling often reverberating along the corridors of Argyle House as a friendly notice he would be popping by a few seconds later wearing his trademark short-sleeved shirt and a dashing, almost mischievous smile to tell us, tongue firmly in cheek, how good looking he was before moving on to the main reason for his visit. For us in the media department, Sandy was a trusted go-to source when we had a spread which needed filled in a magazine or were looking for someone to talk on camera about the latest news – and not just because he was so accessible and easy to turn to. With what he achieved in the game himself, his views were always relevant and I appreciated his forthright honesty. As friendly and approachable as he was, Sandy stood up for his opinions too and whether they were the same as or different from yours, he would still tell you what he thought and why. I had a lot of respect for that. Likewise, he was an ideas man and some of our better work spawned from Sandy planting a seed and encouraging us to let it grow.

"Occasionally lost in the aftermath of his Ibrox departure at the end of 2014 is Ally McCoist's excellent contribution to keeping Rangers going in the first few months after administration and demotion to the old Third Division. Regardless of where Ally ultimately got things wrong as a manager, his role as a pillar of stability for people at all levels within the club in those early days of financial ruin should neither be understated nor forgotten – and Sandy's part on that front was just as significant. In the few meetings the club's administrators held to update staff on developments during that period, Sandy spoke without fear when others worried saying the wrong thing might cost them their jobs. I have no doubt he already knew the answers to the questions he was asking and simply did it for the benefit of others who didn't feel they could speak up without fear of it having a detrimental effect on their own future. That selflessness, above all else, is what I will remember Sandy for and for me, nothing illustrates his good nature more than what was said the last time I saw him. It was in Argyle House before a game at Ibrox in the early part of 2014 and just as Sandy had cancer, my father had also had surgery to remove a tumour in his oesophagus a few weeks earlier so Sandy asked me how he was progressing. 'He's doing well, he walked just over a mile yesterday,' I told Sandy before he hit me with a reply which will always live with me. 'Tell him I'm doing two a day now,' he said with that cheeky smile and a glint in his eye, stopping just short of winking. I didn't know it then and his body language hid it well but Sandy had already learned by that point his own illness was terminal and he passed away three months later. Nevertheless, his message was to keep pushing my dad on to better health, even then, and that said everything about him. I'm told by those who watched him every week that Sandy Jardine was one hell of a footballer. In my experience, he was a very special man too."

32

GOLF, GARDENING AND GRANDCHILDREN

Sandy Jardine knew how to switch off from the stresses and strains of life at Rangers, even in the most testing periods of financial meltdown. Sandy simply got into his car, headed east along the M8 and by the time he had passed Harthill Services on his way home to Edinburgh, he had transformed from Sandy Jardine, Rangers legend, to Billy Jardine from Balgreen – husband, father and grandfather. He was a genuine family man. His family was so important to him, as were his friends. And Sandy had fantastic friends – genuine friends for life. John Greig at Rangers, for so long his traveling companion on his daily commute to Ibrox, Alex MacDonald or Doddie as he only ever called him, had a bond that had been developed in their time together at both Rangers and Hearts and more recently on matches at Rangers when Alex would also be regularly involved in the corporate hospitality activities. Alex Ferguson was also considered a close pal long before he became a knight of the realm. But back in Edinburgh, it was Rossie (David Ross), Murph (John Murphy) and Cookie (Ian Cruikshanks) that Billy was really at home with – three guys that had been together since primary school. It is quite incredible to think that all four played professional football, though Sandy's career by far eclipsed that of his three pals.

One ritual Billy, David, John and Ian made sure was a fixture in their calendar was their annual trip to France for a boys' golfing holiday. David, who made a personal fortune in the world of high finance, owned a flat near Cannes and would organise everything for the boys including chartering a private jet to and from Cannes. For twelve years, the four lads enjoyed each other's company in the south of France for their golfing break but only David has returned since Sandy died.

Golf again was the theme when David Ross decided to celebrate his sixtieth birthday in style in April 2010, but this time instead of the south of France, Rossie treated Billy, John and Ian to a trip to Augusta for the Masters!

David cherishes memories from those golfing trips with his special friends: "No matter what was going on or where we were, Billy would be the driver. He never bothered about having a drink and was happy for the rest of us to have a few beers and Billy would abstain although after dinner and when we were back in the apartment with the car parked for the night, Billy would often pop a bottle of champagne and sit on the balcony quite content to enjoy his glass of fizz and watch the sun go down. However, despite France being famed for its haute cuisine, it just wasn't for Billy Jardine who really was a man of simple tastes. He thought French food was 'bowff' and stuck to his no-nonsense steak and chips or cheeeeeeps as he would ask the waiter for in an attempt to get his message across in his own style of Anglo-French."

Ian Cruikshanks, who also worked with Billy at Hearts in a scouting role, recalls a trip that the foursome made to the London Olympics in 2012: "We somehow managed to get tickets for the 100-metres final and were seated right on the finishing line. As Usain Bolt flashed past us to take the tape and another gold medal, I'll never forget Billy shouting, 'forty-five years ago I would have given him a run for his money!' We all immediately retorted as one: "Aye Right!" but that was Billy, always quick with a joke and not for a minute was he being serious. He was just terrific company and generous to a fault. I remember when he got his first ever Rangers bonus, which had been paid in cash, he went straight out and bought his mum Peggy a fur coat."

David Ross also confirms how patient and accommo-dating Sandy was with fans wherever they were in the world: "Nothing was ever too much trouble as he would pose for photographs and sign autographs and listen to the fans chat even when they were obviously often under the influence of a few pints. It didn't matter to Billy when he was in 'Sandy mode', he appreciated that he had responsi-bilities and was always respectful that he was representing Rangers, the Scottish national side or Hearts and their good standing meant everything to him."

On another occasion, Sandy arranged a visit to Ibrox with directors box tickets for David, John and Ian. David laughs as he recalls: "I can't even remember who Rangers were playing but it was before the club fell into adminis-tration and it was being reported that the club had serious financial issues, while manager Walter Smith had admitted that the Halifax Bank of Scotland were actually calling the shots at Rangers. Anyway, the next day the Sunday papers published a photograph of myself, Murph and Cookie suited and booted in the front row of the box in front of Walter, Martin Bain and John McClelland claiming we three were the financial power brokers from the bank making sure Rangers were being run prudently! How we laughed at that one – a few times!"

When Sandy wasn't golfing he loved to spend time in his garden. Ian Cruikshanks couldn't believe the time his friend devoted to his garden. "Billy loved his garden. It was immaculate and would have won competitions I am sure, had he tried, but it wasn't about that for him. It was more of a distraction but like everything Billy did, he did it well and he was incredibly proud of the way he had laid out his various flowerbeds and how when in bloom they all complimented each other while the lawn was like a bowling green. Even when his health was failing, Billy would be in his garden making sure it was always looking its best and when he had visitors, he took great pride in walking them around the garden explaining what he had recently planted or what was due to blossom next."

David Ross, John Murphy and Ian Cruikshanks were all ushers at the wedding of Billy to Shona in 1969.

Billy and Shona had two children – Nickolla and Steven – and now have seven grandchildren. There are three boys – Storm, Alfie and Zander – and four girls – Honey Bee, Milly, Daisy and Hannah.

It's Hannah who has excelled in football so far, winning a scholarship to the USA in 2014 and a four-year degree course to play for Mississippi college Valley State in Itta Bena. Like her granddad, Hannah is a defender and before heading across the Atlantic, Hannah excelled while playing with Hearts ladies' team. Grandma Shona is proud of all their grandchildren. "Hannah maybe is the footballer but the three boys are Billy's double. They have their grand-dad's colouring and all take after him so much."

Shona was Sandy's rock and she showed incredible courage to care for her husband and to make his final eighteen months as comfortable as possible as he faced his battle with cancer.

As a family, Shona herself admits sometimes they had to take second place to football. "Yes, it's true football was Billy's first love but he was devoted to the family and, of course, holidays were always arranged to fit in with what was happening with football. We used to go to Tenerife or Majorca, usually with my Mum Irene and the kids, but no matter what we were planning, Billy would drag us all off to a sports bar somewhere if a game was on. It didn't even need to be a big game, any game and Billy would be looking for a front-row seat.

"Billy loved his holidays to Spain and loved the sun but

I'm not convinced the sun loved him, with that sandy fair hair and pale complexion, he didn't need much exposure and even when he had plastered on the factor twenty he soon turned pretty red, although he himself thought he looked great with what he called a healthy tan. I remember one holiday in the Canary Isles and a fellow came over, recognising 'Sandy' and said, 'Sandy, look at you – you are bright red – have you spent the night in a deep fat fryer?' My mum and I thought it was hilarious but Billy wasn't impressed but he was still happy with his sun tan.

"The family environment was so important to Billy and he liked nothing better than getting us all together and firing up the barbecue. Billy wasn't the best of chefs but the barbecue was his domain – chops, steaks, burgers and sausages, the grill would be loaded and often the food would be burnt to a crisp but Billy proudly served them up to whoever was around and while I don't recall any of our grandkids being overly keen on grandad's culinary efforts, they would all eat whatever he served up to them, usually just to please him."

Shona knew that home cooking was her husband's favourite, recalling: "Even when Billy was spending ridiculous hours at Rangers, he would never dream of staying in a hotel no matter how late he was working or how early he had a meeting the next day, Billy would drive home and he was always ready for a three-course meal whenever he got home. Billy had a habit of not eating much during the day, often making do with cups of tea and maybe a banana but when my phone went and it was Billy from the car to alert me that he was nearly home, that was my cue to get the soup on. Billy loved soup and it had to be homemade. That would be lapped up and then a big plate of mince or any kind of steak followed up with a dessert. Billy always had room for a pudding. He certainly made up for his moderate intake during the day when he got home but every meal had to start with his soup."

As Sandy's health deteriorated, family and friends

became even more important to him. Golf, his garden and his grandchildren were three topics of conversation for the many visitors to the Jardine household that were always welcome as far as he was concerned and his face lit up every time they were brought up.

Billy's son Steven sums up his dad William Pullar Jardine particularly well. "He was simply the best husband, dad and granddad anybody could ever wish for. He's my hero and remains a true legend of a man in everything he did."

33

SANDY'S SUPER STRIKES

In his Rangers career, Sandy Jardine notched ninety-one goals including two against Celtic.

For Hearts, he managed three goals in 238 appearances while in the dark blue of Scotland, Sandy scored one goal from thirty-eight appearances.

His Scotland goal came from the penalty spot on the 14th May 1974 in a 2-0 win against Wales. Kenny Dalglish had opened the scoring at Hampden Park that day with the clock showing twenty-five minutes, and with only one minute remaining of the first half, Sandy Jardine converted from the spot sliding the ball into the net one way as Welsh goalkeeper Gary Sprake dived the other to double Scotland's lead.

Sandy did score some much more memorable goals, and he even scored one goal and had no memory of his strike at all!

One goal that perhaps signalled Sandy's arrival on the big stage was in his first match against Celtic. Gerry McNee, football writer and broadcaster, recalled Jardine's strike in his tribute to Sandy in his testimonial match programme against Southampton a decade and a half after the event.

"Like most people in Scottish football I first saw Sandy Jardine exactly fifteen years ago. The scene was a vital Old Firm match and was such that the crowd of 78,000 was quite oblivious to the driving rain which battered Glasgow before, during and after the game. Manager Scot Symon had no qualms about catapulting his eighteen-year-old player into what was a baptism of fire. In the Ibrox stand was the wily Helenio Herrera, an urchin from the streets of Casablanca who had risen to the position of Europe's highest paid coach with the great Inter Milan. He was spying on Celtic just weeks before the teams would meet in the European Champions Cup final and on a heavy pitch which pulled at every muscle, he saw a star born against the same eleven men who would lift that trophy. The young Jardine, a mop of reddish hair, a beacon on that grey overcast day, showed not a trace of nerves. From his midfield role he confidently carried the ball to the Celtic defence and in a match which ended 2-2 he scored straight from the pages of *Roy of the Rovers*. He unleashed a shot from fully thirty-five yards which left Ronnie Simpson clawing the air – the ball travelling into the net at the junction of post and crossbar. If you asked me to name a top ten goals from Scottish football it would be one of them. It was a fabulous start to a fabulous career for a man who went from strength to strength thereafter."

Sandy Jardine's only other counter against Celtic came twelve years after his first Old Firm game goal, with the national stadium of Hampden the venue as Rangers faced their oldest enemy in the Drybrough Cup final. It was a game that was to yield not one but three spectacular strikes from Rangers during the course of the ninety minutes. Sandy Jardine was playing in the sweeper role that day. It was a genuine solo effort from Jardine as he majestically strolled out of defence with the ball at his feet before continuing his run deep into Celtic territory, evading a number of Celtic challenges along the way before blasting the ball beyond Peter Latchford and into the net to put Rangers two in front with twenty-eight minutes played. Allan Herron, in his report for the *Sunday Mail* wrote: "The toast is Sandy Jardine – and you can stash away the beer mugs (in reference to the tournament sponsors Drybrough brewers) for it was a champagne goal by the Rangers skipper that paralysed Celtic. When he whipped the ball from Roy Aitken at the edge of the Rangers box in the twenty-eighth minute, there was a murmur of approval from one end of the ground. Several seconds later the referee would have shouted – last orders please – because you were never going to get anything better than the Jardine goal – one of the most spectacular goals ever at Hampden – in this Drybrough Cup final. Jardine operating as a sweeper alongside Colin Jackson moved forward with the ball, resisted two Celtic challenges as he made the half way line – then decided to go all the way. He moved from left to right, took Tom McAdam on on the inside at the edge of the Celtic box then hammered the ball with his left foot. Peter Latchford, who must have been hypnotised by Jardine's mazy 100-yard sprint, got nowhere near the ball as it exploded into the net. What a magnificent goal!"

The Drybrough Cup was in effect a pre-season tournament and many believed they had actually witnessed the goal of the season before it had even started in earnest!

John MacDonald who was just eighteen years old and scored Rangers first goal that day, has vivid memories of a very warm August afternoon at Hampden. "We never gave Celtic a look in that day and the goals were real class. I got the first one and it was only my second Rangers goal. I had scored at the start of my debut season, a year before down at Kilmarnock in a testimonial match for Ian Fallis, but to score against Celtic was something else. I might have had a year to wait to be more involved with the first team but it was worth the wait when the goal went in!

"I was playing wide left, Davie Cooper was playing wide right and Derek Parlane was through the middle. I cut in from the wing and Coop came over to show for it and we worked a one two that left me on top of the goalkeeper and I just slipped it under him. I ran behind the goals to celebrate and sank to my knees and was physically sick! Right there in front of the Rangers end! Wee Doddie (Alex MacDonald) came over to congratulate me on my goal and said, 'That's it wee man get it all up!'. What a welcome to Old Firm football!

"I was just delighted to break into that team and there had been next to no changes from Greigy from the season before, so to become part of the squad and to play alongside Sandy Jardine was a dream come true. We were really on top after my goal when Sandy scored that spectacular solo second. In fact when he struck it, I had to get out the way as it scorched my backside on the way into the net. Sandy's was some goal but then so was Coop's. Everybody just looked on in astonishment as he lofted it over a succession of Celtic defenders before picking his spot, but after he beat the first man I'm thinking shoot, after the second I'm screaming for Davie to hit it, but no he wasn't finished yet as he showboated and then supplied a sublime finish. Do you know what is strange too, everyone knew that Coop could do that but it wasn't something he did in training as it used to be wee games where you were only allowed two or three touches maximum, so to do it at the national stadium against your biggest rivals really rubbed salt in the wound after Sandy's goal had already taken the stuffing out of Celtic."

That Saturday's Drybrough final was sandwiched between a four team tournament at Ibrox involving hosts Rangers, Kilmarnock, West Ham United and Brighton and Hove Albion. It was a regular pre-season feature in those days with Tennent Caledonian Brewers sponsoring the event. So while Rangers enjoyed the glory against Celtic and took the honours from one beer brand on the Saturday, they were beaten in the tournament final sponsored by Drybrough's competitors just twenty-four hours later, Kilmarnock taking the honours in a penalty shoot-out after the game ended 2-2.

John MacDonald went on and had an excellent season bagging nine goals to finish second to top scorer Derek Johnstone who finished on twenty-one. MacDonald left Rangers in 1986 for Barnsley and later played with Scarborough, Airdrie and Dumbarton before ending his career in the Highland league with Fort William and Inverness Caledonian Thistle.

The strike that was least memorable to Sandy Jardine was scored in a match towards the end of 1974 when Dundee United came to Ibrox, and the game was allowed to go ahead despite the playing surface being a sheet of ice! Rangers ran out 4-2 victors with Sandy Jardine lobbing the goalkeeper for one of the goals but he knew nothing about it. It was a goal purely fashioned out of instinct! Sandy had converted a penalty earlier in the game before taking a tumble and collecting a nasty bang on the head along the way. After a bit of treatment and although the medics had reservations, Sandy convinced them he was fit to continue. And continue he did with a second goal that was a measured lob from thirty yards with the United goalkeeper only a few steps off his line. It was a goal that had precision and technique that could only be executed by a real top player. After the ball nestled in the net, Sandy stood arms outstretched to take the applause of the Ibrox crowd and teammates alike with an expression that said "don't be surprised – I do that all the time", but that wasn't arrogance, it was more ignorance as after the game he knew nothing about it when it was confirmed he was suffering concussion from the earlier fall on the frozen surface.

Derek Parlane, unlike Sandy, remembers the occasion well. "I scored and Tommy McLean was also on target. The game probably should never have taken place but in those days you just got on with it. Sandy scored a peach. A real jaw-dropping finish. It looked as if nothing was on with players struggling just to stay on their feet, making movement, and any change of direction a real challenge, but Sandy took a touch, took another, then as the ball sat up from the icy pitch he just measured and delivered the perfect lob that sailed over the keeper's head as if in slow motion and landed in the back of the net with one bounce after it crossed the line.

"It took special skills particularly in those conditions to do that! We all looked in Sandy's direction to congratulate him but he was already acknowledging the reaction and joy from the fans with a massive grin on his face. We won the game and when we went back to the dressing room, Sandy's goal was still being talked about by everybody as a potential goal of the season. We were all taken aback when Sandy with a kind of glazed expression, said, 'What goal? What was the score?' He had no recollection of any of the match at all and even asked who we had been playing! By the look on his face you could see he wasn't kidding and after a quick check over by physio Tommy Craig, and then further examination by the club doc, both diagnosed concussion and Sandy was in need of further medical attention! We all laughed but Sandy couldn't understand what the rest of the dressing room found so amusing. He was our match winner that night but didn't know anything about it!"

Not many players forget about goals they score, particularly when they are as spectacular as Sandy's strike against Dundee United in 1974 was, but he can be forgiven given the circumstances that led to his amnesia and the fact that in typical Jardine style, he still remembered to smile!

Another jewel in the Jardine goalscoring crown came in an 8-1 trouncing of Kilmarnock. His goal that day was more about a goalkeeping blunder as Rangers demolished Killie at Rugby Park in September 1980. Colin McAdam opened the scoring for Rangers and had it cancelled out by a close-range finish from home striker John Bourke. Rangers hit back in style to send them in at half-time with a scoreline of 3-1 in their favour, John MacDonald getting the second with a header and Ian Redford claiming the third with a rocket from the edge of the box. Into the second half and Rangers took Kilmarnock, who were wearing a very unfamiliar red and white vertical striped kit, apart. Rangers went on to score five more goals to see the match end 8-1 in their favour with Sandy Jardine scoring the first goal after half-time. It wasn't so much a thing of beauty from Jardine but a howler of an error from the Killie goalie Jim Brown. John MacDonald scored a hat-trick that day. "Everything we hit went in. Killie couldn't handle the direct style and strength of big Colin McAdam up top and the rest of us just played off him. I got three, Reddy (Ian Redford) two, big Colin got the opener, Jimmy Bett also scored as did Sandy but it was a real howler by their goalie.

"I linked with Sandy to start the move then he played a one-two with Davie Cooper and as it opened up in front of him, he had a swing at the ball with his left foot from more than thirty yards but the effort had no pace on it and it was straight down the keeper's throat, or rather his belly to be more accurate. It should have been an easy save but somehow the goalkeeper let it squirm out his grasp after he seemed to have it safely gathered in his gloves and clutched to his midriff and he basically dropped it over the line!

"Honestly, Sandy gave a look that suggested he didn't know whether to celebrate or go over to give the Killie keeper a cuddle. But, they all count!"

That goal and the other seven he conceded that day all but finished Jim Brown's Kilmarnock career as he drifted out of the first team within weeks of his nightmare against Rangers, before leaving Rugby Park and joining Auchinleck Talbot in the Ayrshire Juniors.

Indeed, it is goals that count they say, and the most crucial and probably the most personally satisfying goal scored by Sandy Jardine in his career takes us back to that European Cup Winners' Cup semi-final win against Bayern Munich. Legendary broadcaster Archie Macpherson is in no doubt Sandy's goal that night will always have a very worthy place in Rangers' history. "Almost 160,000 people watched two massive European games in the city of Glasgow that night," he recalled. "Celtic were entertaining Inter Milan on the same night Rangers took on Bayern. It probably will never ever happen again.

"Sandy Jardine's goal laid down a marker for the action that was about to unfold but it was the manner of the goal that was special. It was a coordinated goal. A beautiful goal indeed. But throughout Sandy Jardine's career he did things with grace, poise and balance. In the opening minutes of that semi-final tie against Bayern Munich, those traits and signs of genius in fact were never better demonstrated. Bayern were in a comfortable position deep inside their own half of the field when they played a speculative forward ball in search of Müller, but Derek Johnstone, playing in a deep midfield role for Rangers, saw the loose ball and pounced upon it eagerly before sliding it with absolute precision into the path of Sandy Jardine. Jardine's first touch was exquisite and with the German defence expecting the Rangers full-back to head down the line, Sandy's deft touch took him inside and clear of his marker – with perfect balance he measured his shot and it must have been fully thirty yards out – before curling the most delightful of strikes beyond Sepp Maier in the Bayern goal and into the net.

"The game was less than one minute old and utterly stunned the Germans – the goal gave Rangers latitude and yes, they were on their way. I suspect the Bayern defenders underestimated Sandy Jardine and doubted whether a full-back, any full-back, playing in Scotland, had the technique or composure to execute such a finish on what would have been considered his 'wrong foot', but Sandy Jardine was no ordinary full-back.

"I had the pleasure of commentating on many matches involving Sandy in domestic competition, Europe and in the international arena over decades and I was always taken by his style and intelligence. Sandy was elegant in everything he did, even if it was just taking a throw-in but more than that, he was always looking for something, always on the move looking to come forward and create. He had an antenna that could seek out errors by defenders before they made them, almost like a cougar or a lion stalking its prey and knowing exactly when to pounce. That was Sandy. That memorable night of a football festival in Glasgow was probably Sandy's finest strike and one that had the highest possible importance to his club. Sandy Jardine may not have been a noted goalscorer, but his goal against Bayern Munich in that European Cup Winners 'Cup semi-final tie will live long in the memory of those that witnessed it. It was a sensational strike and then some."

SANDY IN ROYAL BLUE

Afterword by Jim Hannah

I have worked at Rangers FC for going on thirty-five years and I can honestly say with my hand on my heart that Sandy Jardine was the nicest, most helpful, funny, dedicated person I have ever met. My earliest recollections of Sandy Jardine were back to 1967 when he was drafted into the Rangers team that had just been knocked out of the Scottish Cup in the first round by a Berwick Rangers team who had a certain Mr Jock Wallace in goal. I was seventeen years old at the time so Sandy would have been eighteen and he was playing for the Rangers first team. I suppose I looked at him as one of the young team and he was carrying the banner for all of us teenagers, as a Rangers first team player, amazing. Sandy played the rest of that season, establishing himself as a first team player and you could see he didn't look out of place and appeared not to be overawed by playing for the biggest club in the world. At the end of that season Sandy went on to be the youngest player to play in the 1967 European Cup Winners' Cup final.

I remember interviewing him about five years ago and he talked about himself being too young to be nervous about playing in the first team and playing in a European final, but the experience was to stand him in good stead for the rest of his footballing career as a Rangers player. It was Sandy's fitness and ball skills I admired most. He wasn't a fierce tackler, he didn't need to be, when you had the likes of John Greig in the team looking after you.

I remember being disappointed when he was out of the team the following season, but he got his chance again to feature for the first team, this time as a centre forward and he was a huge success, scoring eleven goals in twelve games, a great return and it was obvious he had a nose for scoring goals. Rangers bought Colin Stein from Hibs for £100,000 – a Scottish transfer record at the time – and Sandy never really featured as a striker again.

In came Willie Waddell as manager. This was to be Sandy's third manager in as many years. Scot Symon and Davie White had now gone, and Waddell came in with fresh ideas. He had a clearout of some of the older players, including the great Jim Baxter. Rangers right back Kai Johansen retired from football, which left the Gers without a regular right back. In stepped Sandy, and the rest is history as they say …

I remember a schoolmate of mine from Govan High also broke into the first team as goalkeeper. Bobby Watson was his name. I brought along my Super 8 cine camera to film Bobby coming out of the tunnel, but it was Sandy who made it into most of the clips in my five-minute video. He scored a goal against Dunfermline from almost thirty yards, something he was to go on to do several times throughout his career.

I can remember climbing the walls at the old Albion training ground to watch the first team train, and my memory was of Sandy getting the ball from Peter McCloy and starting a mazy dribble for about eighty yards leaving players in his wake and at the same time he was giving a running commentary of himself beating every player in the process. He became a regular in the Scotland set-up, and Danny McGrain of Celtic had to move to left back to accommodate Sandy being in the team.

Like most Rangers Fans at the time, we were so proud of him being the only Rangers player to play in the 1974 World Cup for Scotland.

Sandy went on to become a fantastic sprinter, taking part and winning races at Powderhall in Edinburgh, which no doubt helped his football career, because he turned out to be the best right back in British football, well certainly the best I have ever seen playing for Rangers. It wasn't a surprise when he was voted into the greatest ever Rangers Eleven, years later.

I couldn't believe it when Sandy left the Club and went on to Hearts as a player-coach, with Alex MacDonald as manager, you just knew the move would come back to haunt us. He went onto win the Scottish Football Writers' Player of the Year award for the second time in his career. I'm sure most Rangers fans and players would agree he should have remained at the club till he eventually hung up his boots.

I had met Sandy a few times when he worked at the club with Scottish Brewers and eventually he came back to the club to work on a full-time basis in the Commercial department. When I moved over to Argyle House to work in our Marketing department, I became friendly with the legend that was Sandy Jardine. From the first day we hit it off, talking every day about Rangers teams and players past and present. I couldn't believe I was working with and sitting down with a coffee and discussing football with such a Rangers legend.

Sandy was so easy going and an absolute gentleman not just to me, but to everyone he met. We became close working colleagues and we bounced all sorts of ideas off one another. We sometimes travelled to Europe to see the Rangers and also to Supporters Conventions with other ex-players. Sandy always made sure you were never left out of any conversations, in fact he treated you like one of his old teammates.

I have many, many funny stories and great memories of our trips, but one of the funniest was a trip to a NARSA Convention with big Ronnie Mackinnon and Alex MacDonald. Ronnie turned up at Glasgow Airport wearing a Tee-shirt, a polo neck jumper, a Harris Tweed Jacket and a raincoat. Sandy and Doddy gave him pelters, it was eighty-five degrees Fahrenheit in Florida. Big Ronnie never even had a pair of shorts with him. Wee Doddie said: "I was waiting on you coming down to the swimming pool wearing a pair of Harris Tweed swimming trunks!"

Sandy loved meeting up with his ex-Rangers footballing colleagues. They all worked in the Hospitality and before every home game, they would meet up to find out where they were working etc. I was privileged more than once to listen to the banter between them all, the laughter coming from that room was deafening, as well as the serious discussion about the current team.

There was Peter McCloy, Sandy, Eric Callow, Big Davy Provan, Tom Forsyth, Alan McLaren, Willie Henderson Colin Stein, Alex McDonald, Willie Johnston, and the fabulous duo Jimmy Millar and Ralph Brand, some of the greatest Rangers players who I was privileged to watch over the years following the Rangers.

Sandy ended up in the Players Liaison and I was the Fans Liaison, therefore we worked closely together. He would come into my office every morning with his china tea cup and we'd talk about everything and anything but mostly about Rangers and the history of the club.

He had a passion about showing the club's memorabilia to the Rangers fans and his work can be seen in the Blue Room, Trophy Room, old Managers' Room etc. I like to think a bit rubbed off on myself. He had faith in me taking over from him. I've done my best but I'm not Sandy.

A lot of the fans do not know how much he did for our great club, he was a great ideas person, and he used to bounce some of his ideas off me and vice versa. He totally transformed the Blue Room into what it is today with the wonderful murals and all the framed medals which are all significant in the club's history.

The International cap collection that he amassed on behalf of the club, is nothing short of stunning and something all

Rangers fans should be proud of. You will not see a collection anywhere in the world like it. It is on display in the corridor leading to the trophy room.

I simply idolised the man. He was always there for me through some rough times and I was there for him when he had some problems, we could tell one another anything. I used to love listening to his stories about his days playing for Rangers and Scotland, he had a great sense of humour. Once we both took some Rangers fans who had came over from USA, Canada, Australia, the Middle East and the UK, on a tour around Hampden. Our tour guide didn't recognise Sandy and he started to tell us the story about Jimmy Johnstone ending up in the Firth of Clyde in a rowing boat without any oars. Sandy waited till he had finished telling his PC version of the story, then he piped up to say, now I'll tell you the real story. We told the guy he was Sandy Jardine of Rangers and the look on the guy's face was priceless. The story was hilarious, but the guide said 'I better stick to the PC version!' Sometimes when I'm sitting in my office and thinking of him, I have a smile on my face, because even now, I can still hear him walking along the corridor humming a tune that only he knew, and snapping his fingers in time to that tune. He is missed so much by the staff, ex-players, friends, and fans, but first and foremost his family, which he loved to talk about every day.

There was something I didn't want to hear, and that was the day he walked into my office and closed the door. I knew something was wrong but when he said he had something serious to tell me, he just blurted it out that he had cancer. I wanted to be strong for him, but I burst into tears, and God knows how he felt, but my head was buzzing with what he had just told me. Then I heard him ask me if I was ok. That was Sandy – always thinking about others.

One day not long after our conversation, we were talking on the phone and I mentioned the cancer and how he should never give up, I heard him choking up and he said he had to go, then he hung up. He called me back about fifteen minutes later, and made me promise never to speak about it again, all he wanted to talk about was Rangers and football and work. We could talk on the phone for hours.

I visited him about a week and a half before he passed away and he all he wanted to do was ask about the club's situation, and how the staff were being treated, and was everyone still in a job. If he could, he wanted to be able to help out with advice etc.

When I informed him that the Rangers fans had raised the money to commission a bronze bust of him, and that the club had given us permission to have it sited on the level up from the legendary Bill Struth, on the marble stairway, he was taken aback. He said it was a really proud moment for him and his family. I then told him the club were renaming the Govan Stand, as the Sandy Jardine Stand in his honour, for all he did for the club as a player, a leader for the fans and ambassador during the club's hardest time ever, and he had a tear in his eye.

That was the last time I spoke to Sandy face to face, but I will never forget him and I'm really proud to have been able to call him a friend. I will remember the young lad who broke into a great Rangers team in 1967 and went on to become a Rangers legend, a great friend and true Rangers man, Sandy in Royal Blue.

Saturday 6th August 2016 and Rangers welcomed Hamilton Academical FC as their first opponents back in the Scottish Premiership.

A crowd of just short of 50,000 were inside Ibrox as Chairman Dave King prepared to fly the Championship flag ... the journey was complete ...

At the same moment as the flag caught the wind, Amanda Millar, Rangers Football Administration Executive, noticed something significant as she watched the ceremony: "It was a very emotional moment and many people had Sandy in their thoughts. Oh how he would have enjoyed this day ... then ... as the flag unfurled, a beautiful butterfly took flight from the Directors Box ... and I had to think ... maybe ... just maybe ... ?"

Sandy Jardine

The Statistics

Rangers Record

League :	451 Appearances 42 goals
League Cup:	107 Appearances 25 goals
Scottish Cup	64 Appearances 8 goals
Europe:	52 Appearances 2 goals
Total Competitive:	674 Appearances 77 goals
Other Matches:	105 Appearances 14 goals
Overall Total:	779 Appearances 91 goals

Three League Championships (1974/75, 1975/76,
1977/78)
Five Scottish Cups (1972/73, 1975/76, 1977/78, 1978/79,
1980/81)
Five League Cups (1970/71, 1975/76, 1977/78, 1978/79,
1981/82)
One European Cup Winners' Cup (1971/72)

Three Glasgow Cups (1968/69, 1970/71, 1975/76)
One Drybrough Cup (1979/80)

SFWA Footballer of the Year (1974/75)

Hearts Record

League :	187 Appearances 3 goals
League Cup:	29 Appearances 0 goals
Scottish Cup	19 Appearances 0 goals
Europe:	3 Appearances 0 goals
Total Competitive:	238 Appearances 3 goals

SFWA Footballer of the Year (1985/86)

Season	Club	League Apps	League Goals	League	Final Pos	Scottish Cup	League Cup	Europe	Scotland caps/gls
1965-66	Rangers	0	0	Scot Div 1	2nd	Winners	Final	-	-/-
1966-67	Rangers	14	2	Scot Div 1	2nd	Round 1	Final	CWC Final	-/-
1967-68	Rangers	9	0	Scot Div 1	2nd	Round 3	Section	Fairs Quarter	-/-
1968-69	Rangers	18	4	Scot Div 1	2nd	Final	Section	Fairs Semi	-/-
1969-70	Rangers	14	0	Scot Div 1	2nd	Round 3	Section	CWC Round 2	-/-
1970-71	Rangers	32	1	Scot Div 1	4th	Final	Winners	Fairs Round 1	1/0
1971-72	Rangers	31	5	Scot Div 1	3rd	Semi	Section	CWC Winners	3/0
1972-73	Rangers	34	2	Scot Div 1	2nd	Winners	Semi	Super Cup*	3/0
1973-74	Rangers	34	3	Scot Div 1	3rd	Round 4	Semi	CWC Round 2	12/1
1974-75	Rangers	34	9	Scot Div 1	Champions	Round 3	Section	-	8/0
1975-76	Rangers	25	2	Scot Premier	Champions	Winners	Winners	EC Round 2	-/-
1976-77	Rangers	36	2	Scot Premier	2nd	Final	Semi	EC Round 1	3/0
1977-78	Rangers	32	5	Scot Premier	Champions	Winners	Winners	CWC Round 1	4/0
1978-79	Rangers	35	0	Scot Premier	2nd	Winners	Winners	EC Quarter	-/-
1979-80	Rangers	35	3	Scot Premier	5th	Final	Round 3	CWC Round 2	4/0
1980-81	Rangers	32	3	Scot Premier	3rd	Winners	Round 2	-	-/-
1981-82	Rangers	36	1	Scot Premier	3rd	Final	Winners	CWC Round 1	-/-
	TOTAL -	451	40						
1982-83	Hearts	39	2	Scot Div 1	2nd	Quarter	Semi	-	-/-
1983-84	Hearts	33	0	Scot Premier	5th	Round 4	Section	-	-/-
1984-85	Hearts	34	0	Scot Premier	7th	Quarter	Semi	UEFA Round 1	-/-
1985-86	Hearts	35	0	Scot Premier	2nd	Final	Quarter	-	-/-
1986-87	Hearts	34	1	Scot Premier	5th	Semi	Round 2	UEFA Round 1	-/-
1987-88	Hearts	9	0	Scot Premier	2nd	Semi	Quarter	-	-/-
	TOTAL -	184	3						

*Rangers banned from Europe but contested the inaugural European Super Cup against European Cup winners Ajax.

Further Breakdown of the Seasons at Ibrox:

Season	League	League Cup	Scottish Cup	Europe	TOTAL
1965/66	-	-	-	-	-
1966/67	14(2)	-	-	5	19(2)
1967/68	9	6(1)	1	1	17(1)
1968/69	18(4)	2(3)	-	4(1)	24(8)
1969/70	14	4(1)	1(1)	3	22(2)
1970/71	32(1)	10(1) C	5	2	49(2)
1971/72	31(5)	6	7	9(1) C	53(6)
1972/73	34(2)	11	6 C	2	53(2)
1973/74	34(3)	11	2	4	51(3)
1974/75	34(9) C	6 (5)	2	-	42(14)
1975/76	25(2) C	7 (5) C	3 C	2	37(7)
1976/77	36(2)	11(6)	5(2)	2	54(10)
1977/78	32(5) C	7(1) C	5 C	4	48(6)
1978/79	35	10(1) C	9(1) C	6	60(2)
1979/80	35(3)	4	6(2)	6	51(5)
1980/81	32(3)	4	6	-	42(3)
1981/81	36(1)	8(1)	6(2)	2	52(4)
	451(42)	107(25)	64(8)	52(2)	674(77)

Scotland Internationals

11 Nov 1970 Scotland 1 Denmark 0
13 Oct 1971 Scotland 2 Portugal 1
10 Nov 1971 Scotland 1 Belgium 0
1 Dec 1971   Holland 2 Scotland 1
19 May 1973 England 1 Scotland 0
22 Jun 1973 Switzerland 1 Scotland 0
30 Jun 1973 Scotland 0 Brazil 1
26 Sep 1973 Scotland 2 Czechoslovakia 1
17 Oct 1973 Czechoslovakia 1 Scotland 0
14 Nov 1973 Scotland 1 West Germany 1
27 Mar 1974 West Germany 2 Scotland 1
11 May 1974 Scotland 0 Northern Ireland 1
14 May 1974 Scotland 2 Wales 0   (1 goal)
18 May 1974 Scotland 2 England 0
1 Jun 1974   Belgium 2 Scotland 1
6 Jun 1974   Norway 1 Scotland 2
14 Jun 1974 Zaire 0 Scotland 2   (World Cup Finals,
                                         played in Dortmund)
18 Jun 1974 Scotland 0 Brazil 0   (World Cup Finals,
                                         played in Frankfurt)
22 Jun 1974 Scotland 1 Yugoslavia 1 (World Cup Finals,
                                         played in Frankfurt)
30 Oct 1974 Scotland 3 East Germany 0   *captained Scotland
20 Nov 1974 Scotland 1 Spain 2
5 Feb 1975   Spain 1 Scotland 1
16 Apr 1975 Sweden 1 Scotland 1   *captained Scotland
13 May 1975 Scotland 1 Portugal 0   *captained Scotland
17 May 1975 Wales 2 Scotland 2   *captained Scotland
20 May 1975 Scotland 3 Northern Ireland 0   *captained
Scotland
24 May 1975 England 5 Scotland 1   *captained Scotland
27 Apr 1977 Scotland 3 Sweden 1
15 Jun 1977 Chile 2 Scotland 4
23 Jun 1977 Brazil 2 Scotland 0

21 Sep 1977 Scotland 3 Czechoslovakia 1
12 Oct 1977 Wales 0 Scotland 2   (played in Liverpool)
13 May 1978 Scotland 1 Northern Ireland 1
7 Jun 1978   Scotland 1 Iran 1   (World Cup Finals,
                                                        played in Córdoba)
12 Sep 1979 Scotland 1 Peru 1   *captained Scotland*
17 Oct 1979 Scotland 1 Austria 1
21 Nov 1979 Belgium 2 Scotland 0   *captained Scotland*
19 Dec 1979 Scotland 1 Belgium 3   *captained Scotland*

Record v Celtic

Overall Total (League, League Cup, Scottish Cup)
Played: 49   Won: 16   Drawn: 10   Lost: 23

At Ibrox
Played: 20   Won: 8   Drawn: 5   Lost: 7

At Celtic Park
Played: 21   Won: 3   Drawn: 5   Lost: 13

At Hampden
Played: 8   Won: 5   Drawn: 0   Lost: 3

Other Games v Celtic:
Played: 6   Won: 3   Drawn: 2   Lost: 1

Of the 'Other Games' four were played at Hampden resulting in one win each and two draws and two were played at Celtic Park, both won by Rangers.

Cup Finals played in

31 May 1967 – European Cup Winners' Cup Final – Att: 69,500 – Stadion am Dutzendteich, Nuremberg
Bayern Munich 1 (Roth 109) Rangers 0
Rangers team – Martin, Johansen, Provan, Jardine, McKinnon, Greig, Henderson, A.Smith, Hynd, D.Smith, Johnston

15 Apr 1969 – Glasgow Cup Final – Att: 21,000 – Ibrox Stadium
Rangers 2 (Johnston 17, Persson 60) Partick Thistle 2 (Divers 45, Duncan 70)
Rangers team – Martin, Johansen, Mathieson, Jardine, Jackson, Smith, Conn, Penman, Ferguson, Johnston, Persson

11 Aug 1969 – Glasgow Cup Final replay – Att: 19,000 – Firhill Park
Partick Thistle 2 (Bone 51, Flanagan 88pen) Rangers 3 (Persson 30, Jardine 77, Provan 78)
Rangers team – Neef, Johansen, Provan, Greig, McKinnon, Smith, Conn (Jardine), Watson, MacDonald, Johnston, Persson

10 Aug 1970 – Glasgow Cup Final – Att: 58,144 – Hampden Park
Celtic 3 (Gemmell 3, 19, Quinn 47) Rangers 1 (Greig 27)
Rangers team – Watson, Jardine, Mathieson, Greig, Jackson, Smith, Henderson, Conn, Stein, MacDonald (Miller), Johnston

24 Oct 1970 – League Cup Final – Att: 106,263 – Hampden Park
Rangers 1 (Johnstone 40) Celtic 0
Rangers team – McCloy, Jardine, Miller, Conn, McKinnon, Jackson, Henderson, MacDonald, Johnstone, Stein, Johnston

16 Aug 1971 – Glasgow Cup Final – Att: 12,500 – Ibrox
Stadium
Rangers 2 (Stein 17, 70) Clyde 0
Rangers team – McCloy, Jardine, Mathieson, Greig, McKinnon,
Jackson, McLean, Conn, Stein, Johnston, Henderson

24 May 1972 – European Cup Winners' Cup Final – Att:
45,000 – Camp Nou, Barcelona
Rangers 3 (Stein 24, Johnston 40, 49) Dinamo Moscow 2
(Eschtrekov 59, Makovikov 87)
Rangers team – McCloy, Jardine, Mathieson, Greig,
Johnstone, Smith, McLean, Conn, Stein, MacDonald,
Johnston

16 Jan 1973 – European Super Cup, 1st leg – Att: 58,000 –
Ibrox Stadium
Rangers 1 (MacDonald 41) Ajax 3 (Rep 34, Cruyff 45, Haan
76)
Rangers team – McCloy, Jardine, Mathieson, Greig,
Johnstone, Smith, Conn (McLean), Forsyth, Parlane,
MacDonald, Young

24 Jan 1973 – European Super Cup, 2nd leg – Att: 40,000 –
Olympisch Stadion, Amsterdam
Ajax 3 (Haan 12, Muhren 37pen, Cruyff 79) Rangers 2
(MacDonald 2, Young 35)
Rangers team – McCloy, Jardine, Mathieson, Greig,
Johnstone, Smith, McLean, Forsyth, Parlane, MacDonald,
Young

5th May 1973 – Scottish Cup Final – Att: 122,714 – Hampden
Park
Rangers 3 (Parlane 34, Conn 46, Forsyth 60) Celtic 2 (Dalglish
24, Connelly 54pen)
Rangers team – McCloy, Jardine, Mathieson, Greig, Johnstone,
MacDonald, McLean, Forsyth, Parlane, Conn, Young

3 Aug 1974 – Drybrough Cup Final – Att: 57,558 – Hampden Park

Celtic 2 (Murray 30, Wilson 94) Rangers 2 (Scott 38, Parlane 116) *Celtic win 4-2 on penalties*

Rangers team – Kennedy, Jardine, Mathieson, Greig (Young), Jackson, Johnstone, McLean, Scott, Parlane, MacDonald (Denny), Fyfe

21st Aug 1974 – Trofeo Joan Gamper – Att: 100,000 – Camp Nou, Barcelona

FC Barcelona 4 (Miller 23og, Marcial 36, 58, 85) Rangers 1 (Fyfe 16)

Rangers team – Kennedy, Jardine, Miller, Forsyth, Jackson, Johnstone, McLean, Parlane, Young, Fyfe, Scott

10 May 1975 – Glasgow Cup Final – Att: 70,494 – Hampden Park

Celtic 2 (Wilson (2)) Rangers 2 (Stein, McLean)

Rangers team – Kennedy, Jardine, Greig, McKean, Jackson, Forsyth, McLean, Stein, Parlane, MacDonald, Johnstone

25 Oct 1975 – League Cup Final – Att: 58,806 – Hampden Park

Rangers 1 (MacDonald 67) Celtic 0

Rangers team – Kennedy, Jardine, Greig, Forsyth, Jackson, MacDonald, McLean, Stein, Parlane, Johnstone, Young

1 May 1976 – Scottish Cup Final – Att: 85,354 – Hampden Park

Rangers 3 (Johnstone 1, 81, MacDonald 45) Hearts 1 (Shaw 83)

Rangers team – McCloy, Miller, Greig, Forsyth, Jackson, MacDonald, McKean, Hamilton (Jardine), Henderson, McLean, Johnstone

10 Aug 1976 – Glasgow Cup Final – Att: 60,000 – Celtic Park

Celtic 1 (Edvaldsson 42) Rangers 3 (Jardine 4, Jackson 10, Miller pen)
Rangers team – McCloy, Miller, Greig, Forsyth, Jackson (McKean), MacDonald, McLean, Jardine, Parlane, Munro, Johnstone

7 May 1977 – Scottish Cup Final – Att: 54,252 – Hampden Park
Celtic 1 (Lynch 20pen) Rangers 0
Rangers team – Kennedy, Jardine, Greig, Forsyth, Jackson, Watson (Robertson), McLean, Hamilton, Parlane, MacDonald, Johnstone

18 Mar 1978 – League Cup Final – Att: 60,168 – Hampden Park
Rangers 2 (Cooper 38, Smith 117) Celtic 1 (Edvaldsson 84)
Rangers team – Kennedy, Jardine, Greig, Forsyth, Jackson, MacDonald, McLean, Hamilton (Miller), Johnstone, Smith, Cooper (Parlane)

6 May 1978 – Scottish Cup Final – Att: 61,563 – Hampden Park
Rangers 2 (MacDonald 34, Johnstone 58) Aberdeen 1 (Ritchie 85)
Rangers team – McCloy, Jardine, Greig, Forsyth, Jackson, MacDonald, McLean, Russell, Johnstone, Smith, Cooper (Watson)

31 Mar 1979 – League Cup Final – Att: 54,000 – Hampden Park
Rangers 2 (A.MacDonald 77, Jackson 90) Aberdeen 1 (Davidson 59)
Rangers team – McCloy, Jardine, Dawson, Johnstone, Jackson, A.MacDonald, McLean, Russell, Urquhart (Miller), Smith, Cooper (Parlane)

12 May 1979 – Scottish Cup Final – Att: 50,610 – Hampden Park

Rangers 0 Hibernian 0
Rangers team – McCloy, Jardine, Dawson, Johnstone, Jackson, A.MacDonald (Miller), McLean, Russell, Parlane, Smith, Cooper

16 May 1979 – Scottish Cup Final replay – Att: 33,504 – Hampden Park
Rangers 0 Hibernian 0
Rangers team – McCloy, Jardine, Dawson, Johnstone, Jackson, A.MacDonald, McLean (Miller), Russell, Parlane, Smith, Cooper

28 May 1979 – Scottish Cup Final, 2nd replay – Att: 30,602 – Hampden Park
Rangers 3 (Johnstone 42, 61, Duncan 110og) Hibernian 2 (Higgins 16, McLeod 78pen)
Rangers team – McCloy, Jardine, Dawson, Johnstone, Jackson, Watson (Miller), McLean (Smith), Russell, Parlane, A.MacDonald, Cooper

4 Aug 1979 – Drybrough Cup Final – Att: 40,609 – Hampden Park
Rangers 3 (J.MacDonald 12, Jardine 27, Cooper 78) Celtic 1 (Lennox 84)
Rangers team – McCloy, Miller, Dawson, Jardine, Jackson, Watson, Cooper (Smith), Russell (Johnstone), Parlane, A.MacDonald, J.MacDonald

10 May 1980 – Scottish Cup Final – Att: 70,303 – Hampden Park
Celtic 1 (McCluskey 107) Rangers 0
Rangers team – McCloy, Jardine, Dawson, T.Forsyth (Miller), Jackson, Stevens, Cooper, Russell, Johnstone, Smith, J.MacDonald (McLean)

9th May 1981 – Scottish Cup Final – Att: 53,346 – Hampden Park

Rangers 0 Dundee United 0
Rangers team – Stewart, Jardine, Dawson, Stevens,
T.Forsyth, Bett, McLean, Russell, McAdam (Cooper),
Redford, Johnston (J.MacDonald)

12 May 1981 – Scottish Cup Final replay – Att: 43,099 –
Hampden Park
Rangers 4 (Cooper 10, Russell 20, J.MacDonald 29, 77)
Dundee United 1 (Dodds 23)
Rangers team – Stewart, Jardine, Dawson, Stevens,
T.Forsyth, Bett, Cooper, Russell, Johnstone, Redford,
J.MacDonald

28 Nov 1981 – League Cup Final – Att: 53,777 – Hampden
Park
Rangers 2 (Cooper 74, Redford 88) Dundee United 1 (Milne
48)
Rangers team – Stewart, Jardine, Miller, Stevens, Jackson,
Bett, Cooper, Russell, Johnstone, Dalziel (Redford),
MacDonald

22 May 1982 – Scottish Cup Final – Att: 53,788 – Hampden
Park
Aberdeen 4 (McLeish 33, McGhee 92, Strachan 103, Cooper
110) Rangers 1 (MacDonald 15)
Rangers team – Stewart, Jardine (McAdam), Dawson,
McClelland, Jackson, Bett, Cooper, Russell, Dalziel
(McLean), Miller, MacDonald

10 May 1986 – Scottish Cup Final – Hampden Park
Aberdeen 3 (Hewitt 5, 48, Stark 75) Hearts 0
Hearts team – Smith, Kidd, Whittaker, S.Jardine, Berry,
Levein, Colquhoun, Black, Clark, G.Mackay, Robertson

Goals (League, League Cup, Scottish Cup, Europe)

1966/67 (2):   1 v Ayr (a, 4-1); 1 v Celtic (h, 2-2)
1967/68 (1):   1 v Aberdeen (h, 3-0, LC)
1968/69 (8):   1 v Partick (h, 2-1, LC), 2 v Morton (a, 5-0, LC),
                2 v Partick (h, 2-0), 1 v Vojvodina (h, 2-0, FC),
                1 v Kilmarnock (h, 3-3),
                1 v Dunfermline (h, 3-0)
1969/70 (2):   1 v Airdrie (a, 3-0, LC), 1 v Forfar (a, 7-0, SC)
1970/71 (2):   1 v Dunfermline (h, 4-1, LC),
                1 v Cowdenbeath (a, 3-1)
1971/72 (6):   1 v East Fife (h, 3-0), 1 v Dundee Utd (a, 5-1),
                1 v Motherwell (h, 4-0),
                1 v Airdrie (h, 3-0), 1 v Kilmarnock (a, 2-1),
                1 v Bayern Munich (h, 2-0, CWC)
1972/73 (2):   1 v Dundee Utd (a, 4-1),
                1 v Motherwell (h, 2-1)
1973/74 (3):   2 (2 pens) v Hibernian (h, 4-0),
                1 (pen) v Dundee (h, 1-2)
1974/75 (14): 1 v St. Johnstone (h, 3-2, LC),
                2 v St. Johnstone (a, 6-2, LC),
                1 v Dundee (a, 2-0, LC),
                1 (pen) v Dundee (h, 4-0, LC),
                1 (pen) v Ayr (a, 1-1),
                1 (pen) v Kilmarnock (a, 6-0),
                1 v Clyde (h, 3-1), 1 (pen) v Hearts (a, 1-1),
                2 (1 pen) v Dundee Utd (h, 4-2),
                2 (1 pen) v Airdrie (a, 3-4),
                1 (pen) v Ayr (h, 3-0)
1975/76 (7):   3 (2 pens) v Airdrie (h, 6-1, LC),
                1 v Motherwell (a, 2-2, LC),
                1 v Montrose (Ham, 5-1, LC),
                1 v St. Johnstone (a, 5-1), 1 (pen) v Ayr (3-0, h),
1976/77 (10): 2 v St. Johnstone (h, 5-0, LC),
                1 v Montrose (h, 4-0, LC),
                1 v Hibernian (h, 3-0, LC),

1 v Montrose (a, 3-0, LC),
1 v St. Johnstone (a, 1-0, LC), 1 (pen) v
Falkirk (h, 3-1, SC),
1 (pen) v Hearts (Ham, 2-0, SC),
1 (pen) v Hearts (a, 3-1),
1 (pen) v Partick (h, 2-1)

1977/78 (6): 1 v St. Mirren (a, 3-3),
1 (pen) v Aberdeen (h, 3-1),
1 (pen) v Hibernian (a, 1-0),
1 (pen) v Dunfermline (a, 3-1, LC),
1 v Partick (h, 2-1),
1 (pen) v Dundee Utd (h, 3-0)

1978/79 (2): 1 (pen) v Celtic (Ham, 3-2, LC),
1 (pen) v Dundee (h, 6-3, SC)

1979/80 (5): 1 (pen) v St. Mirren (h, 1-2),
1 (pen) v Clyde (a, 2-2, SC),
1 (pen) v Hearts (h, 6-1, SC),
1 (pen) v Aberdeen (h, 2-2),
1 (pen) v Dundee Utd (h, 2-1)

1980/81 (3): 1 v Partick (h, 4-0), 1 v Kilmarnock (a, 8-1),
1 v Kilmarnock (h, 2-0)

1981/82 (4): 1 v Raith Rov (h, 8-1, LC), 1 v Airdrie (h, 4-1),
2 v Dumbarton (h, 4-0, SC)

Goals for Rangers by Club (League, League Cup, Scottish Cup, Europe)

8 v Airdrie
7 v St. Johnstone
6 v Dundee Utd, Partick
5 v Kilmarnock
4 v Ayr, Dundee, Hearts, Hibernian
3 v Aberdeen, Dunfermline, Montrose, Motherwell
2 v Celtic, Clyde, Dumbarton, Morton, St.Mirren
1 v Bayern Munich, Cowdenbeath, East Fife, Falkirk, Forfar, Raith Rov, Vojvodina

Goals for Rangers in other games

4 v Queen's Park*
2 v Amal Alliance, Ayr, Celtic, Partick
1 v Chelsea, Everton, Athletic Bilbao, Estoril

*scored all four against Queen's Park in the same game (14 October 1968, Glasgow Cup).

Three goals for Hearts – 1 (pen) v Clydebank, 1 (pen) v Airdrie, 1 v Hamilton